G.L. MEHTA
A Many Splendoured Man

About the Author

Aparna Basu, Ph.D. (Cantab) was Professor of History, University of Delhi. She is the UGC Convenor of the national subject panel on History and Archaeology. She is the author of several books including *Growth of Education and Political Development in India Women's Struggle : A History of All India Women's Conference, Rebel With a Cause: Biography of Mridula Sarabhai, From Indepedence to Freedom : Women and Fifty Years of India's Independence* and a *History of Delhi University* on the occasion of its Platinum Jubilee. She is on the Editorial Advisory Board of *Gender and History, Indian Economic and Social History Review, Indian Journal of Gender Studies* and *Women's History*

G.L. MEHTA
A Many Splendoured Man

Aparna Basu

CONCEPT PUBLISHING COMPANY, NEW DELHI-110059

ISBN 81-7022-891-3

First Published 2001

Published and Printed by
Ashok Kumar Mittal
Concept Publishing Company
A/15-16, Commercial Block, Mohan Garden
New Delhi-110059 (India)
Phones: 5648039, 5649024
Fax: 091–(11)–5648053
E-mail: publishing@conceptpub.com

For
My sisters – Nilanjana and Uma
And our children and grandchildren

GREAT SON OF TYDEUS, *why do you ask of my birth? The generation of men is just like that of leaves. The wind scatters the leaves on the ground but the living wood puts out others as the season of spring comes around. So it is with men: one generation springs up as another passes away.*

Homer The Illiad

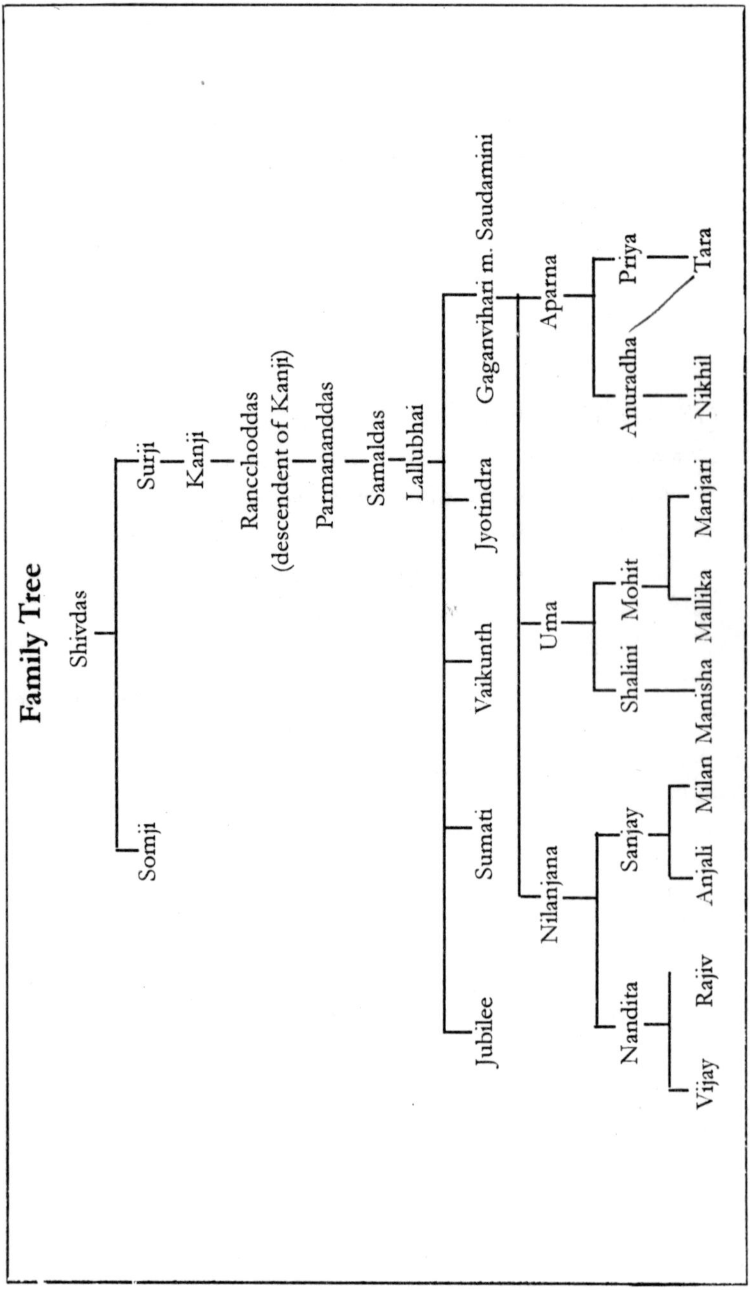
Family Tree
Shivdas
Somji
Surji
Kanji
Rancchoddas
(descendent of Kanji)
Parmananddas
Samaldas
Lallubhai
Jubilee
Sumati
Vaikunth
Jyotindra
Gaganvihari m. Saudamini
Nilanjana
Uma
Aparna
Nandita
Sanjay
Shalini
Mohit
Anuradha
Priya
Vijay
Rajiv
Anjali
Milan
Manisha
Mallika
Manjari
Nikhil
Tara

Foreword

As Chairman of the G.L. Mehta Centenary Celebration Committee and as a personal friend of Mr. Mehta's for over twenty years, I am happy to write this Foreword to his Biography.

I shall mention here a few personal anecdotes to highlight his keen insight, breadth of vision, his idealism interwined with amazing pragmatism, his personal charm and his delicate humour.

I came to the Provisional Parliament in 1950. Shri G.L. Mehta, after a distinguished career in the Private Sector joined as a Member of the Planning Commission. At that time, there was a raging controversy whether India should have a planned economy or only priorities selected for implementation. Dr. John Mathai, who was the Finance Minister, strongly supported the latter point of view. Among the Gandhians, there was a genuine apprehension that Planning will lead to regimentation, rigid controls and re-enactment of the rigours of the Soviet System. Prime Minister Nehru was sold out on a Planned Economy and was nervous of an opposition building up against Planning. I was a fairly vocal member of the Provisional Parliament which then consisted of a Single Chamber with 250 Members. Youngsters had plenty of opportunity to speak in the House. I was a Member of the Standing Finance Committee which in those days, used to approve proposals for expenditure and therefore, well acquainted with Dr. Mathai, the Finance Minister. At the same time, I was a strong supporter of Nehru's Social Legislation, the Special Marriages Act, the Hindu Code Bill and one of the vociferous shouters of the 'Hindi-Chini Bhai Bhai'.

In those days, the Members of Parliament and the Finance Minister used to have a Dinner together on the nights of the Standing Finance Committee and Dr. Mathai spoke to me about his objection to total planning. I was in a fix. I supported the idea of a planned economy. I mildly remonstrated that having missed the Industrial Revolution, we had to accelerate development. A meaningful dialogue was cut short by some other Member intervening at this stage. Soon after Dr. Mathai dissenting from the proposal of a Planned Economy resigned from the Cabinet. Nehru, the true democrat that he was, immediately organised an informal meeting in the Parliament House between the Planning Commission and Members interested in the subject. I met Dr. Deshmukh and G.L. Mehta and others. These two created a deep impression in my mind. G.L. Mehta had a dignified presence, with a suppressed smile all the time on his face with easy and fluent expression, enlivened by soft humour. The Gandhians voiced their familiar views that priority should be given to Cottage and Rural Industries, and Village Development Programmes and expressed their objection to large scale industries. It was G.L. Mehta's turn to take up the issues. Though coming from the large industries sector, Mehta did not take a confrontationist line but soothingly agreed with the Gandhians saying that all these will be taken care of in the Plan and added that a large scale sector is necessary in areas which were beyond the capacity of the rural sector. He said we all want Railways for transport of rural products but engines could not be made in the rural industries sector. He quoted Gandhiji's own statement regarding the railway engines. This is a sample of the manner in which he handled even irate opponents. When it came to my turn, I said we should have a composite industrial policy where large, small and cottage industries should have their appropriate place. This established a rapport between me and G.L. Mehta which ripened to mutual respect and friendship.

In the early fifties, the U.S. Secretary of State, Dulles visited India to persuade India to join the SEATO. India's refusal invited Dulles' wrath and he made a caustic remark that India cannot be non-aligned between Right and Wrong. American hostility towards India took root. The Balance of Power theory equating India and Pakistan in International and in all U.N. affairs, became a sheet anchor of American policy. It was in this climate that G.L. Mehta became the Indian Ambassador to the United States in 1952. His was an uphill task. To sell India to a prejudiced customer is no easy task.

In September 1953, I was chosen as a delegate to the United Nations General Assembly in which Mrs. Vijayalakshmi Pandit was elected President of the General Assembly. During one-week end, I went to Washington and promptly Ambassador Mehta called me for Lunch. Then a very interesting conversation lasting almost an hour ensued. I had kept brief notes of the talk. In substance, G.L. Mehta conceded that he had a difficult task that notwithstanding the sullen hostility, he was pushing on visiting various centres and delivering talks. He found that the people were not as much against India as the Government and that he was relentlessly carrying on his campaign. This assignment put to test all the fine qualities that G.L. Mehta possessed. He was true to the definition of a '*Karma Yogi*' who performed his duties regardless of the results achieved. I met him a few more times when G.L. Mehta was Ambassador. I noticed that during his six years in Washington, he was slowly but surely gaining ground. This is borne out by what *Washington Post*, by no means a friendly paper to India wrote about G.L. Mehta: "When he (G.L. Mehta) arrived here in September, 1952, there was much mutual mistrust between the United States and India. A great deal of that mistrust was dispelled as Mr. Mehta travelled extensively throughout the country.

He not only made a number of speeches in which he interpreted India and its policy of neutrality in the troubled Asia of that period to Americans, but also grasped the meaning of American life and aspirations and in turn interpreted them to India.

On his return, he became the Chairman of the ICICI and established the Institute of Financial Management in the then Madras State and I had become the Industries Minister of Madras and our dialogue continued. He was impressed with my composite industrial policy of promoting large medium and small rural industries.

G.L. Mehta was a man of rare charm and wit. He was master of elegant humour which had no trace of malice or britterness. He had the gift of spotting talent and promoting it. H.T. Parekh who was in close touch with me later when I became Finance Minister, had generously acknowledged how much he owed to Sri G.L. Mehta for his success in life.

The lives of great men remind us, we make our life sublime. Shri G.L. Mehta was one such great man of who could make our life sublime.

It is appropriate that a biography of his has been written in the centenary year of his birth by his daughter who is an eminent historian.

R. VENKATARAMAN
Former President of India

New Delhi
Dated: 17-04-2000

Preface

This is primarily the story of an individual, whose life spanned three quarters of the twentieth century during which India experienced a most remarkable transformation in the political, economic and social spheres. In a way it is also the story of the Indian intelligentsia, the urban middle classes, who came of age and went to school and universities in the thirty years between 1917, the emergence of Mahatma Gandhi on the Indian political scene and 1947 when India attained independence. These young men joined the new professions opened by British rule, entered government service or went into business. The avenues open to them however were limited. My father, Gaganvihari Mehta, or Bapu as we called him (and as I shall refer to him in this book) belonged to this generation and was a product of this transformation . Through his work in business, in government, and in civil society, he was deeply involved in this process of transformation both as an observer and as a participant.

Bapu was born in 1900, at the 'high noon of the Empire' when Queen Victoria was still Empress of India and in the last year of her reign. Lord Curzon was the Viceroy of India. In a life that spanned three quarters of the twentieth century, he witnessed many changes. He was a child before the Wright brothers left the ground at Kittyhawk and lived to see men land on the moon. In the year of his birth Marconi took out his patent for wireless telegraphy. Electricity, telephones and motorcars had barely come to India when he was born. Bapu lived through two World Wars, the Russian Revolution and the complete dissolution of British imperial power.

English education was officially introduced in India in 1835 by Macaulay's famous minute and Bentinck's Resolution that henceforth all government funds would be spent on promoting Western education through English medium. This exposed many Indian families, like my father's, to European thought, literature, philosophy and science. To synthesise Western culture and ideas with one's traditional beliefs and customs was not always easy. Those belonging, for instance, to the 'Young Bengal' group in Calcutta in the 1820s and 1830s, under the influence of Vivian Derozio[1], a young teacher at Hindu College, were completely swept off their feet by Western thought and culture and rejected everything Indian. Rammohun Roy[2], the first social reformer of modern India and the founder of the Brahmo Samaj, accepted Western education and values such as rationalism and humanism but at the same time emphasised the basic truths of Hindu religion and philosophy, discarding all irrational beliefs, idolatry, superstitions and rituals. Orthodox Hindus rejected Rammohun Roy's reformist programme, though they did not oppose British rule or even English education. The encounter with the West thus produced different reactions among different groups. Westernisation was more complete among communities such as the Parsis in Bombay or some Brahmo families in Calcutta. It was less so among the educated Hindus in South India and Western India.

My grandfather, Sir Lallubhai Samaldas joined Elphinstone College, Bombay, the first institution in western India to offer higher education in English but did not complete his graduation.

1. Henry Louis Vivian Derozio (1809-1831), a talented Eurasian teacher of Hindu College, Calcutta; writer, poet; one of the pioneers of the Young Bengal Movement and the Bengal Renaissance.

2. Rammohun Roy (1773-1833), first Indian social reformer in the nineteenth century, often called the 'father of modern India'. Founder of the Brahmo Samaj. Great advocate of women's rights and education. Led the campaign for prohibiting *Sati*.

He was, however, a highly cultivated person. He was an avid reader, built up an excellent personal library of English books and subscribed to The *Guardian*, *Nation* and *Punch*. He and his sons read Shakespeare, nineteenth century English novelists, the Romantic poets, books on politics and philosophy and ordered the latest publications from London. But they did not adopt Western dress, food, manners or habits. Macaulay's education system succeeded in making them Western in intellect and in their political opinions but not, as he had hoped, in their tastes or in their morals, nor in making them eat with cutlery made in Sheffield or wearing clothes made in Manchester. Though steeped in Western literature, Bapu remained quintessentially an Indian and his pride in India and everything Indian was deep. He sincerely cared about what was happening in the country and its progress. If he was depressed about many things in the country towards the end of his life, he was equally proud of any achievements by Indians individually and collectively. In this sense, he characterised a whole class of the Indian intelligentsia whose values represented a synthesis of the old and the new, of Western and Indian thought.

From the late nineteenth century with the foundation of the Indian National Congress in 1885, nationalist ideas began to influence educated Indians. Bapu lived through the various phases of India's independence movement. He was of course too young to remember the *swadeshi* movement against the partition of Bengal in 1905. He, however, accompanied his father to the session of the Indian National Congress held in Karachi in 1913. He remembered being present at the Congress session in Bombay in 1915 where he heard Mahatma Gandhi speaking for the first time. He was a student of Elphinstone college in Bombay when the Home Rule movement was launched by Annie Besant and Lokmanya Bal Gangadhar Tilak in 1917 and he attended public meetings where Annie Besant spoke and was greatly impressed by her oratory. He was still in college when the Rowlatt Bill was passed in 1919 and the *satyagraha* against it was started by Mahatma Gandhi. He was horrified by the Jallianwala Bag massacre in Amritsar, Punjab, where hundreds of unarmed men and women were shot down on General Dyer's orders. In 1921, when Bapu left for England, the *Khilafat* and non co-operation movement was going on. From London, Bapu keenly observed political developments in India. He got from India Gandhiji's weekly journal, *Navjivan* and read it regularly.

Educated Indians were greatly attracted by the industrial and scientific progress made in the West, and admired the English legal system and modern education and held that association with England could bring about progress. On the other hand, they wanted a greater say in the political and economic decision-making process in their own country. Nationalist sentiments became stronger after the coming of Mahatma Gandhi on the political scene in the 1920s. There were conflicts and differences of opinion within families. My grandfather, a close friend of Gopal Krishna Gokhale, was a 'moderate' in his political views, i.e., he believed that India could gradually achieve self government through constitutional means by co-operating with the British, working through the institutions introduced by British rule. In this, he represented an important stratum of Indian opinion which admired the new concepts introduced into the Indian polity by the British, namely, equality before the law, freedom of speech and worship and the maxim that state did not exist for the aggrandisement of a family or caste. Foreign rule, with all its drawbacks, struck them as a necessary stage in the training of the country for self government. My father and his brothers were much more sympathetic to Gandhi's non-co-operation and civil disobedience movements. My father's eldest brother, Vaikunthbhai, Batuk Kaka as we called him, and as I shall refer to him henceforth, was a devoted follower of Gandhi and dedicated his life to

Gandhian constructive work, particularly to *khadi* and village industries. Two of his closest friends were Mahadev Desai[3], Gandhi's Private Secretary and Syed Abdulla Brelvi[4], also an ardent follower of Gandhi.

My parents did not actively participate in any of the *satyagrahas*, but they were deeply emotionally involved in the civil disobedience movement of the 1930s and the Quit India movement in 1942. They had taken to wearing *khadi* and foreign goods never entered our house. They were jubilant and full of hope when India attained independence in 1947. My father was a member of the Constituent Assembly which was drafting a new constitution for a free India. I was fortunate to accompany him to Delhi to witness the historic transfer of power ceremony on 15 August 1947, 'at the stroke of the midnight hour' in the hall of Parliament House and see 'India awake to life and freedom'. At dawn on 15 August we saw the Union Jack being lowered and India's national flag being hoisted on the Red Fort by Jawaharlal Nehru. Batuk Kaka, who was by then Finance Minister of Bombay, was present at the Gateway of India to bid farewell to the last British regiment as it left India. Though my parents never went to jail, their sympathies had been entirely with the national movement. They had close personal relationships with Gandhiji, Sardar Vallabhbhai Patel, Jawaharlal Nehru and many other leaders of the Indian National Congress.

Bapu had a vision of a free, industrialised, modern India. He shared the nationalist view that British rule had stifled the growth of Indian business and industry. In the pre-independence period, he took up the cause of Indian shipping. As President of the Indian Chamber of Commerce in Calcutta in 1939-40 and of the Indian Federation of Commerce and Industry in 1942-43, he urged for greater control by Indians in shaping the

3. Mahadev Desai, (1892-1942), Private Secretary of Mahatma Gandhi.
4. Syed Abdulla Brelvi (1891 - 1949), Editor, *Bombay Chronicle*, a nationalist Muslim.

country's economic policy. While he had refused to accept any government post under British rule, he accepted the chairmanship of the Tariff Board after independence in 1947. In 1950 he became a member of the first Planning Commission. In the 1960s and 1970s, he became somewhat sceptical of the license permit *raj* and bureaucratic controls over the economy. After his return from the United States in 1958, where he had served as India's Ambassador for six years, he took up the chairmanship of ICICI and helped in setting up the first industrial development bank in the country. He was also the first chairman of Indian Investment Centre.

This book incidentally also shows how a traditional family gradually transformed itself and was inducted into the modern world. This pattern was repeated in many families, reflecting the emergence of a new urban middle class under British rule. My grandfather's horizon widened when he moved from the princely State of Bhavnagar to Bombay and started participating in numerous public activities. His business associates as well as personal friends were drawn from various castes, communities and religions. My father's ideas and attitudes changed even more because he spent a year in London, two years in Rangoon, twenty in Calcutta and nearly six in Washington. My mother came from a family of social reformers. While higher education for boys came to be gradually accepted as the common pattern rather than an exception among urban middle class families, my parents encouraged the higher education of their three daughters and sent them abroad for studies, two to the United States and one to Cambridge, England. They did not object to their marrying outside their caste and community.

The book has also something to say about the world of business and politics in India of the 1920s, 1930s and 1940s. The connection between businessmen and the Indian National Congress has been the subject of considerable historical interest. Bapu's views and activities show the close and intimate relationship between businessmen and Congress leaders. With the growing clash of interests between British and Indian business after the First World War and the increasing strength of Indian nationalism, Indian businessmen and nationalists depended on each other for many things. The book also throws light on the growth of the Indian press and of English language newspapers and magazines edited and published by Indians that were critical of British rule and played a crucial role in the freedom movement. The book touches upon the setting up of the Tariff Board and the Planning Commission in independent India. It deals with Indo-U.S. relations in the 1950s and the establishment of the first development bank in India.

This attempt to write a biography of my father is perhaps the most challenging task I have ever ventured to undertake. I hesitated for some time after the idea was first suggested to me. To write a dispassionate biography of one's own father is a difficult task. The material available was also limited. There were some letters written by Bapu to his father and brothers from London and later from Delhi and Calcutta. The diary he kept during his Washington days is unfortunately rather dull and mostly a record of his appointments. He recorded an interview with the Oral History Section of the Nehru Memorial Museum and Library but it covers the period only until 1947. Despite all this, eventually my interest in the subject overcame my caution and the presumption of the task. Moreover, Bapu never wrote his own autobiography. "Many people ask me why I did not write my reminiscences," he wrote, "I do not think I have done anything so extraordinary as to record the events of my life. Not that ordinary people cannot also write their memoirs; they might at times be even more interesting. Nor have I the necessary leisure. I am so absorbed in my present activities, whatever their worth, that I hardly find time to recall the past except spasmodically."

I undertook the task of writing this biography, in the centenary year of Bapu's birth, because I felt that it would be interesting for his grand-children whom he loved so dearly, and for his great grand-children, who never saw him, to discover their roots. As a historian, I was also interested in portraying Bapu's growing up in pre-Independence India and subsequently his life and work in the post-Independence era. I believe that this book will, in a way, contribute to our understanding of modern India.

I am grateful to the Nehru Memorial Museum and Library for all the help I received while consulting the private papers of my father, my uncle, V.L. Mehta and S.A. Brelvi which are lodged in the manuscript section there. I must also thank the World Bank for allowing me to look at some records in its archives in Washington. I also consulted some Congressional records in the Library of Congress, and the printed volumes and files of the 'Foreign Relations of the United States' in the State Department Archives in Washington. Bapu's conversations with John Foster Dulles, U.S. Secretary of State, is in the Dulles Archives. The Chapter 'Foundation of Planning Commission' is based on an interview Bapu gave of his experience with the Planning Commission, which I found, among his papers. The Chapter 'Building a Financial Institution' is almost entirely in Bapu's own words from a piece be wrote entitled 'My years with ICICI'. I am grateful to Mr. William Diamond for sharing some of his memories of ICICI with me and for allowing me to quote from an article he wrote about Mr. H.T. Parekh. The quotations in the book are from Bapu's letters, diaries, articles, U.S. State Department archives, World Bank archieves, Brelvi Papers, V.L. Mehta Papers and U.S. Congressional Records, though they have not been cited in footnotes.

I must thank my husband, Prahlad, my sisters Nilanjana and Uma, my brother-in-law Dr. Subhas Dhar , my daughters Anuradha and Priya and my nephew Ashish Mehta for reading the manuscript and for their valuable suggestions. I am most grateful to Shri Ashok Kumar Mittal of Concept Publishing Company for offering to publish this book in such a short time. I am well aware that this biographical account of my father's life and times is sketchy and incomplete.

APARNA BASU

New Delhi
28 November, 2000

CONTENTS

1

Growing Up

Gaganvihari was the youngest of the three sons of Sir Lallubhai Samaldas who belonged to the princely state of Bhavnagar in Kathiawar or Saurashtra, now part of Gujarat. Bhavnagar was a state in the Kathiawar Political Agency of Bombay Presidency with an area of 2,860 sq. miles. It was bound in the north by Ranpur, Ahmedabad district and the Panchal; on the east by the Gulf of Cambay and the Dhandhuka taluka of Ahmedabad; on the south by the Arabian Sea and on the west by Sorath and Halar. The city of Bhavnagar was named after Maharaja Bhavsingh I who founded it in 1723. He belonged to the *chandravanshi* – moonborn – Rajput warrior clan that had moved to these parts from the northern regions almost a millennium earlier and his ancestors had been rulers of the area for hundreds of years. Bhavnagar was fortunate in having two enlightened rulers in the latter part of the nineteenth century. The Samaldas family had an unbroken connection with the state for nearly a hundred years. Lallubhai's elder brother, Vithaldas, their father, Samaldas and grandfather, Parmananddas had all served as Dewans (Chief Ministers) of Bhavnagar. Parmananddas's father Rancchoddas was a *karbhari* of the state, the position and function of which office was similar to those of the Dewan of later days. So for four generations the family had supplied Dewans to Bhavnagar. The family was known as the *das* (meaning servant or subordinate) family, possibly because they were servants of the state. Lallubhai's sons adopted the surname Mehta as it was customary among the British to have surnames. Mehta literally means a teacher in Gujarati. My father's two elder brothers addressed him as Gagandas. Lallubhai's was one of the leading families of Bhavnagar and their *haveli* (family house) was located in Dewanpura, the best residential locality in the city. The Percival Fountain was in Dewanpura close to the *haveli*.

The family was Vadnagra Nagar by caste. Traditionally there are four *varnas* or castes among the Hindus, viz., Brahmins (priests), Kshatriyas (warriors), Vaishyas (traders) and Shudras (peasants and other low castes). However, within each of these, there are innumerable *jatis* or sub-castes, often linked to occupation or place of origin. The castes are ranked hierarchically according to their ritual purity. Members of a higher caste will not marry or eat with those from lower castes. In Gujarat, Nagars are ranked as the highest caste. There are five kinds of Nagars– Vadnagra, Visnagra, Prashnora, Sadhodra and Krashmora. The first two came from the towns of Vadnagar and Visnagar which are about fifteen miles apart from each other in northern Gujarat. The roots of Nagars are clouded in mystery but they possibly gelled as a culturally identifiable group sometime after Alexander the Great's invasion of India in early 4th century BC. A group of Nagars camped in Vadnagar near Mehsana around 140 A.D., although it was not known by that name till much later. From the end of the first millennium, living here became unsafe as invaders coming from the west and north-west passed through the town. As a result the Nagars began to move to safer cities. They sought jobs in various professions, which required good education, an asset they possessed even then. Vadnagra Nagars considered the highest among the Nagars, are again divided into two sub castes – *Grihastha* and Brahmin, who could inter-dine but not inter-marry. Rancchoddas' family was *Grihastha* and was considered superior to the Nagar Brahmins who in Bhavnagar were traditionally cooks and priests. In Rancchoddas' family the cooks were always Nagar Brahmins right upto the time of Lallubhai and his two elder sons. The cooks could also act as priests and were treated with great respect. Nagars were the most literate caste in Gujarat. Since they served in the courts of Muslim princes, they learnt Persian and later when English became the official language, they switched to learning English.

Many Nagars from Vadnagar moved to Ghogha, an ancient port on the Gulf of Cambay (Khambhat or Kutch), in the Dhandhuka taluk of Ahmedabad about ten miles from Bhavnagar. It was a busy port on the Western coast of India from which sailing vessels carried men and goods far and wide across the Indian Ocean to Africa and the Persian Gulf. The natives of the town were reckoned to be the best sailors in India. Ever since Ghogha became a flourishing port, Nagars had settled there. There is a saying in Gujarati '*Lanka ni ladli ne Ghogha no var*' (a bride from Lanka and a groom from Ghogha) which indicates that men from Ghogha married girls from the different countries they visited. After Surat became the chief port of Gujarat, the Cambay ports, including Ghogha, suffered.

The earliest ancestor of the Samaldas family whose name we can trace is Shavdas who had two sons, Somji and Surji, both of whom acquired fame in the Mughal army. It used to be said that Nagars were skilled in *kalam*, *kadcchi* and *barcchi*, i.e. writing, cooking and fighting. Surji had three sons, the youngest of whom was Kanji. Rancchoddas was a descendant of Kanji and was born in 1723 in Ghogha, then a part of the Mughal Empire. He had heard that Damanji II, Gaekwad, ruler of the princely state of Baroda, had a high regard for Nagars as administrators and soldiers and so he left for Baroda, joined Damanji's army, fought bravely in many battles and impressed the Gaekwad by his courage, skill, intelligence and loyalty. The Gaekwad's army included many Arab soldiers and he needed officers whom both the Marathas and the Arabs could trust. The Arab General, Abud Manani suggested to Damanji that this difficult task should be entrusted to Rancchoddas. Apart from his various other duties, Rancchoddas was asked to deal with and maintain the accounts of payment made to Arab troops, a task, which he performed with great success and earned the trust and respect of both the king and the Arabs. He was appointed a member of the Council of Ministers which advised Damanji and in 1762 was offered the Dewanship of Baroda at a time when the Gaekwad's power in Gujarat was more than that of the Peshwas, the rulers of the Maratha Empire after the death of Shivaji. But Rancchoddas declined. In 1768, Damanji died and when a dispute over his succession broke out, Rancchoddas resigned and returned to Ghogha.

Bhavnagar, in the 1760s, was a small state ruled by Bhavsinghji's son, Rawal Akheraji, who in order to increase the prosperity of the state invited some Nagars from Ghogha to come and settle there. In 1772, Bhavsinghji's grandson, Wakhatsinghji succeeded to the chiefship. Among those he invited was Rancchoddas who came and settled in Bhavnagar around 1778-1780. He built houses for himself and his brothers in the *Nagarpol*, near Himja Mata's temple. His house was eight or ten minutes distance from the sea and across from his house was the *Hatkeshwar* temple, *Hatkeshwar* or Shiva being the deity Nagars worshipped. He, together with his family and friends, tried their very best to increase the trade and prosperity of Bhavnagar.

In 1783, a strange incident took place in Rancchoddas' house in Bhavnagar. The Arab General, Abud Manani, whom Rancchoddas had known in Baroda came to visit him together with many of his Arab soldiers on their way to Mecca to perform *haj*. As they were sitting in the courtyard, Abud Manani took out his sword and started waving it around to everyone's amazement and fear. He then got up and struck the sword against a wooden pillar, took out a piece of wood, smelt it repeatedly and nodded his head. When asked what he was doing, Abud replied that he had been told in Baroda that Rancchoddas had made so much money that he had sandalwood pillars in his house and so he had wanted to find out whether this was true. He offered a large sum of money to Rancchoddas to apologise for doubting his honesty but the latter refused saying that he had enough money for himself and his family and needed no more. He introduced Abud to the Maharaja who wanted Arab soldiers to fight the *Kolis* (tribals) who were raiding villages and harassing traders.

Rancchoddas thus served as a close adviser to the rulers of Baroda and Bhavnagar and revealed his talents as a soldier, diplomat, administrator and trader. He died in 1796 leaving behind a daughter and two sons, the younger of whom was Parmananddas.

Parmananddas was born in Ghogha in 1794. His mother died when he was a mere child and his elder sister, Juthibai, who like many Nagar women was a very capable woman, brought him up. Nagar women did not observe *purdah*. A great deal of lawlessness prevailed in Saurashtra at this time, with the result that indigenous schools had declined. In any case village schools imparted only an elementary knowledge of reading, writing and arithmetic. The wealthier classes in the cities – business and professional families – employed Brahmin teachers for their boys. English education had not yet come into vogue. Juthibai took great pains to see that her brother got the best education possible and employed a Qazi to teach him Persian. When he was 14, Parmananddas was married to Rajula, the sister of Gaurishankar Udayshankar Oza, C.I.E., a distinguished Dewan and administrator, who built up Bhavnagar State. Parmananddas had four sons, the youngest of whom was Samaldas.

Parmananddas was a shrewd businessman and a farsighted administrator. Ghogha came under British rule after the defeat of the Marathas by the British and the Treaty of Bassein in 1818. The East India Company tried to revive its trade, which had collapsed under Peshwa rule. Parmananddas played an important role in this and his own firm prospered in Ghogha and Bhavnagar. Bhavnagar faced many problems and the young ruler, Maharaja Vajesinhji often consulted Parmananddas and borrowed money from him as well as other shroffs (indigenous money lenders) from Baroda and Ahmedabad in return for which he gave them land, the revenue from which was theirs.

Bhavnagar was under great financial pressure as the British were raising their revenue demands. In addition, the Koli attacks continued. In these troubled times, the Maharaja made Parmananddas the Dewan in 1828 and he held this office till his death in 1850. There is a family lore that once when Parmananddas and a wealthy friend from Ahmedabad, were riding on horseback together, along a practically deserted road from Bhavnagar to a neighbouring city, on a hot summer afternoon, they heard a cry for help from the wilderness. At some distance from the main highway, they found an old woman, a *charni*, belonging to the community of royal bards, in great pain lying on the ground and wanting water. As they had just enough water for themselves, the friend was reluctant to share any with this woman. But Parmananddas gave up his share without any hesitation. Thereupon the woman looked at him with a great sense of kindness and foretold that for this humane act his progeny would gain fame for several generations to come. The story goes that in later years, fortune slipped away from the wealthy friend who spent his last years in dismal poverty and loneliness in Ahmedabad.

Parmananddas took away some villages from the *Bharvatias* (tribals) of Khuman as punishment and a warning for those tribes who were attacking native states. He introduced a new system of revenue farming as a result of which farmers started growing cash crops like cotton and sugar and soon a class of rich peasants emerged. Parmananddas played an important role in the financial negotiations between the Bombay government and the princely state of Bhavnagar when the former was continually raising its revenue demands. He also tried to develop the port of Bhavnagar. Parmananddas was gifted with the art of settling disputes between different parties whether between the British and the Indian Princes, between business partners or between caste members. On his death, his brother-in-law, Gaurishankar Oza succeeded him as Dewan. When Oza retired, instead of recommending his son as Dewan he selected his nephew, Parmananddas' son, Samaldas to be Dewan. Samaldas was thus appointed Dewan in 1877 when Takhtsinghji was on the throne. His son Bhavsingh II succeeded him. Much of Bhavnagar's early civic works – administrative buildings, roads, railways – were built during the rule of these two princes who did much to modernise the state. In Samaldas' time Bhavnagar was a small but proud 'jewel in the crown' and boasted of a three hundred strong cavalry which was with stately pride called the Imperial Service Lancers!

It was a matter of great pride among the Nagar community that Samaldas' head coachman was a European. When the family went to Ahmedabad for his son Lallubhai's wedding, the neighbourhood turned out *en masse* to see not only the handsome bridegroom and his beautiful wife but also the European coachman This was the talk of the town especially in *lakha patel ni pol* where most Nagars of Ahmedabad lived in those days.

Samaldas was educated at first in a local school in Ghogha and later in a school started by the British government under the supervision of a 'trained' teacher. He became a great Persian and Sanskrit scholar and when he died in 1884 and a memorial had to be erected for him, his son Lallubhai suggested that the best memorial would be a college and it was at his suggestion that Samaldas College was established in Bhavnagar. An Englishman, R. Proctor Sims who was the Public Works Councillor, constructed the college. The Maharaja gave Samaldas the village of Jalalpur as a gift for the services he had rendered to the state. Lallubhai's sons surrendered this village voluntarily to the government after independence, without demanding any compensation, as they were opposed to the *zamindari* system and absentee landlords.

Samaldas' elder son, Vithaldas succeeded him as Dewan and held this office till 1900. His younger brother, Lallubhai entered the service of the rulers of Bhavnagar at the age of 18 when his father was still Dewan and his elder brother was Chief Revenue Commissioner. At first, he was assigned the task of helping the Dewan and the Private Secretary to the Maharaja in various tasks. He took special interest in the political and revenue departments and when his brother became Dewan, Lallubhai was elevated to the post of Revenue Commissioner or what we would today call Revenue Minister in charge of agriculture and land revenue, a post which he held for fifteen years. That was the beginning of his deep interest in revenue matters, famine relief and agricultural problems that later blossomed into his interest in the co-operative movement. He was one of the pioneers of the co-operative movement in India and was responsible for establishing one of the earliest co-operative societies in Kheda district in Gujarat. Under his supervision, vast tracts of wasteland were brought under cultivation and he encouraged the cultivation of sugarcane. Under the revised land revenue settlement and a new revenue code introduced by him, the revenue of Bhavnagar State increased.

Lallubhai studied at Samaldas College while serving as a state officer. He went to attend classes in a carriage drawn by two horses in great style. He then went to study at Elphinstone College in Bombay, then the premier educational institution in Western India but never obtained his B.A. degree. The Maharaja feared that if Lallubhai obtained a university degree he would leave Bhavnagar and go away to British India and so he asked him not to appear for his examination and return home. Lallubhai had filled up his examination form but such was their loyalty to the state that he could not think of disobeying the Maharaja's wishes. Lallubhai, however, continued his interest in classical Sanskrit literature as well as in English literature and built up an excellent library.

In 1899, when Lallubhai was still Revenue Commissioner, he had some differences with the new Maharaja Bhavsinhji. Lallubhai wrote: "October 25, 1899 is engraved in my memory. We were in the midst of the 'severest famine of the century', as Lord Curzon called it. As Chief Revenue Officer, I was in charge of relief measures to help agriculturists tide over the difficulties of scarcity of food, fodder and water. I had done office work from 7 in the morning and was resting after my morning meal at 11 a.m. A man came with a message from His Highness that he wanted me immediately. The Maharaja spoke appreciatively of the services rendered by the Samaldas family to the state but said that the good relationship between the family and the state could continue if I resigned." Without even asking why he was being asked to resign, Lallubhai simply handed over his letter of resignation. Vithaldas, who had served as Dewan for fifteen years, refused to sign his brother's resignation letter and handed over his own resignation. Thus ended the family's official connection with Bhavnagar that had begun in the 1780s. Bapu thus never lived in Bhavnagar but all through his life he had a deep sense of affection and loyalty to it and in his early years often visited it. Lallubhai had never dreamt of leaving Bhavnagar or of any career outside state service. At 36, he felt that the world had crashed at his feet. He had a choice between moving to Ahmedabad, which he knew a little because of his wife's family being there or to Bombay that was quite unknown. The existence of his father's estate meant that he had no financial troubles. He could have retired to a life of leisure. But he was young and full of ideas. He chose to go to Bombay as he felt that it offered a greater challenge and wider opportunities. It was initially in Bombay that capital, accumulated through trade mainly with China, found a fruitful outlet in a genuinely capitalist indigenous textile industry. Raw cotton was easily available from the Deccan that was opened up by railways and British businessmen in India showed little interest in a textile industry that would compete with Manchester. The rise of textile mills in Bombay, owned and managed by Indians, was causing acute alarm in Lancashire, and the unfair excise policies imposed from London formed one of the major stimuli for the growth of patriotic consciousness among the businessmen and intelligentsia of Bombay.

Lallubhai moved to Bombay in 1900, the year Bapu was born. He hardly knew anyone in Bombay but had an introduction from his brother, Vithaldas, to Vijbhukandas Atmaram, regarded as a 'merchant prince' (father of Sir Chunilal Mehta[1], who later became a close friend of the family). Vijbhukandas introduced him to the business community of Bombay and it was on his advice that he took up the business of a banker and a guarantee broker to Gyzi and Kleinjing, a Swiss firm established in Manchester. One of Lallubhai's earliest ventures was to import cotton piecegoods. He soon became a well-known figure in Bombay's commercial world. There were hardly any Indian banks then and Lallubhai and a few others felt the need for it as it was difficult for Indian entrepreneurs to secure loans from British banks. The Bank of India was, therefore, started and Lallubhai was one of its founder directors. For about five or six months he worked in the Bank every day in an honorary capacity. Lallubhai and his colleagues wanted to prove that a bank managed by Indians could be efficiently and successfully run. Lallubhai remained a Director of the Bank of India till he resigned in 1921-22 to become Chairman of the

Bank of Baroda, a position that he held till 1935. Like banking, insurance was another sector exclusively European. Lallubhai wanted Indians to enter this area also and was founder Director and Chairman of the Bombay Life Insurance Corporation, originally called Swadeshi Life Insurance Corporation. Its name was changed after the *swadeshi* movement in Bengal (launched in 1905 against Curzon's partition of Bengal), perhaps because it was felt that this might give the impression that it was revolutionary in character.

Lallubhai established one of the earliest cement companies in India in Porbunder in 1913. That company still exists as part of the Associated Cement Company. He started the Bhavnagar Electric Supply Corporation which till today supplies electricity to Bhavnagar. He established the Nura Valley Sugar Company near Poona in 1921-22. Unfortunately, sugar was not a protected industry and the factory had to close down. He thought of setting up a paper factory in Burma in 1916-17 and went to Rangoon for this purpose. The scheme did not materialise but in Calcutta he met Sir Rajendra Nath Mukherjee[2] of Martin Burn and Company who was obviously very impressed by Lallubhai and made him a Director of two of their Light Railways, one in Assam and the other in Bihar. Through Fardunji M. Dastur, Professor of Mathematics at Samaldas College, Bhavnagar and later at Elphinstone College, Bombay, Lallubhai came to know Barjorji Padsha, a close confidante of Jamshedji Tata. Barjorji introduced him to Tata who made Lallubhai a Director of Tata Iron and Steel Company, of all three Tata's Hydro Electric projects which supply power to Bombay, as well as of Tata's Textile Mill in Ahmedabad. During the First World War, Lallubhai established an India Industrial Syndicate but it did not progress much. Lallubhai together with Sir Manmohandas Ramji, Chairman of the Bombay Native Piecegoods' Association, Sir Dinshaw Wacha[3], Sir Ibrahim Rahimtoola[4], Sir Vithaldas Thackersey[5], Sir Fazalbhoy Currimbhoy[6] and Sir

Purshottamdas Thakurdas[7] established the Indian Merchants' Chamber in Bombay in 1907.

Till the end of the First World War, Indian shipping as such did not exist. The War had, however, brought home to all maritime companies the importance of building their own shipping power. Moreover, the ideal of economic nationalism and the spirit of national enterprise had stirred the hearts of Indian entrepreneurs to build up new industries in India. Lallubhai had a vision of India's commercial and industrial development and dreamt of the country's industrialisation. He wanted to increase India's productive powers and develop the technical skills of Indians. This was a dream shared also by his youngest son.

Walchand Hirachand[8], a contractor, who later became Chairman of Premier Construction Co. Ltd. and of Premier Automobiles Ltd. and a leading industrialist of Western India, came to know that His Highness the Maharaja Scindia of Gwalior had decided to sell the hospital ship, S. S. Loyalty at the end of the First World War. He rushed to Lallubhai's office and told him in confidence that the ship could be bought for Rs. 25,00,000 and that he intended to form a syndicate of four consisting of himself, Lallubhai, Narottam Morarji and Kilachand Devchand. Lallubhai consulted two of his business friends, Sir David Sassoon and Sir Shapurji Bharucha, both of whom advised him to stay out of the syndicate. Lallubhai, however, excited by the idea of an Indian shipping company, disregarded the advise of his two friends, and in a spirit of adventure agreed to join. Thus the first and what was to become the biggest Indian shipping company, the Scindia Steam Navigation Company, was launched on 27 March, 1919.

Lallubhai's own business ventures did not succeed because of his lack of business acumen, faulty judgement of people and reposing confidence and trust in wrong men. He lacked the ruthlessness of a capitalist entrepreneur and was too kind to sack incompetent men. He had the vision but lacked the practical qualities necessary for running a successful business venture. Government policy also did not make it easy for Indian industries to flourish.

Lallubhai's business friends were drawn from all communities, Parsis, Jews, Jains and Hindus. They included Barjorji Padshah, Shapurji Bharucha who were Parsis, David Sassoon, a Jew, Chunilal Mehta, Purshottamdas Thakurdas, Hindus and many others. By the time of his death, he was director of 40 to 50 companies. Industrialists eagerly sought him partly because of his contacts with rulers of Indian princely states who had ready cash for investment. He was widely respected for the integrity, honesty and gentility that he brought into Bombay's commercial life. Jokingly, he used to say that even though he was in business, he could look upon it as a Brahmin and not as a Vaisya.

Lallubhai's interests were not confined to business and industry. Among his close friends were K. Natarajan[9], editor of the *Indian Social Reformer* which Lallubhai helped financially and which he and his sons regularly read, Fardoonji Dastur, Professor of Mathematics and later Registrar of Bombay University and Barjorji Padshah. Natarajan, Dastur and Padshah all stayed in Bandra, then a quiet suburb of Bombay. Lallubhai also moved to Andheri, another suburb, in 1911 after Gaganvihari had typhoid and also perhaps he wanted a change of scene after his wife Satyavati's death in 1907. These friends formed a study circle and used to meet every Sunday to read and discuss books. They read the plays of Shaw and Ibsen, the poems of Browning, Tennyson and the works of many other authors, playwrights and poets.

As noted above, another of Lallubhai's interest was the co-operative movement and he served on the Indian Co-operative Committee appointed in 1914 by the Government of India under the chairmanship of Sir Edward McLagan who was afterwards

Lt. Governor of Punjab. Lallubhai was Chairman of the Co-operative Committee appointed by the Mysore state in 1920-21. He was one of the promoters and later Chairman of the Bombay Provincial Co-operative Bank. He was also an active member and President of the Bombay Provincial Co-operative Institute and the first President of the National Co-operative Union in 1929.

Politically, Lallubhai was a liberal moderate, a follower of Gopal Krishna Gokhale[10] (1866-1915), a great patriot, whom Gandhiji described as his political *guru*. Gokhale had faith in the British system of justice, its upkeep of law and order and the administrative unity that the *Raj* had helped to achieve. The best course open to the country, according to him, was to utilise the opportunities offered by British rule, such as Western education and democratic institutions, before graduating to the goal of self-government. Gokhale became a close friend of my grandfather. Among his political associates was Sir Chimanlal Setalvad[11], a distinguished lawyer. He knew Pherozeshah Mehta[12] though he opposed him on the Land Revenue Amendment Bill for the purpose of restricting the agriculturists' right of alienating their land. Lallubhai tried to understand Pherozeshah's views but with his own experience of land revenue affairs in Bhavnagar could not agree with them. Pherozeshah regarded this as a grave defection by one of his followers.

Lallubhai attended the 1905 session of the Indian National Congress in Benares over which Gokhale presided. In those days an Indian Industrial Conference used to be held along with the Congress session. Ramesh Chandra Dutt[13], ICS, who was later Dewan of Baroda, presided over the Industrial Conference in 1905. Bapu, together with his father, attended the session of the Indian National Congress held in Karachi in 1913. In that year Lallubhai presided over the Indian Industrial Conference and in his speech said, "There never was a time when there was greater need for a strong and informed expression of Indian opinion." My father recalled: "I remember we went by steamer from Bombay and that was my first sea voyage...That was the first time I saw Jinnah. He was on the steamer and I was very young – only 13 years old – and was very struck by the immaculate way in which he used to dress in Western attire. He would not talk much to anybody. He had always a kind of hauteur. But what we found most amusing was that at 5 O'clock when he would come out after his nap and tea, he used to put on an evening hat on the steamer!" He also recalled that "Lala Lajpat Rai[14], who had just returned from America was supposed to speak and his name was on the programme. But instead of him, through some error, Rambhuj Dutt Chaudhuri, an Arya Samajist and nationalist leader of Lahore and husband of Sarla Devi Chaudhurani[15], niece of Rabindranath Tagore, was asked to speak. He received such a tremendous ovation that for some time he did not understand the reason till he realised that people had mistaken him for Lajpatrai. I heard Lajpatrai speak for the first time here."

The second time Bapu attended a Congress session was again with his father in 1915 in Bombay where he heard Gandhiji speaking for the first time. "I was a student but we attended the Congress meeting which was presided over by Lord Sinha[16]. I still remember how thrilled I was when I heard Surendranath Banerjea[17] speak. He said that the reception the President of the Congress had received was something which even kings might envy. Gandhiji had just returned from South Africa after his heroic struggle and received a tremendous ovation. In those days there were no microphones or loudspeakers. Gandhiji spoke almost inaudibly and we were all disappointed by his speech. We wondered whether this was the man of whom we had heard so much...Subsequently I went along with my father to see Gandhiji and I remember that Gandhiji was trying to explain his ideas about the amelioration of the condition of the Depressed Classes. I think he said that it was C.F. Andrews[18] who had suggested that they were not the Depressed Classes; it was not the correct term to use and he added, I would rather call them the suppressed classes. We sat on the floor with Gandhiji and listened. That was my first meeting with Gandhiji."

While Lallubhai had the greatest personal regard for Gandhiji, he did not approve of the non co-operation movement, which was launched by Gandhiji in 1921 that advocated the boycott of government schools and colleges, law courts and offices. He, therefore, did not attend Congress sessions after 1920. But he gradually changed his political opinion and in 1930 during the Civil Disobedience movement and Salt Satyagraha his sympathies were with Gandhiji. He went out of his way to help several families whose breadwinners had gone to jail. He would regularly visit them and see what could be done to assist them. Mahadev Desai and Syed Abdulla Brelvi who were his son Vaikunthbhai's closest friends and were like members of Lallubhai's family were in jail and Lallubhai wrote to them and visited them. Lallubhai went to Guruvayur temple in Kerala at the time of Gandhiji's fast for allowing *Harijans* (untouchables) entry into the temple and met the Zamorin, the ruler of Calicut there. On his return, he reported to Gandhiji who was very pleased by this and said "If an orthodox Hindu like Lallubhai, who was old in years and occupying such an eminent position could be converted to such an extent, then my efforts on behalf of Harijans have not been in vain."

The Morley Minto Reforms of 1909 abandoned the official majority in the provincial legislatures and enlarged them as well, and provided that most of the non-official members should be elected directly, for Muslims and landholders, or indirectly by recognised local interest groups such as trade associations and universities. Lallubhai was a nominated member of the Bombay Legislative Council from 1910-1912. In 1920, under the new constitution introduced by the Montague – Chelmsford reforms he stood for a seat in the Imperial Council of State as an

Independent Candidate and was elected. He together with Sir Pheroze Sethna, a Parsi industrialist and Mr. Kamath, a lawyer represented Bombay. In the Imperial Council he was an Independent and did not join any party. Soon after he was elected, he moved a resolution, which created quite a stir. It was a resolution on fiscal autonomy demanding that fiscal policy should be determined not by the British but by the Indian Central Legislature. The government opposed the resolution and so did Sir Srinivasa Sastri[19] who was then a member of the Council of State. Though the resolution was defeated, the nationalists and the Indian press welcomed it.

Lallubhai was a member of the Bombay University Senate and Syndicate. He was one of the founders of the Sydenham College of Commerce. He was one of the earliest members of the Deccan Education Society which was started in 1884 "to promote the cause of private independent education adapted to the wants of the community, and so cheapened as to come within the reach of children even the lower middle classes." Gokhale was a life member of the DES and when he went to Saurashtra to collect money, Lallubhai helped him.

Thus Lallubhai had a wide range of interests–business, the co-operative movement, banking, insurance, education, social service, literature and politics.

In 1926, Lallubhai went to England to place order for a ship to be built at Glasgow. Previously, Scindias had purchased only second-hand ships. On his arrival in Southampton, he got the news that he had been knighted and received his knighthood in person in Buckingham Palace from King George V. Lallubhai later recalled that he felt that the King was rather amused by his dress. In Europe he wore trousers, a long coat and a turban.

Though Lallubhai was knighted, was a member of the Council of State, mixed with European officials and had business associates and friends from different castes and communities, his personal life was orthodox and traditional. Though 'modern' in his thinking, he was not anglicised. He did not adopt British ways of eating or drinking. At home, the family members spoke Gujarati, ate their meals sitting on wooden stools on the floor (not on a dining table and chairs) and the food was strictly vegetarian, cooked and served by Nagar Brahmin cooks. He sat down for his meals, after a bath, wearing a silk *abotiya (dhoti)* and the sacred thread (*janoi*) which only Brahmins can wear. He never adopted the Western dress but wore a spotless white *dhoti*, a long coat, *dupatta* over it and a Bhavnagree turban – red with a narrow gold border. Once when he was in Calcutta, Sir Rajendra Nath Mukherjee took him to Calcutta Club where in those days only men in suits and ties were allowed. But Lallubhai's presence and personality were so distinguished that the club authorities did not raise any objection despite his Indian dress.

Lallubhai married Satyavati, grand-daughter of Bholanath Sarabhai.[20] Her photographs show that she was beautiful and petite, with fair skin and dark hair. They had seven daughters of whom only two survived into adulthood and three sons. The children had a sheltered life in Bhavnagar belonging as they did to the Dewan's family. They were educated at home by private tutors and each child had a servant attached to him or her. Jubilee, the elder of the two daughters was born in 1887, the year of Queen Victoria's Diamond Jubilee. She was married into a family which did not approve of girls reading and writing and young Jubilee, who had a liberal upbringing and was fond of reading was miserable and died of tuberculosis at the age of 17. The fate of her younger sister, Sumati, born in 1890, was equally tragic. She had little formal education but was taught Sanskrit and English at home by her father and brother,Vaikunthbhai. She was also married into a family where there was great prejudice against women's education. Orthodox Hindus of those times kept their women illiterate since there was a firm belief that the educated woman was destined to be widowed. In such families feelings ran so high against women's education that women were despised and derided if they were found reading. It is indeed surprising that Lallubhai agreed to his two daughters to be married into such families. Apparently it was under pressure from his elder sister or sister-in-law. Ramabai Ranade recalls in her autobiography how all her in-laws made fun of her when her husband, Madhav Govind Ranade, the great social reformer, taught her to read and write at home. Unfortunately, Sumati's husband did not share any of her literary and intellectual interests. Gokhale was very fond of her and introduced her to the plays of Ibsen. Sumati translated 'Doll's House' into Gujarati and dedicated it to Gokhale. Barjorji Padshah introduced her to Browning and she translated 'Saul' into Gujarati and dedicated it to Barjorji. As her married life was unhappy, she started living in her father's house after the death of her mother. To divert her mind, she read Shelley, Keats, Byron, Tennyson, Wordsworth and the Brownings. Apart from 'Doll's House', she adapted four plays of Ibsen into Gujarati, wrote five or six novels, two plays and several poems all between the age of 16 and 21. At the age of 16, she developed intestinal tuberculosis and died when she was only 21. A collection of her poems *Hriday Jharna* (Springs from the Heart), dedicated to her three brothers was published posthumously.

The eldest of the three sons, Vaikunthbhai (1891-1964) was ten years old when the family moved from Bhavnagar to Bombay. In his family circle and by intimate friends, he was called Batuk, meaning short, an appropriate name for him since he was short in height. We children called him Batuk Kaka. He studied at the New High School (later called the Bharda Murzban New High School) where he did exceedingly well in his studies. He always used to top his class. He also got both the junior and senior good conduct medal at school for the best-behaved student. After passing his Matriculation , he joined Elphinstone College. In his Previous (First Year) examination he got a first class and won a college scholarship. Soon after, however, he learnt that there was another student, Mahadev H. Desai, who came from some village near Surat and was in poor circumstances. Batuk Kaka went up to Principal Covernton and told him that his scholarship might be transferred to Mahadev Desai. The Principal appreciated this gesture very much. Mahadevbhai got the scholarship but did not know till many years later that the scholarship had been transferred by Batuk Kaka who never mentioned it to him because of his innate modesty. In B.A., Batuk Kaka took up mathematics which was his favourite subject and studied under Prof. Furdoonji M. Dastoor. In the final university examination, he did not get a first class but he got the Ellis Prize for standing first in the university in English.

After leaving college, Batuk Kaka did not join his father's business but undertook to work with Sir Hormusji Wadia on a famine relief committee which had been set up after the 1912 famine in Bombay Presidency. My father felt that if Gokhale had lived, Batuk Kaka would have joined the Servants of India Society, which had been founded by Gokhale in 1905 "to spiritualise public life and fill the heart with love for the country." Its first three members, N.A. Dravid, A.V. Patwardhan and G.K. Devdhar shared these ideals. The objective was to bring together and train a band of selfless and dedicated young men, 'national missionaries', as Gokhale called them. But instead of joining the Servants of India Society, Batuk Kaka joined as manager of the Bombay Provincial Co-operative Bank that had been started by Sir Vithaldas Thackersey and Lallubhai and remained there for 34 years from 1912 to 1946. Batuk Kaka's whole life was dedicated to the co-operative movement and to rural development. In 1916, he was awarded the Kaiser-i-Hind medal for his services to the co-operative movement. However, in 1930, during the Civil Disobedience movement, he returned the medal to the Government of India. He used to send press clippings from nationalist newspapers about the movement to friends in

England such as Agatha Harrison[21]. The CID discovered this and he was called to the office of the Police Commissioner of Bombay for interrogation. It was expected that he might be arrested but no action was taken against him presumably because he had not committed any cognisable crime. He did not go to jail, perhaps in deference to his father's wishes, but worked for *swadeshi* and Harijan uplift. Gandhiji's constructive work programme evoked in him an instinctive response. Gandhiji developed affection and regard for him and assigned to him the work of the khadi and village industries association. Gandhiji wrote an article on him in *Harijan* (11.9.1946) describing him as '*Shruchari* Vaikunth Mehta'. When Mr. B.G. Kher wanted Batuk Kaka to be Finance Minister of Bombay in the Ministry constituted in 1946, he was most reluctant, indeed positively unwilling to take up this assignment. He wrote to Bapu and asked him to go and see Gandhiji, who was then in Calcutta, and try and explain to him why he did not wish to join the Ministry and request Gandhiji not to insist. His contention was that he was a constructive worker and Gandhiji was against constructive workers going in for parliamentary work. He also argued that he had not gone to jail during the various Congress movements and preference should be given to those who had. Bapu went to see Gandhiji at the Khadi Prathishthan Ashram at Shodepur, just outside Calcutta, early one morning. Gandhiji told him that he had received Batuk Kaka's letter but he thought that he should at least stand for election. In 1946, when elections were held to the provincial assemblies, much against his will, Batuk Kaka contested. He wrote to Gandhiji that he had no money to fight an election and the latter asked him to contest without spending anything. He did so and won. Actually, B.G. Kher[22], who became the Chief Minister of Bombay, had already got the consent of Gandhiji and Sardar Patel and Vaikunthbhai's name was included in the panel of Ministers without consulting him. Vallabhbhai told Bapu in Delhi on April 9, 1946, "We have forced Vaikunthbhai to assume office much against his will." Mr. Ramakrishnan, at present Director of the Bharatiya Vidya Bhavan, who was then working as Sardar's Secretary recalls that Batuk Kaka went to Vallabhbhai and asked, "What wrong have I done that you want me to be a Minister?" He was an extremely successful Finance Minister. Sir John Matthai, who for a brief period was Finance Minister at the Centre, told Bapu that Batuk Kaka was the ablest state Finance Minister and could have no doubt continued as a minister but he was genuinely averse to holding any office or wielding power and refused to contest elections a second time. In 1952, he was appointed a member of the Finance Commission and next year of the Taxation Enquiry Commission. When Sir John Matthai was Chairman of the State Bank of India, he appointed Batuk Kaka as Vice-Chairman (1955-57) and from 1957 onwards he was Chairman of the Khadi and Village Industries Commission till his death in 1964. When Batuk Kaka was Finance Minister, he gave away his whole salary for charitable purposes and did not retain anything himself. He did not accept any remuneration as Chairman of the Khadi and Village Industries Board or Commission.

Batuk Kaka's closest and most intimate friend was Syed Abdulla Brelvi , editor of *Bombay Chronicle*. Brelvi, Mahadev Desai and Batuk Kaka were a trio in Elphinstone College and were friends throughout their lives. The friendship between him and Brelvi was something extraordinary. Pandit Motilal Nehru[23] called Brelvi "the fourth son of Sir Lallubhai". When Brelvi passed away, Kher remarked that "Vaikunthbhai and Brelvi were one soul in two bodies". They used to meet almost every evening after office hours and until Brelvi married, he used to go to Andheri every evening by train and after a game of bridge or billiards and sometimes dinner, go back to the *Chronicle* office for work. Brelvi was a Muslim and the eating habits of the family being orthodox, he was served his dinner outside the dining room in a plate on a table. But everyone, as a matter of course, accepted this. Whenever Batuk Kaka or Brelvi were out of Bombay they wrote to each other regularly. After Brelvi's death, he made it a point to visit his widow and children almost every other day and help them in every way he could.

The second brother, Jyotindra (called Khandubhai and Khandu Kaka by us) was quite different in temperament from his elder and younger brothers. He was not interested in politics or public life. He was shy and introvert by nature and basically a family man who was happiest at home. He worked all his life as Manager of the Bombay Life Insurance Corporation. He was fond of reading, painting, astronomy and sports and played tennis, billiards and also bridge.

The three brothers were very close to each other and corresponded regularly when away from each other. After their father died, Batuk Kaka and Khandu Kaka who both lived all their lives in Andheri, kept in touch with Bapu and us in Calcutta through weekly letters. There was a deep sense of family loyalty. When my father had his appendicitis operation in 1940, Batuk Kaka came especially from Bombay for this. From Calcutta we came to Andheri every year during our Diwali holidays. When we moved to Bombay in 1948 as Bapu became President of the Tariff Board, Batuk Kaka who was then Finance Minister of Bombay, came at least two or three times a week in the evening, after office, to see us and the two brothers would often go for a walk. Batuk Kaka would telephone every morning and my father would ring up Khandu Kaka. We went to Andheri almost every weekend when we lived in Bombay.

Bapu was born on 15th April 1900 (on Chaitra Purnima, full moon in the month of Chaitra, according to the Hindu calendar) in Ahmedabad in the *haveli* of Bholanath Sarabhai Divetia, his mother, Satyavati's grandfather. Bholanath Sarabhai's was a distinguished family of Gujarat. Bholanath served in the East India Company as a judicial officer and rose to the rank of a district munsiff, the highest position an Indian could aspire to in those days. After retiring from service, he turned his attention to religious and social reform and became one of the most eminent social reformers of Gujarat and a founder of the *Gujarat Prarthana Samaj*. In 1848, together with Alexander Forbes, a Sessions Judge, he founded the Gujarat Vernacular Society, which served as a pivotal vehicle for education and social reform for decades. The Society opened the first girls' school in Ahmedabad in 1849. It also started a journal, *Buddhi Prakash* which carried articles on subjects pertaining to education and social reform. Bholanath himself was a Sanskrit and Persian scholar and also learnt English. One of his sons, Narsinharao Divetia was a well-known Gujarati poet and literary critic. Another son, Bhimrao, Satyavati's father, was a reputed writer and the author of a long epic poem called *Prithvi Raj Raso* which deals with the story of Prithviraj and Samyukta but the first portion of which is really an eloquent summary in poetry of the early history of India. My father claimed that he inherited his literary talents, particularly his interest in Gujarati literature and ability to write in Gujarati as well as his rational approach, lack of belief in superstitions, rituals, and idol worship from his mother's family.

Though born in Ahmedabad, Bapu grew up in Bombay. His father moved to Bombay the year he was born. "We stayed first is Girgaum, in Chunabhati Lane, what later became Lamington Road, on the first floor of a house on the corner of Lamington Road and Vithalbhai Patel Road. From there we moved to *Saubhag Mahal* one of the first houses on the sea on Walkeshwar Road"; he was to recall later. The building was still there in the 1970s and Bapu often pointed it out to us as we drove along Walkeshwar Road. He remembered how thrilled they were as children to see the rays of the morning sun dancing on the sea waves. "There were little windows in the drawing room which looked like a ticket office and we played train train there."

In those days, almost every year Bombay had a plague epidemic from January to June and those who could afford it went away to the suburbs – Santa Cruz, Bandra, Andheri, etc. which were regarded as health resorts. Local trains to the suburbs had started in 1881. Lallubhai's family moved to Andheri. In those days, Andheri had no electricity, no sewage, schools, shops or telephones. In the evenings when the masters of the house returned from the city by train, their servants used to receive them at the station with lanterns in their hands and they had to cross open fields and walk through woods. Lallubhai purchased a motor car when few people in Bombay had one, its number was 504.

The bungalow in Andheri in which the family lived was huge with a large garden with jack fruit, banana and mango trees and a well. They had a tennis court and a billiard table. The house had a warm and friendly atmosphere and its doors were always open to relatives and friends. Lallubhai was generous to a fault. Cousins, nephews and other relatives from Bhavnagar parked themselves there, some for short periods, others for years while they studied. Relatives came to spend their summer vacations. Everybody was always welcome. Among Lallubhai's friends, Gokhale came frequently, Bapu called him Goklu and used to make him play cricket with him. G.K. Devdhar of the Servants of India Society, Natarajan, Dastoor and Padshah were frequent visitors. Batuk Kaka's friends, Brelvi and Vakil came almost daily.

Bapu's mother died when he was only 7 years old. He remembered this sad occasion till his last days, particularly his sister Sumati's heart rending cries as Satyavati's body was being taken away – "Satyavati, speak once, answer me once". Being young, Bapu could not quite comprehend what was happening and when his father returned from the cremation ground, with tears in his eyes, he clung to him and said "Take me back to Bombay, I don't like it here." He used to say that he did not miss his mother so much because of the affection he got from his father and bothers and also because the house was always full of people and he was never lonely. Despite his very busy public life, Lallubhai had always time for his family and as Bapu was the youngest, he was particularly fond of him and was both father and mother to him.

My father began his schooling in Delvadkar's Kindergarten School and then went to New High School, later called Bharda Murzban New High School. He never liked going to school and frequently complained of stomachache to be excused from going. He went by the local train to school and if he saw any school boys going in the opposite direction from him, hoped that some dignitary had died and it had been declared a holiday! Because of his sister Sumati's illness, they frequently went to Panchgani, Poona or Nasik, as a result of which he missed school and was taught by teachers at home. He, however, developed great regard for Mr. J.D. Bharda, the headmaster of New High School. He heard the news of Bharda's death on board S.S. Morena on his way to England. Feeling very sad, he went out on the deck and gazing at the sky saw Taurus the Bull with the Pleaides "like a swarm of fireflies tangled in a silver braid" as Tennyson called it in 'Lockley Hall'. He wrote home "Bharda who taught us all this and made us feel the immensity of the starry heavens above is no more. No more will he lecture there in the New High School talking on equal terms with the boys, laughing and making them laugh, humble on account of his knowledge, reverencing his pupils as they reverenced him, with no cant in his life – a second father to every student. Pardon me these sad thoughts but I cannot help having them when I think of the beautiful starlets I saw last night after such a long time. Perhaps there is some consolation in the thought that the good he has done will never be destroyed–it remains and will be propagated for all time. He did more good in his life, improved Bombay more than any politician did or capitalist has done. Its fruits may not be visible and so demonstrative but like all educational work, it is slow, permanent and lasting....I felt as if I had lost a beloved and respected member of my family." Later, he was to write, "Bharda Master as we affectionately called him was not only an educationist with ideas and imagination but a stimulating teacher who wanted to prepare students not only for examinations but for life...Bharda was an outstanding educationist and a great teacher which is not the same thing. Along with his colleague the late Mr. K. Marzban, Bharda built up one of the best educational institutions in the city. As a teacher he stimulated the thinking of his students, aroused their intellectual curiosity and inspired them to new heights. Bharda was particularly fond of astronomy. He taught students to gaze at the stars, to recognise constellations and planets and told us about literary allusions about the heavens. I recollect his mentioning the constellation of Pleaides and quoting from Tennyson"

Bapu joined Elphinstone College in June 1917. In those Days, Elphinstone College together with Deccan College, Poona offered the best that was available in Western India in the way of English education. The Principal was then J.C. Covernton. Professor Sisson taught English, Professor Wilkinson, mathematics and Professor Faren, an Irishman, taught history and politics. But the professor who left the most lasting impression on him was J.C. D'Andrade who taught them logic in Intermediate Arts. "D'Andrade asked students to shoot higher, to be interested in the process of thought and insisted on clarity and precision of expression – not cramming for passing examinations. It was not until I was in Intermediate Arts that I loved studying. Until them I liked some subjects like English or History and detested others like Mathematics as taught in First Year in College....One amusing incident I recall is about a class we used to have from 3.45 to 4.30 p.m. to do some exercises in Algebra, Geometry and Trigonometry. Most students did not like this additional class nor I suspect did the tutors who were assigned to supervise. On one occasion, I was on the last bench and instead of doing my work was reading a play by Bernard Shaw. Shri Junarkar who was then our tutor...caught me. But from the Second Year in College, I became interested in ideas as such and wanted to know and learn more. I was excited by debate....In my Intermediate Arts Examination, I stood first in Logic in the University". It was in Elphinstone College that he acquired a taste for English poetry and cultivated an elegant English style, which was to prove a great asset to him in later life.

"When I was in the First Year, a Social Service League was organised which was named after the Principal and called the Covernton Social Service League. One of the persons who was active in organising it was an Assistant Professor, the late M.M. Gidwani. Many of us participated in its activities. We used to go on Saturday afternoons to the Indian Soldiers' Hospital Camp near Marine Lines, where there were wounded Indian soldiers with whom we used to talk and for whom we used to take gifts..." Bapu became Joint Secretary of the League

He writes, "The first year that I joined college was an exciting one, not merely because it was thrilling to be in college but also because of the happenings in the country. The First World War was then going on. Mrs. Annie Besant[24] started the Home Rule Movement[25] and the Government of India interned her along with Mr. B.P. Wadia[26] and Dr. George Arundale[27]. The Government of Bombay issued a circular prohibiting students from attending political meetings. Some of us, however, did not obey this order. I remember having attended some political meetings including one held at China Bag (now Sikkanagar at Vithalbhai Patel Road) which was addressed by several Bombay leaders of those days. We also went round with small Home Rule flags on our coats. We were noticed and this was reported to our Principal but no action was taken against us. I also attended the first Gujarat Provincial Political Conference held at Godhra, which was presided over by Gandhiji. This was indeed Gandhiji's debut in Indian politics after his return from South Africa. Even then no action was taken against me...." Annie Besant had in those years become the idol of the nationalists in India. Bapu, like many others, went to her public lectures and was deeply impressed by her oratory. They used to call her Besant saheb.

The Jallianwala Bag[28] massacre moved him deeply and he wrote to Brelvi, "The curfew has tolled in the streets of Amritsar and Lahore and it has tolled the knell of the world's lasting hope (sounds like the beginning of an editorial – eh?)"

In BA, he took Economics Honours. Prof. Beri taught them Economics. He read a great deal of English literature and among his favourite authors were Shakespeare, Thomas Hardy, Galsworthy, Dickens, Shaw, Goethe and the Romantic poets, Wordsworth, Shelley, Keats, Browning, Byron and Tennyson. In a holiday in Mahabaleshwar, he writes, "After a walk or set of tennis, at night we all of us read Morley's Recollections". He also read the plays of Oscar Wilde which he enjoyed enormously. In fact Wilde became one of his favourite authors and he knew 'The Importance of Being Ernest', 'The Ideal Husband' and 'Lady Windermere's Fan' almost entirely by heart.

"In many respects, these were the most fruitful years of my life at college....Some of us organised a History and Economic Association and invited some prominent people to address us on important political and economic subjects. My father presided over a lecture given by Ewbank, Registrar of Co-operative Societies on the co-operative movement. We had a debate on whether economic reform should have precedence over political reform...I moved this proposition and was opposed by S.V. Deshpande, a brilliant student...Deshpande subsequently left the college because of the non co-operation movement and joined the labour movement.....I also read a paper in this

Association on 'The State in the Future'. I used to read a lot about Guild Socialism and had been impressed by it... I used to write quite frequently in *The Elphinstonian*. He wrote an article on 'What is Wrong with History' in the December, 1918 issue of the magazine and expresses views, which seem almost contemporary. "The last and greatest charge against history as it is written today is that it is the biography of a few great personalities. It is in no sense the real history of the world. How little do we know of the ideas, the beliefs, and the customs of the man in the street at any particular period of the history of the country! Historians write about warriors, senators and courtiers. An ideal historian must acquaint us with the common man of the period for it is here that history is being made." In the September, 1920 issue he wrote an article entitled 'Towards the Pinnacle' which discussed the idea of progress.

At a meeting of the History and Economics Association, D.B. Diwanji read a paper on 'The League of Nations and the Peace of Versailles' and the Elphinstonian records that "Mr. P.L. Mehta spoke at length on the subject." Bapu was then called Prabuddha, Gaganvihari being his other name.

Among his contemporaries in Elphinstone were A.D. Shroff, the businessman and industrialist and C.C. Desai and A.D. Gorwalla who both joined the ICS. Two promising students and friends of his were Dilkhush Diwanjee and Hemant G. Nilkanth both of whom left college to join the non co-operation movement. "When I was in College, there were very few girls studying with us. One promising graduate student was Miss Mitha Tata (later Mrs. Mitha Lam)...

"The last year of my college was even more full of excitement than the first one. Gandhiji launched the non co-operation movement...I was not fully convinced of the desirability of quitting college and did not do so...." They had endless discussions at home and in the college arguing for and against non co-operation.

"The college had a prize for the student who stood first in History and Economics in all the 4 examinations of the two years of junior and senior BA. I won this prize but failed by just a few marks to get a first class at the final examination. This disappointed me."

REFERENCES

1. Sir Chunilal V. Mehta, b.1881. A leading businessmen and public figure of Bombay; millowner; chairman, Century Spinning and Weaving Mills; elected to Bombay Legislative Council by Corporation in 1916, Minister in Bombay government, 1921-23. Member, Executive Council of Government of Bombay, 1923-28.
2. Sir Rajendra Nath Mukherjee, b. 1854. A leading industrialist of Bengal; senior partner in the firm of Martin Burn & Co.; Member, Indian Industrial Commission, Sheriff of Calcutta, 1911.
3. The Hon. Sir Dinshaw Edulji Wacha, (1844-1936). Member, firm of Morarji Goculdas & Co., mill agent, Member, Council of State. Served Bombay Municipal Corporation for 31 years. President of 17th Indian National Congress, Calcutta, 1901.Governor, Imperial Bank of India.
4. Sir Ibrahim Rahimtoola, b. 1862. Member, Executive Council of Governor of Bombay; President of Bombay Legislative Council, 1923.
5. Sir Vithaldas Thackersey, (1873-1922). Millowner, one of the founders of the Co-operative movement in Bombay. S.N.D.T. Women's University is named after his mother, Shrimati Nathubai Damodardas Thackersey.
6. Sir Fazalbhoy Currimbhoy, b. 1872. Merchant, millowner; member, Bombay Legislative Council and Imperial Legislative Council. Sheriff of Bombay, 1926. Represented Bombay Millowners' Association in Bombay Provincial Council.
7. Sir Purshottamdas Thakurdas (1869-1916). A leading industrialist. One of the founders of FICCI. Member, Imperial Legislative Assembly.
8. Walchand Hirachand, (1882-1953). Chairman, Premier Construction Co. Ltd. One of the founders of Scindia Steam Navigation Co. and its Chairman. Chairman, Premier Automobiles Ltd. Director, Associated Cement Co. Ltd., Tata Chemicals. President Indian Merchants Chamber, Bombay, 1927. President FICCI, 1932-33. Vice President, International Chamber of Commerce, Paris, 1923-35 and 1936-37.
9. Natarajan, Kamakshi, (1868-1948). Editor, *Indian Social Reformer*, President, National Social Reform Congress, 1921.

10. Gopal Krishna Gokhale, (1866-1915). Social reformer and leader of moderate nationalists; founder of Servant of India Society. President of Indian National Congress 1905 session.
11. Sir Chimanlal Setalvad (1866-1947). Member, Southborough Franchise Committee, 1918; member, Hunter Commission, 1919; member, Bombay Governor's Executive Council, 1921-23. Vice Chancellor, Bombay University, 1917-29. Leading liberal and lawyer of Bombay. Knighted in 1919, made a KCIE in 1924.
12. Pherozeshah Mehta (1945-1915). One of the founding members of Indian National Congress. Leading moderate politician.
13. Dutt, Ramesh Chandra, ICS (1848-1909). Joined ICS in 1871. Retd. 1897. Dewan of Baroda. Author of *Bengal Peasantry* and *Economic History* of India
14. Lala Lajpat Rai, (1865-1928). Arya Samajist. Leading nationalist.
15. Sarla Devi Chaudhurani (1872-1945). Daughter of Swarna Kumari Devi, editor of *Bharati*, first women's magazine in an Indian language; neice of poet Rabindranath Tagore; writer, poetess and nationalist.
16. Lord S.P. Sinha, (1863-1928), the first Indian Advocate General of Bengal; member, Viceroy's Executive Council.
17. Surendranath Banerjea, (1848-1925). One of the founders of the Indian National Congress and its President in 1895 and 1902. Resigned from the ICS in 1874. Founded Ripon College. Proprietor of nationalist newspaper *Bengalee*. Autobiography–*A Nation in the Making.*
18. C.F. Andrews, (1871-1940)). Member of Cambridge Mission, attached to St. Stephen's College, Delhi. Close associate of Rabindranath Tagore and Mahatma Gandhi.
19. V. Srinivasa Sastri, (1869-1946). President, Servants of India Society. Represented India at the Imperial Congress 1921. Member Privy Council, agent general to South Africa, attended RTC. Member of Council of State. Liberal, Moderate leader.
20. Bholanath Sarabhai, (1822-1886). Social reformer. One of the founders of Gujarat Prarthana Samaj.
21. Agatha Harrison, (1883-1954). Member, Society of Friends; worked for C.F. Andrews; became Secretary of India Conciliation Group; friend of Mahatma Gandhi.
22. B.G. Kher (1888-1957). Chief Minister of Bombay, 1937-39, 1947-1952. India's High Commissioner to U.K.
23. Motilal Nehru, (1861-1931). Leading lawyer of Allahabad. President of Indian National Congress, Amritsar, 1919. Father of Jawaharlal Nehru. Formed Swaraj Party and dominated Legislative Assembly as leader of opposition.

24. Annie Besant (1847-1933): Social reformer, theosophist and Indian Independence leader. She became President of the Indian National Congress in 1917. She based herself in India from around 1895, living at Adyar, near Madras, the headquarters of the Theosophical Society.
25. Home Rule Movement, (1917). Two Home Rule Leagues were started in 1917, one by Annie Besant and another by Bal Gangadhar Tilak. Both were demanding home rule for India.
26. B.P. Wadia, Theosophist, originally follower of Annie Besant. Later founded United Lodge of Theosophists in Bombay.
27. George Sydney Arundale, President Theosophical Society. Husband of Rukmini Arundale. Organising Secretary, Home Rule League. Detained under Defence of India Act, 1917.
28. Jallianwala Bagh. The year 1919 was a turning point in the colonial history of India. The repressive government legislation recommended by the 1918 Rowlatt Report – a recommendation to carry the emergency powers of wartime into peacetime triggered off tremendous agitation. It became law on 21st March 1919, having been forced through the Imperial Legislative Council on a vote split along purely racial lines. This caused Gandhi to launch an all India campaign of passive resistance, which immediately led to loss of life, culminating in the shooting of nearly four hundred people and the wounding of two thousand more – all of them unarmed – at Amritsar's Jallianwala Bagh on 13 April, 1919.

2

London School of Economics—1921-22

Bapu was the first member of his family to go abroad. He sailed from Bombay by the P&O boat S.S. Morena in July, 1921, travelling First Class with a cabin on the promenade deck as befitted a son whose father was a member of the Council of State and a well known figure in the world of Indian business and industry. Having lost his mother when he was only seven, Bapu was deeply attached to his father. As the ship sailed from Bombay harbour, he was desperately homesick with a feeling of guilt about having left his father. He wrote: "I have often asked myself during the last month whether I was not doing a wrong thing in giving you so much pain by my departure. Chunilal wrote to me that you were ready to part with me for my evolution. I replied that I owed so much to you that though this act of self sacrifice comes at the top, it did not appear much to me...I have a father who never refuses anything..."

On the boat with him were Kamaladevi Chattopadhyaya[1] (who was going to join her husband, Harindranath), and the Mukherjee family – Satish Chandra Mukherjee, I.C.S., his wife Charulata (daughter of Mr. and Mrs. P.K. Ray), their two sons, Shanto (later Member, Railway Board) and Subroto (later, Air Marshall) and their two daughters, Lata (later Mrs. Renuka Ray,

MP and Minister, West Bengal Government) Nita (later, wife of Dr. Sushanto Sen). The Mukherjee family and Bapu became good friends and the friendship continued in later life. As both Bapu and Kamaladevi were vegetarians, they were put on the same table and when they parted in Marseilles, he wrote that Kamaladevi had tears in her eyes. Brought up in an orthodox Brahmin household, he did not know much about Western food and was grateful to Brelvi for having made him familiar with some European vegetarian dishes, which were very few in those days.

My father joined the London School of Economics that was then very different from the ancient universities of Oxford and Cambridge. Between the two World Wars it was the only institution to take all the social sciences seriously. There, the majority of students came from Grammar schools and many of the students who were to rule India in the thirty years after independence had studied there. Bapu decided to go to LSE partly because he had heard about it from some Indian friends who had studied there earlier, among them Manu Subedar[2], N.M. Mazumdar, and K.T. Shah. He had also read in the London *Nation* articles by Harold Laski, reviews of his books as well as articles by Sidney Webb. He had been told that there was a freer and more liberal atmosphere in the LSE and an absence of stuffiness and a greater concentration of international eminence. He took courses in Social Philosophy, Social Psychology, History of Political Ideas, and Local Government. He later wrote: "There was little or no teaching at the School at that time which was not inspired by the spirit of search and discovery." He had energetic discussions in the surrounding tearooms and elsewhere with friends. He attended the lectures of Harold Laski (1893-1950) which were brilliantly delivered and based on great erudition and a memory of extraordinary power. Laski's lectures were always crowded and his personal popularity with students from Britain as well from countries of Asia and Africa, who regarded him as their *guru*, was unparalleled. Bapu found his lectures, "brilliant, there was no other word for it. I was almost mad with joy at hearing him and felt what an intellectual treat it must be to be associated with such men", he wrote home. "He talks at such a terrific speed. Heaven knows how many words a minute and talks so brilliantly that I am simply bewildered. He has been everywhere, knows everybody, has read everything...I have hardly met a man more active minded and intellectually vigorous...He was at times distinctly and sincerely eloquent and at other times full of delicate and subtle humour. Undoubtedly he is today what Bentham was in his own generation, whose devoted student and opponent he is. He represents the 20th century reaction against the comfortable Benthamite conception of human nature which in a sense is at the basis of representative government...This morning I had my usual fight with Laski in the class." He was very pleased when Laski mentioned his essay in the course of his lectures as "the most admirable one among those presented – the result being that I was congratulated by some at the end of the lecture....I cannot tell you what a great encouragement I have received by Laski's appreciation of my work. He is really very kind to me." Laski gave him a certificate, when Bapu was applying for a post in Lucknow University in 1925, in which he said, "I have the highest possible opinion of Mr. G.L. Mehta. I saw a good deal of him at the LSE and learned to respect him greatly. He is a man of quite first rate ability, of high character and of great personal charm. I have little doubt but that he would make a really successful university teacher. I have no hesitation in warmly recommending him to the University of Lucknow." In our house we had every book written by Laski and Bapu frequently reviewed his books.

He also enjoyed the classes of Edward Alexander Westermarck[3], one of which "was turned into a cross examination of myself by him regarding village panchayats, Hindu-Muslim unity, Islam and Moplahs, caste system, language problem in India and education". He attended the lectures of Graham Wallace[4] and of L.T. Hobhouse[5].

As he read and listened to the lectures, he felt more and more that "there was no panacea for human ills and the evils one can cure in one's own lifetime are too few. Again all study of history makes one conservative for one is oppressed with a sense of complexity and far reaching characters of all events and of the ultimate futility of all efforts."

In the 1920s, Indian students mostly mixed among themselves and had few English friends. Bapu's close friends were also mostly Indians but one English student with whom he developed a life long friendship was Lionel Robbins[6]. Of their first meeting, he wrote home: "On Friday, I lunched with one Mr. Robbins who is one of the most brilliant, if not the most brilliant student in our School; – a favourite student of Laski's.... We talked for two hours at a stretch on various subjects and I was really benefited by it." They both attended a summer school in Vienna. In later life, whenever Bapu was in London, he made it a point to meet Robbins and they usually went to the theatre or ballet or opera together. Robbins, was a Professor at LSE and an eminent economist. He was also chairman of the boards of the Financial Times and the National Gallery, and he sat on the boards of the Tate Gallery, the Royal Opera House and the Royal Economic Society. He served as President of the British Academy and was a life peer.

Vera Anstey[7], the Economic Historian, was initially Bapu's advisor in studies and Clement Attlee[8], one of his tutors. In 1960 after Bapu became the first Indian Honorary Fellow of LSE, at a dinner of the Honorary Fellows of LSE in London, where Bapu spoke on behalf of the Fellows, Attlee also spoke. Attlee told him that he remembered him as a student. Bapu's affection for LSE lasted a lifetime. He was the President for many years of the Friends of the London School of Economics, a Society started for the alumni of the

LSE in India. As Dr. I.G. Patel former Governor of RBI and first Indian Director of LSE, recalled at a lecture delivered in Delhi on 17 April 2000, on the occasion of the birth centenary of G.L. Mehta, several of Bapu's colleagues in later years happened to be from LSE. Among them were Dr. Tarlok Singh and Dr. K.N. Raj in the Planning Commission, Mr. B.K. Nehru in Washington. Shri H.T. Parekh in ICICI, and Shri Ravishanker Bhatt in the Indian Investment Centre. He would have been delighted and proud that his grandson, Sanjay Dhar went to LSE and obtained a First Class B.Sc. degree in Economics.

Apart from the lectures at LSE, he went to various other lectures. He heard Bertrand Russell for the first time in the autumn of 1921 when Russell delivered three lectures on China after his visit to that country. Bapu wrote to his father that he found Russell's "liberal mind, freshness of approach, gentle and subtle irony all captivating.... I cannot tell you what a joy I felt at hearing him and seeing a man who was a true lover of freedom. His personality is not at all appealing. He is neither aristocratic looking nor good looking.... His delivery is not forceful, vigorous and direct like Laski's but much more intellectual, subtler, deeper...coming out I was mad with joy and for the first time after coming to London threw away my money on two books of his...."

Thus began Bapu's life long admiration for Russell. He purchased and read every book of Russell, wrote many articles on him, reviewed his books and his MA thesis for Bombay University was on the Social Philosophy of Bertrand Russell.

He also admired George Bernard Shaw and did not miss any opportunity to see a play of his or hear him speak. After hearing a lecture of Shaw, he wrote home:

"Shaw was not merely sane and balanced which he always is; he was full of human tenderness and sentiment and sympathy which he so shrewdly conceals behind his apparent fanaticism and brutal realism."

He attended lectures given by G.D.H. Cole[9], R.H. Tawney[10], Rivers, the social anthropologist[11], Professor Herman Finer[12], Lord Robert Cecil[13] and many others. He heard Philip Guedella[14] on 'Politics in Fiction and Fact' and was most impressed by his wit and sharpness of irony and wrote home: "I have never heard anything that surpasses it." Guedella's speeches retained all the epigrammatic glitter of his Oxford Union days and were marked by verbal fireworks and, like Lytton Strachey, a lack of reverence for established reputations.

In his weekly letters to his father, Bapu gave detailed accounts of the lectures he attended, the synopsis of the lectures and his own critical comments. He also wrote about the people he met and the gist of the conversations he had with them, the plays he saw, and the places he visited. These letters were circulated and read by all members of the family and friends.

The letters to his brother, Jyotindra, were more light-hearted and frivolous. In one of this he wrote: "The mail is as terrible to us as is the Dail[15] to England. I watch the next morning mail for news from the time I receive one mail's letters and how disappointing it is! If we could only send ourselves by post and yet remain here. Really God has no imagination. I would like to be his Secretary and rather improve life. I do not get any news about the Ali brothers..."

To begin with, Bapu stayed in a boarding house on 22 Oxford Road in Putney where he got vegetarian food. In the same house, stayed for a short time, "the famous Prof.C.V. Raman... He has come for the Science Congress at Oxford and is experimenting on various things, one of them being about the whispering gallery which he is going to try in St. Paul's in a few days." Raman, then the Palit Professor of Physics at Calcutta University, was doing research in many fields, including vibrations and sounds. In 1933, he received the Nobel Prize. Bapu later moved to 2 Fulham Park Road as a paying guest of the Laytons, who, he wrote home, "were liberal in politics, pacifists in international affairs and non conformists in religion." For him, the important thing was that they were vegetarians and could provide him with vegetarian meals. Of one of his Indian friends, he wrote approvingly, "He is as shy and good as ever and I am pleased to see that he has not picked up any English vices at all. He has remained a vegetarian, does not drink and smoke and is as simple as before."

All his life, Bapu loved seeing plays and the love of the theatre began during his stay in London. He saw plays of Shakespeare, Shaw, Ibsen, and Galsworthy and wrote home detailed comments on each. "John Bull's Other Island is the third play I have seen in a month, but the temptation was irresistible", he wrote.

Apart from plays, he made frequent visits to the British Museum, National Gallery, Victoria and Albert Museum and other art galleries. Bapu had seen from an early age, many deaths, including that of his mother and sisters, and perhaps because of that, he had a sense of the tragedy that lay at the heart of life. Walking through Westminster Abbey over the tombs of Dickens, Browning and other great men, he wrote that he felt "the infinite melancholy of history and the pathos of human life...It is for this that we strive and suffer, love and hate. It is for this that politicians lay out their schemes and conquerors are ambitious. Tread softly, I said to myself, for on whom do I tread? So many times greater than myself and yet are today no better than the dust beneath our feet...I felt however, that their dead are alive in their monuments and one feels as if Gladstone's and Milton's ashes are still pregnant with a celestial fire and continue to dream below us..."

Similarly, "the gloom of all history" in the British Museum produced in him "a profound awe and pessimism. What a tiny atom is man and how immense is the universe! Ah the mystery of it."

Bapu had a passion for reading newspapers. In London,

apart from the *Times*, *Guardian* and *Daily Herald*, he also read the *Nation* and *Punch*. His father in India also subscribed to the last two. *Nation*, a radical paper, edited by H. W. Massingham, was on the whole, sympathetic to India's struggle for freedom. His father sent him from India, Gandhi's *Navjivan* and the *Indian Social Reformer*. Bapu felt that except for the *Daily Herald* no English newspaper, Liberal, Tory or Coalitionist, understood or even attempted to understand the truth of the Indian situation. By 1920, Gandhi's plan of non-co-operation had taken a definite shape and he envisaged a strategy whereby a systematic campaign would be waged against the government. Initially he proposed the return of decorations and honours awarded by the British, the withdrawal of children and students from government-supported schools and colleges, the boycott of law courts by lawyers and litigants, and the boycott of elections to the new legislative councils under the Montague-Chelmsford reforms. If these steps did not yield the desired results, all government officials would be asked to leave their offices, and soldiers would be asked to lay down their arms. A massive refusal to pay taxes would take care of the rest of his programme of 'progressive non-violent non-co-operation'. While in London, Bapu constantly followed the exciting events in India. He wrote to his father, "I have read in the *Times* that the Congress had adopted a resolution declaring Gandhi to be the sole spokesman and adopting civil disobedience...I hope there will be no bloodshed and violence." In 1921, Gandhi launched the non-co-operation movement. Parallel to it, the Khilafat movement had begun to make inroads among the Muslims. It gained its name from opposition to Britain's policy towards the Sultan of Turkey, the Caliph, who was effectively a prisoner of the British in Constantinople. Many Muslims regarded the Caliph as their temporal and spiritual head. An All India Khilafat Committee was formed with the brothers Mohammad Ali (1878-1931) and Shaukat Ali (1873-1938), both journalists and politicians from

United Provinces, as leaders and Gandhi agreed to support the movement as long as it remained non-violent.

In February 1922, peasants who had volunteered to pursue the policy of non-co-operation murdered twenty-one Indian policemen and rural watchmen at Chauri Chaura in the Gorakhpur district of U.P. After the men had been murdered, their bodies were doused in petrol and set on fire. As a token of regret, Gandhi went on a fast. On 10 March 1922, in view of this violence, Gandhi suspended the movement and was arrested. At his trial, Gandhi made an extraordinary confession and declaration of faith, which won him great respect from many of his most tenacious British critics. Bapu was deeply moved by Gandhi's arrest and for two days could think of nothing else. He wrote: "I have read and re-read the comments on Gandhi's arrest. I am only filled with dismay and disappointment.... Between the Tories condemning even the mild Montague policy and the Liberals defending the 'Reforms Act'[16] which for serious purposes is discredited.... Sir Michael O'Dwyer[17] and his friends carry on a campaign of vilification and misrepresentation that makes me merely amazed at their capacity of deliberately lying...." He felt that in the face of this, "the faith of the Moderates in British democracy (though they have no faith in the capacity of their own people to rule themselves) is, to say the least, extremely simple minded and pathetic. Excepting a sane article by H.N. Brailsford[18] in the *Daily Herald*, where Gandhi is compared to Jesus, I have not seen one article in any English paper that touches the heart of the matter..."

Bapu felt that while the Irish leader, De Valera[19] was not arrested though he openly advocated violence, "it does not reflect much to the of credit on the world and its rulers that its greatest man is now in prison." He found the description of Gandhi's parting farewell from the people in Sabarmati ashram, before his arrest, very touching and it brought tears to his eyes, "as I have not the courage to do anything more, I cursed the rulers of our country with all my heart. May they perish soon. For if there is justice in the universe and providence above, how long can this oppression and injustice last – how long!.... How great Gandhi appears even through all their vilifications, misrepresentations and misunderstanding!"

Bapu kept on thinking and writing about India. From Nice, on a holiday, he wrote to Brelvi, "I have thought for hours at a stretch, mostly about the Indian political situation ...I cannot enjoy myself here while Mahadev Desai is harshly treated in prison, while Pandit Motilal Nehru's son goes to jail, while non-co-operators are flogged and while the honour of the country is at stake." Though he lacked the courage or conviction to join the movement, his sympathies were clearly with Gandhi. He wrote to his father, "The second act in the drama of the new Indian nationalism (begun since the War) has ended – the first ending (not with the death of Tilak as the *Servant of India* says) but with the close of the Punjab episode in the June of 1919. Then people lost faith not so much in British justice but in their own power of constitutional agitation. We saw with despair that it is only by grace that we are allowed to agitate and even live in our own country and that British rule rests on conquest rather than on co-operation...At last there was a light on the ocean, a star across the firmament and a man arose who said that he for one would not bear the insult. He did not stop to enquire how big was the British Empire, how huge its army and navy...He relied on his conscience which is ultimately greater than the greatest government... How much has one man done to transform such a huge mass within three years!" Bapu blamed himself for being "a coward, a lover of ease and comfort, the talker and not the doer... which prompts me to give intellectual justification for my inactivity and sacrifice...This is what stings our conscience...Is it not one's duty as an Indian to see that the challenge of the government meets with a universal response and prisons are filled till they are overfull? Sitting as I am miles away, I can literally think of nothing else...of what use am I to my country, to the cause we all have at heart." He felt that he lacked the courage, faith and endurance to go to jail. He wrote, "Day by day my intellectual conviction in Gandhi's principles and his movement grows stronger...There is no alternative to non-co-operation...It is once in a century that a man is born who says 'I will not tolerate this government, this system. I will see the end of it or die!...Gandhi has definitely broken with the traditional mode of politics for good or evil."

Despite his hatred of British rule in India, like so many of the Indian intelligentsia of his time, he had an admiration for British democratic institutions. He went to the House of Commons and met J.S. Wedgwood[20] whom his father knew. He felt in the House "the atmosphere of the place, the weight of tradition, and the greatness of the place, seldom, if ever in my life have I felt the sensation I then felt when I entered the gallery, saw the Speaker before me and Mr. Churchill speaking."

Bapu made new friends, went for long walks, visited Oxford and Cambridge where he met old friends from Elphinstone College. In Cambridge, he attended a Union debate on the motion 'India should obtain *swarajya* by every possible and proper means'. He also made trips to the Lake Districts, Manchester, Liverpool, Devon, Torquay, Bournemouth, Eastbourne, Glasgow, Edinburgh and various other places. He spent some of his happiest hours with Kamaladevi and Harindranath Chattopadhyaya[21]. He wrote to his father, "When I am with them, I feel that there is after all some joy in life. They are such an intellectual and loving couple. With all his brilliance, cleverness , poetry, dreams and wit, Mr. Chattopadhyaya cannot reach his wife in a certain moral stability, a faith, a sweetness and a depth such as I have never seen in an Indian girl..."

Bapu first saw and heard Dilip Kumar Roy (1897-1980), a poet, writer and musician, sing at an international concert in London in June 1922. Roy was the son of the famous playwright, poet and composer Dwijendra Lal Roy. Dilip Roy studied at Cambridge University where he did a Tripos in music and later studied German and Italian music on the continent. At the concert that Bapu attended, Roy sang two songs and his strikingly handsome personality and melodious voice immediately captivated him. "I remember approaching him with some hesitation after the concert...In November, 1922, when I was returning to India by an Italian steamer from Venice, Dilip Roy joined the steamer from Brindisi. This was one of the most fortunate events of my life; we spent 12 days on board the steamer discussing a variety of subjects from philosophy to politics. He told me of Bertrand Russell's eloquent and moving essay *A Freeman's Worship*, which I have since read and re-read several times... We had two things in common – humour and Bertrand Russell. These were to be our bonds throughout our lives – radically divergent as they have been..."

Bapu was not happy that his father continued to be a member of the Council of State. He wrote to him, "I cannot conceal from you that every day I watch the papers hoping to read of your resignation from the Council since Gandhi's conviction...Do you think there is any useful purpose served by your remaining in the Council?" He asks, "Do you really think that even the most rabid of non-co-operators are worse colleagues than Sir Maneckji Dadabhoy[22], Sir Pheroze Sethna[23] and the Maharajas and zamindars on the one hand and Vincent[24], Shafi[25], Hailey[26], Sapru[27] and company on the other? Would you put even Mr. Srinivas Shastri on a higher moral level than Mahadev Desai? Surely, if the persons who are in the non-co-operation movement are undesirable and unfit to put into practice Gandhiji's lofty principles, it is the duty of all sensible and sincere people to join and improve its tone. One may of course fail. How far have the Councils succeeded on any matter of vital importance and on any issues of principle?" Lallubhai belonged to the old school of Moderates and was a believer in law and order. He held that constructive criticism and co-operation should guide action. Understandably passive resistance and non co-operation did not appeal to him, for as a law-abiding citizen he disapproved of methods that by-passed or defied established authority and inculcated a spirit of indiscipline among the masses. He felt that boycott of British goods and institutions would do more harm than good. He was averse to populist politics and believed that the people had to be educated before they could achieve political reform. While he had great personal regard for Gandhiji, he did not subscribe to the method of non-co-operation and therefore did not resign. He felt that the participants in the non-co-operation movement would largely be the illiterate and the ignorant and this would lead to complete disorganisation and chaos. Bapu visited a theistic church, near London, whose Minister, Dr. Walter Walsh had written a pamphlet entitled 'Gandhi in Gaol'. He immediately bought two copies and sent one to his father and one to Mahadev Desai.

On 21 March, 1922, his eyes fell on these lines of the poet Robert Burns printed on his calendar, "The smiling spring comes in rejoicing, and surly winter flies" but as he looked out of his window, "snow was falling like feathers from the tree on the tennis court" and so he wrote, "I hear nothing but the terrific roar of the biting northerly wind...The sound of the cold, sharp and piercing wind is like the proverbial ghosts singing in wilderness. I rather take consolation in Shelley's words, "The trumpet of a prophecy! O wind, If winter comes, can spring be far behind? Such indeed is one's thought at the condition of India...Though the wind of repression be chilly and cut our countrymen through and through, though the winter of oppression lingers on, can the spring of *swarajya* be eternally delayed or the sun of freedom hidden always from the view?" This was, however, not his style of writing and so he added, "But this is Sarojini-like".

The weather in London continued to be atrocious and he wrote to his father, "Nature like the Government of India wishes to rule by caprice instead of reason and the intolerable repression of cold and damp rather than conciliation of sunshine. Inevitably, my cough, like non-co-operation grew more powerful and Pandit Motilal Nehru in the form of Dr. Nanavati, advised me to try the Round Table Conference called Eastbourne." It was these constant attacks of cough and cold and asthma, which made him and his father anxious about his health. As two of his sisters had died of tuberculosis , it was decided that he should return to India after a year having obtained only a diploma.

REFERENCES

1. Kamaladevi Chattopadhyaya (1903-1988). Freedom fighter. First woman to contest elections to an Indian legislature but was defeated. Member of Congress. Social worker. President All India Women's Conference. Pioneer of revival of handlooms and handicraft in India after Independence. Awarded Magasaysay Award in 1966.
2. Manu Subedar, B.Sc. (London School of Economics, 1st Class Hons.), Barrister-at-Law. Professor of Economics, Calcutta University. Secretary, Sholapur Spinning and Weaving Mills. Financial Adviser to several Indian States. President, Indian Merchants Chamber, 1935.
3. Westermarck, (1862-1939). Professor of Sociology, London School of Economics. Author of *Origins of Human Marriage* and *Future of Marriage in Western Civilisation.*
4. Graham Wallace, (1858-1932). Professor of Political Science, London School of Economics. Author of *Human Nature of Politics* and *The Great Society.*
5. L.T. Hobhouse. Professor, London School of Economics.
6. Lionel Robbins, (1898-1984). Professor and Director of London School of Economics. Later, Baron Robbins.
7. Vera Anstey, Economic Historian. Tutor and Lecturer, London School of Economics.
8. Clement Attlee (1883-1967). Tutor and Lecturer in Social Science, London School of Economics, 1913-23. Labour Party M.P., Prime Minister of England, 1945-51.
9. G.D.H. Cole (1898-1959). Prominent socialist writer. Chichele Professor of Social and Political Theory, Oxford. Advocate of Guild Socialism.

10. R.H. Tawney, (1880-1962). Historian and author of *Religion and the Rise of Capitalism* and *Equality*.
11. Charles Rivers, Social Anthropologist.
12. Herman Finer, (1898-1969). Professor of Political Science, London School of Economics. Author of *Theory and Practice of Modern Government.*
13. Lord Robert Cecil, (1864-1958). Member of Parliament; creator of League of Nations.
14. Philip Guedella, (1889-1944). Author and public speaker.
15. 'Dail' was the name used for the Irish Parliament.
16. 'Reforms Act' refers to the Montague Chelmsford Reforms Scheme which introduced 'dyarchy'.
17. Sir Michael O'Dwyer, (1864-1940). Indian administrator, posted to the Punjab in the Indian Civil Service, 1885. Lieutenant Governor, Punjab 1913-19, approved action of General Dyer at Jallianwala Bagh on 13th April, 1919. Shot by an Indian at a meeting of the Royal Central Asian Society in London, 1913, GCIE 1917.
18. H.N. Brailsford, (1873-1958). Journalist. Author of *Rebel India* and *Subject India.* Friend of Jawaharlal Nehru and Mahatma Gandhi.
19. E. De Valera, (1892-1975). Prime Minister of Ireland. Fought for freedom of Irish Republic.
20. J.S. Wedgwood, (1872-1943). Liberal Party member of British Parliament from Newcastle on Tyne. Toured India and attended meeting of Indian National Congress.
21. Harindranath Chattopadhyaya, writer, poet, actor. Brother of Sarojini Naidu. Husband of Kamaladevi Chattopadhyaya. Studied theatre and acting in England and in Europe.
22. Sir Maneckji Dadabhoy (1865-1953), was elected to the Council of State in 1921; nominated to Council of State in 1928, 1931, 1937; Governor, Imperial Bank of India, Member, Indian Fiscal Commission, Indian Currency and Exchange Commission, etc.
23. Sir Pheroze Sethna (1866-1938), Chairman and Managing Director, Central Bank of India and Director of many leading companies was a member of the Council of State.
24. Sir William Henry Hoare Vincent, ICS. Member of Council of India, 1923. Member of Governor-General's Council of India, 1917. Vice-President of Council, 1921.
25. Sir Muhammad Shafi, Education Member, Viceroy's Executive Council, 1919-1922; Vice-President of the Council, 1922-24; Law Member, 1922-24; Leader of the Council of State, 1922-24.

26. Sir Malcolm Hailey, Governor of U.P. 1928-30. Chief Commissioner, Delhi, 1912-18; Member of Executive Council of Governor General, in Finance and Home Department, 1919-1924. Governor of Punjab, 1924-28.
27. Sir Tej Bahadur Sapru (1875-1949). Advocate, Allahabad High Court. President of Indian Liberal Federation; at one time President of all India Congress Committee, Member of Imperial Legislative Council, 1916-20; Law Member, Viceroy's Executive Council, 1920-23.

3

Bombay Chronicle Days

After his return from England, Bapu was depressed and at a loss as to what to do. "Confusion, indecision, hesitation, diffidence – all drove me hither and thither. All doors seem locked for me and no keys", he wrote to Brelvi. He had a love for journalism but did not want to serve a newspaper like the *Times of India* which in those days voiced the government's point of view. He, therefore, decided to join the *Bombay Chronicle*, a nationalist newspaper, which had been started in 1913 by Pherozeshah Mehta, who was also Chairman of the Board of Directors that included Chimanlal Setalvad, Jehangir Petit[1], Sir Bhalchandra Krishna[2] and W.A.Chambers. It became an influential paper which supported the Home Rule movement and later the non- co-operation and civil disobedience movements. Its first editor was B.G.Horniman[3]. When Horniman was forced to leave, Brelvi became the editor. Bapu was one of the principal editorial writers and regaled his readers with his editorials written in a lighter vein. Among one of his colleagues, with whom he could share his jokes, was Pothan Joseph whom he first met in Brelvi's room in the Taj Hotel in Bombay in July/August, 1924. Bapu wrote," Joseph joined the *Bombay Chronicle* as a joint editor and we had a hilarious time as

Joseph made the editorial side pungent and lively". S.R. Das, then Law Member of the Viceroy's Executive Council, had written a 'letter to his son', then in Cambridge, advocating the philosophy of moderation and arguing against the creed of violence as well as non-violent non-co-operation. "I asked Joseph to make some fun of it", wrote Bapu, but he suggested that the best way to answer was through a letter from the son to the father and asked me to try my hand at it...I did so. The letter was dated St. Leger's Day (a race day in England) and was addressed to 'Reverend Papa'. In the end I had said, 'You might feel like a father to young India', to which Joseph added; 'but fellows here have composed verses in which our family name is made to rhyme with a well known but inferior kind of quadruped!' I had written on the top that through the inadvertence of the post office, a letter addressed to Mr. S.R. Das had fallen into our hands and though we do not vouch for its authenticity, it bears the postmark of Cambridge. Many people thought that this was genuine stuff and that the *Bombay Chronicle* had made an amazing scoop. For weeks afterwards Joseph used to call me junior Das....Joseph contrasted his style with mine by saying that my editorials were like a ship with all sails in full bloom steadily heaving into port while his was like a car driving fast with a lot of backfiring."

"Joseph left the *Chronicle*, so did I but we met whenever I went to Bangalore and we had a roaring time." Joseph wrote a column 'Over a cup of tea' in the *Deccan Herald* and Bapu read it regularly. Joseph used to call him the Stephen Leacock of India and taught him that the secret of style was the ear, how the sentence sounded.

The Government of India Act of 1919, the outcome of the Montague Chelmsford reforms, had been planned as a way of diverting Indian political attention from the national, the all-India stage, and directing it to provincial affairs. The provincial legislatures as well as the Imperial Legislative Assembly and

Council of State were elected on a slightly extended franchise. There were to be Indian ministers in the provinces, in charge of certain specified departments. This was under a system which Lionel Curtis termed as dyarchy, though not all that many Indians knew Greek. Indians were also to be in a majority in the Legislative Assembly in Delhi. The Indian National Congress was split into two groups, the 'no changers' who did not favour joining the legislature and the 'pro changers' who wanted to contest the elections and oppose the government from within the Assemblies and the Council of State. The leaders of the 'pro changers' were C.R. Das[4] and Motilal Nehru who advocated council entry with a view to 'non-co-operation from within'. They believed that the municipal, provincial and national legislatures afforded the most suitable arena in which to obstruct, discredit and change the government. However, several Congressmen such as C. Rajagopalachari[5] and Vallabhbhai Patel[6] vehemently opposed this.

While Gandhiji was still in Yeravda jail, a movement was started under the leadership of C.R. Das and Motilal Nehru, who had recently been released from prison, to withdraw the boycott and to participate in the general elections which were due to be held at the end of 1923. In the teeth of strong opposition to their proposed strategy, C.R. Das and Motilal Nehru, along with a few followers, seceded from the Congress at the beginning of 1923 to form a separate and temporary Swaraj Party. In the ensuing months support for the Swaraj Party increased more than they had expected, and at a special session of the Congress held in Delhi in September a resolution was passed permitting Congressmen to enter the legislatures if they had no conscientious objection against doing so. The Swarajists built up an efficient party machine of their own and their candidates achieved considerable success in the elections. Bapu was deputed by *Chronicle* to cover the first session of the new Legislative Assembly in Delhi where the Swaraj Party made its debut.

Bapu watched with great interest the Legislature at work and covered the sessions every day. To Brelvi he wrote, "Almost every morning I rush to the Legislature and the time I am at home is utilised in reading papers – the *Chronicle* and back numbers of the *Guardian* and the *Nation*." He stayed at 16 Windsor Place, the bungalow allotted to his father who was a Member of the Council of State. This gave him an opportunity to meet national leaders like Motilal Nehru, Vithalbhai Patel[7], Chimanlal Setalvad, Purshottamdas Thakurdas, Kelkar[8], Dewan Chamanlal[9], Rangaswamy[10], Agnihotri and many others. He used to meet N.M. Joshi[11], the labour leader frequently as Joshi knew both his father and brother well. He met Sir Srinivas Shastri – "I saw Shastri once but after that I have ceased to talk to him. These Liberals and Independents and all the rest are anxious to see Byrt and other white reporters but for our people they have no time." He wrote to Batuk Kaka, "In the morning we went to visit various members from Sir Sivaswamy at one extreme to Mr. Niyogi at the other...In the evening we went to Okhla...who should be there but Sir Maneckji Dadabhoy. There I met my old acquaintances – K.C. Roy and Sen of Associated Press...Only one person in Indian dress amongst so many and that too in *khadi* amongst the 'co-operators' as the *Chronicle* would label". Bapu had started wearing *khadi sherwani, chudidar* and a Gandhi cap, a dress he wore all his life, except when he was abroad. My parents wore *khadi* till independence but slowly gave it up after that as they felt that *khadi* was now being worn by corrupt politicians and was no longer a symbol of nationalism.

His letters to his brothers were not as prompt and regular as they should have been and so in his humorous style he wrote, "In a city where everything is done progressively – development of self-government, Indianisation, economic autonomy and social amelioration, you should not wonder if its residents develop idleness also progressively and fail to realise the goal of letter writing...On Sunday I took rest for the simple reason that it is a day of rest while for the rest of the week I take rest for the complex reason that I cannot find suitable employment." This was not quite true as he was working long hours and getting exhausted. He described in his own style a day in the Assembly when Sheshagiri Iyer had given notice to move a resolution "for the repudiation of the repudiation of debts. Iyer had not consulted his party and had done it in a hurry and thus both he and the Assembly were in a fix. He could neither withdraw nor go forward. The extreme moderates were annoyed at his giving importance to such a trifling thing and at his recognising the Congress as a body that counts in the country. The moderate extremists were grieved at this further estrangement between the people and their 'representatives'. As the Congress that has repudiated the debts also repudiates the Councillors, there was no point in these repudiated legislators repudiating the repudiation of debts". The resolution never came off because of other business. He then went over to the Council of State "where the day was given over to two minor but concrete proposals of Indianisation of services where Srinivas Shastri made a really fine and effective speech". He bemoaned the lack of understanding between the Swarajists and the Independents.

At the suggestion of Dewan Chamanlal, Bapu interviewed Sir Joseph Nunan, an Irish Barrister, who had served in various capacities in British Guyana. He did not take any notes during the interview and wrote it up from memory. When he showed it to Sir Joseph, he was very impressed and wrote, "I thought it was excellent and it was wonderful how you remembered all the statements without taking a single note." This bucked up his sagging morale.

Bapu felt that by and large, the Legislative Assembly and Council were not serving any useful purpose and wanted his father to resign, "His giving up", he wrote to Batuk Kaka, "would benefit his health and his work ...you must prevail upon him to give up the Council immediately. It is a sheer waste of time, energy and money and results in no tangible good – either to himself or to the country..."

The weakening of the non co-operation movement had brought the legislatures into greater prominence and strengthened their position to some extent but Bapu found no towering personality in the Legislative Assembly or Council of State either in the power of speaking or debating strength.

In the meantime, his thoughts were elsewhere. He had refused to have an arranged marriage as was the custom in those days in India as well as in his own family. He had expressed a desire to his father and to Gatubhai Dhru, a cousin of his mother, that he wanted to marry an educated girl. Gatubhai introduced him to his niece, Saudamini, daughter of Ramanbhai and Vidyagauri Nilkanth. Ramanbhai was the son of Rao Bahadur Mahipatram Nilkanth, one of the founders of the Gujarat Prarthana Samaj and a well-known religious and social reformer. Mahipatram, a schoolteacher, was the first person from his caste to go to England where he was sent by the DPI to be further trained as a teacher. As a result of his crossing the seas, he was excommunicated from the caste. He was awarded a CIE by the government for his work in the fields of education and social reform. Ramanbhai was a lawyer, a social reformer, a Prarthana Samajist. and a reputed writer and literary critic who was intensely involved in the public life of Ahmedabad. He was a distinguished public figure, respected for his integrity and high moral standards. He was for many years President of the Ahmedabad municipality. In politics, he was a moderate and opposed to the non co-operation movement as he believed that freedom could be achieved gradually in stages through constitutional reform. He was knighted by the British government in 1928 . His wife, Vidyagauri, (1876-1958) was the grand-daughter of Bholanath Sarabhai and thus a cousin of Bapu's mother, Satyavati. Vidyagauri herself was a pioneer in many fields: the first woman graduate of Gujarat, she was a social reformer who throughout her life was actively associated with numerous educational, social reform and philanthropic organisations. She was given a MBE and the Kaiser-i-Hind gold medal by the British government for her social service but she returned these during the civil disobedience movement in 1931. Vidyagauri had five daughters all of whom were graduates. While the family was highly educated, they were very simple in their dress, food and life style and had deep roots in Gujarati literature and culture.

Saudamini writes* : "I was then in my junior BA. One day in our 'Baradari' bungalow which overlooked Sabarmati river, I was reading Carlyle's *Hero and Hero Worship*. Suddenly my uncle, Gatubhai Dhru, entered my room and said, "I have brought Gaganbhai to meet you." I was surprised but happy. I got up from the chair and sat on the edge of the table and asked Gaganvihari to sit on the chair. Gatubhai said, "I am going downstairs to talk to Vidyabhen." At first we talked of Carlyle's *Hero and Hero Worship* and then of various other subjects and so an hour passed away. Then we both went downstairs.... Some time back, I had heard Gatubhai tell my mother, 'what if we arrange a match between Saudamini and Gagandas?' I had been very happy to overhear the conversation. The next day also Gaganvihari came to meet me and we stood on the terrace facing the river and talked for over an hour. Gaganvihari had come from Bhavnagar and was on his way to Delhi where his father was a member of the Council of State. He promised to write to me from Delhi.....

" When I received no letter for some time, I decided to write the first letter. Thus our correspondence began. Gaganvihari did not believe in God and I was brought up in a Prarthana Samaj family and so we discussed about these matters

* Translated from the original *Smaranoni Suvas* by Saudamini Mehta (in Gujarati) by author.

in our letters. But gradually through these letters we became good friends and the nature and content of our letters changed....I received letters from Gaganvihari regularly...At the end of a year, I told my mother about our intention to marry and then my father wrote to Gaganvihari's father...In 1924, I went to Bombay to appear for my BA examination, as the examination was not held in Ahmedabad. After one paper, we used to have an hour's break when Gaganvihari would come and meet me and we had tea in a restaurant opposite the Bombay School of Economics. On the last day, after the examination finished, Gaganvihari and his father came in their car to fetch me and we went for a walk in Hanging Gardens.

"Next day to celebrate my engagement, there was a lunch in Andheri where Gaganvihari's family lived. I stayed for a few days with my sister, Jyotsnabhen in Santa Cruz and every day a car came to fetch me in the afternoon and I went to Andheri to meet Gaganvihari. This was, of course rather unusual.

"In September, I went with Lallubhai to Simla. On the way we stayed in Gwalior as guests of the Maharaja. In Simla, I met Rameshwari Nehru who jokingly remarked 'What are we coming to. You are going around with your would be father-in-law!'

Bapu was overwhelmed with joy by his visits to Ahmedabad. After his second visit, he confided in Brelvi, "Saudamini came both to receive me and see me off at Ahmedabad. All the three afternoons we were together...I walked with her to college and was with her the whole day. In too good to be true."

On December 3, 1924, they were married in Ahmedabad. It was a simple ceremony as my mother's family were Prarthana Samajists and did not believe in many of the orthodox rituals and ceremonies of a traditional Hindu marriage. They had three daughters, Nilanjana, Uma and Aparna.

The happiest years of their married life were spent in Calcutta. Ma wrote to Brelvi on 3rd December, 1934, "To-day is our tenth wedding anniversary. But I feel as if we are newly

Saudamini & Gaganvihari Mehta

married. I cannot tell you how happy these ten years have been. In this respect we have been extremely lucky because I have seen few of our friends so happily married. There has not been a single day when I have regretted marrying." Bapu dedicated his book *From Wrong Angles*, a collection of his humorous essays, published in 1933, to Saudamini, "Owing to whom life to me has been one stream of ringing silvery laughter, But for whose delightful personality and association G.L.M.'s contributions would have been impossible."

Soon after marriage, Bapu left the *Bombay Chronicle*. He wrote to Brelvi, "I love the work immensely and do it more for the sake of the work than for anything else. But my salary has been cut off entirely and has progressively declined instead of rising after two years' sincere and strenuous labour for a paper which I feel is my own." His salary was only Rs.150/- per month. Lallubhai had invested money in a sugar factory and in the Bhavnagar Electricity Works. Both ventures had failed and there was no hope of recovering the money. It was, therefore, imperative for him to earn enough to support himself and his wife. Apart from this financial problem, Ma having been brought up in a reformist, liberal household, was not comfortable and happy in the Andheri house where the atmosphere was more conservative and orthodox. She wanted to live separately in their own house. He tried to get a teaching job in Lucknow University, which had only recently been established. He felt that educational service might give him more leisure and greater opportunity to study. Unfortunately, the Lucknow job did not materialise and most unwillingly he joined the Scindia Steam Navigation Company. He wrote later, "Realising the truth of Lord Northcliffe's observation that journalism is a good profession to get out of, I gave up the *Chronicle* and journalism" but this was not true. He loved journalism all his life and gave it up much against his desire. He had never thought that he would join business and it was with a heavy heart that he accepted his first posting with Scindias in Rangoon.

REFERENCES

1. Jehangir Petit, well known Parsi businessman and industrialist of Bombay.
2. Bhalchandra Krishna, a prominent citizen of Bombay.
3. Benjamin Guy Horniman, English journalist and author; worked with *Manchester Guardian*. He was assistant Editor, Calcutta, *Statesman*. He was appointed editor of *Bombay Chronicle* in 1913. He was a leader of the Home Rule Movement and because of his anti government writings, was deported to England in 1919.
4. Chittaranjan Das (Deshbandhu) (1870-1925); Barrister. His defence of Aurobindo Ghosh in the Alipore Bomb Case brought him great fame. He was a member of the legislative assembly and belonged to the Swaraj party.
5. C. Rajagopalachari (1879-1972), joined national movement after Rowlatt Act and Jalianwallah Bagh. Chief Minister of Madras, 1937-1939. Opposed Congress leaving ministries in 1939 as well as to the 'Quit India' movement 1942. Governor of West Bengal–1947. Governor General of India, 1948-50. Minister in the Central Cabinet.
6. Vallabhbhai Patel (1875-1952). Known as 'Sardar'; associated with Kheda Satyagraha and Bardoli Satyagrahas and Salt Satyagraha. Imprisoned by the British several times.Was boss of the Congress party organisation. Home Minister, Minister for Indian States and Information & Broadcasting – 1947-1952.
7. Vithalbhai Patel (1873-1933), brother of Vallabhbhai Patel. Freedom fighter who was jailed several times. Member of Legislative Assembly.
8. N.C. Kelkar, (1872-1947). One of Tilak's principal aides in the Home Rule movement. Editor of *Maratha* and *Kesari*. Member, Legislative Assembly, 1922 and 1929. President, Poona Municipality.
9. Diwan Chamanlal, b. 1892. Barrister, founded All India Trade Union Congress, 1920. Member, Central Legislative Assembly, 1923-31 and 1945-46
10. Rangaswamy Iyengar, b. 1877. Editor, *The Hindu*, Madras. Elected to second and third Central Legislative Assembly. Secretary, All India Swaraj Party, 1925-37. General Secretary of Indian National Congress, 1926-27.
11. N.M. Joshi (1879-1955). Member, Servants of India Society. Founded Social Service League, 1911. President, Social Service League. 1921.

Founded All India Trade Union Congress. In 1929, left AITUC to form a rival Trade Union Federation. For 26 years (1921-1947), he was the sole nominated member of the Central Legislative Assembly to represent labour.

4

Years in Calcutta: 1928-1947

Rangoon was a long way from Bombay and the young couple felt lonely and unhappy. Moreover, Bapu did not like his work to Brelvi he wrote, "Working under unknown persons of not an agreeable temperament or refinement...you cannot appreciate the difficulty of doing thoroughly distasteful work as a subordinate of people with unusual nature. Still I am making the best of a bad job .If you see me here outside the office or even inside, you would not find me very much less cheerful than in Bombay...Through no fault of mine and despite my undoubtedly honest work and capacity, I have lost the liberty of doing what I choose and love and know, through a conspiracy of malevolent circumstances... I had never dreamt that I would have to earn my living through service of this sort and under such conditions, the shock has been too great."

He tried to keep himself intellectually alive by reading and reviewing books. He thought of rejoining *Bombay Chronicle* but was hesitant and wrote to Brelvi, "You will probably feel that I am complaining about my position and not taking an opportunity to go out of my present uncongenial work. You cannot know how heartily I dislike it and how keen I am to get out of it at the earliest possible opportunity.... But journalism is a precarious, ill paid and exhausting profession and I would not like to go back to it unless it is impossible for me to get into the educational line. Still I am unable to make up my mind."

In 1928, Bapu was transferred from Rangoon to Calcutta as manager and head of the Scindia Steamship office there, then located at 100 Clive Street (now Netaji Subhas Road) the heart of Calcutta's commercial centre. Reminiscing about his Calcutta days, he wrote, "Clive Street then symbolised British commerce and industry and for Scindias, British shipping. It was like Wall Street or Lombard Street. It was the stereotype of alien economic domination and exploitation." He arrived in Calcutta in January 1928 from Rangoon accompanied by their Brahmin cook, Manishanker, whom my mother had brought from her parental home in Ahmedabad. Ma joined Bapu soon with their two daughters, Nilanjana and baby Uma. They rented a small house on Shyamanand Road in Bhowanipur. During their twenty years' stay in Calcutta, they shifted house nine times! For a few years they lived in a house on 24 Ray Street, a house belonging to Shri Jivanlal, the father of the present Governor of West Bengal, Shri Viren Shah. They moved from Bhowanipore, which was a middle class Bengali residential area, where some professional non-Bengalis also lived (most Gujarati and Marwari businessmen then lived in north Calcutta), to the more anglicised residential area between Park Street and Lower Circular Road (now re-named Acharya Jagdish Chandra Bose Road). A 'good address' in Calcutta in those days was 'south of Park Street'. They shifted to 9/1, Hungerford Street, a house belonging to Ajay Dutt, son of Ramesh Chandra Dutt, ICS who had been Dewan of Baroda and a friend of my mother's family. From there they shifted to 3, Loudon Street and finally to 11, Rawdon Street. Hungerford Street and Rawdon Street were named after Lord Hastings in his many guises and Loudon Street after his wife. The houses here were usually two storied, with large rooms, high ceilings and long south facing verandas from which direction the breeze came on summer evenings. They had large lawns. Bapu wrote, "Calcutta, then was much cleaner, brighter, more cheerful, less congested and much more anglicised. The British dominated the city, its commercial and its multifarious social life. Racialism was encountered in Calcutta at various levels. In railway trains, compartments were reserved for Europeans and however crowded the train might be, no Indian was allowed to travel in them though they were empty. An Englishman could take even an unreserved compartment and he would not allow any Indians to enter it. Benches and chairs were also reserved for Europeans in public parks and other places. The hallmark of British colonial culture was the club. Calcutta was dotted with exclusive European clubs whose doors were closed to 'natives'."

Lallubhai Samaldas was a Director of Martin's Light Railway Company and of TISCO and came to Calcutta two or three times a year for Board meetings there or in Jamshedpur. One of the first persons he introduced my parents to was Mrs. Sarala Ray (1859 - 1940) whom he knew because of their common friendship with Gopal Krishna Gokhale. When Mrs. Ray's son died at a young age and she was grief stricken, Gokhale suggested to her that she should start a school for girls and so when she did this, she named it Gokhale Memorial Girls' School. Our parents were against Convent education, which alienated children from their own culture, and so it was to this school that we were sent and my two sisters had almost their entire school education there. Ma took great interest in the management and activities of Gokhale School. (My sister, Uma recalls that when my parents visited the school, she and our elder sister Nilanjana used to feel embarrassed because Bapu wore white *khadi sherwani, chudidar* and a Gandhi cap, whereas the fathers of other girls all wore suits and tie! Ma also always wore a *sari* in the Gujarati way). Mrs. Ray was a great educationist with a vision and in her school all students had to learn three languages – Bengali, English and Hindi, long before the three language formula was adopted officially. The medium of instruction in the primary school was Bengali but English was taught from the kindergarten by English teachers. She employed teachers from different parts of India. Great emphasis was laid on sports and games, on drama, music and other extra curricular activities. The girls sang Tagore's prayer songs in their morning assembly and 'Jana Gana Mana' was the school song long before it became the national anthem. Mrs. Ray was a member of the Calcutta University Senate and a pioneer of women's emancipation. She married P.K. Ray of the Indian Education Service. My parents also met Sarala Ray's sister, Abala Bose (1864-1951), wife of the renowned scientist, Sir Jagadish Chandra Bose. Abala Bose had founded the Brahmo Girls' School and also Bani Bhuvan, an institution where widows from villages and deserted women were trained as teachers. My mother and she had many common interests and became friends. Sarala Ray's daughter, Charulata Mukherjee and her family had been with my father on S.S. Morena on their voyage to England and this friendship was renewed. Through this family, my parents came to know several Brahmo families in Calcutta, such as that of Ramanand Chatterji, editor of *Modern Review.* My mother's family, as mentioned before, was Prarthana Samajist. The idea of a Prarthana Samaj at Bombay was first mooted in the 1840s inspired by the Brahmo Samaj but it was formally organised in 1867 at the instance of Keshub Chandra Sen. The Brahmo preacher and organiser, Pratap Chandra Mazumdar visited Ahmedabad and stayed with my mother's great grandfather, Bholanath Sarabhai. Ma found many things in common with Brahmo ladies in Calcutta and easier to mix with them, as many of them were educated and spoke English. A friendship, she particularly prized, was that of Indiradevi Chaudhurani, (1873-1906), daughter of Satyendranath Tagore, brother of Rabindranath Tagore. Satyendranath, the first Indian I.C.S., had been posted to Ahmedabad as District Judge and had come to know my mother's family there. Indiradevi had married the writer Pramatha Chaudhuri and was best known for her compilation of the notations of Tagore's songs. She was trained in both Indian and Western music. Besides translating from Bengali into English and from French into Bengali, she published several books of her own in Bengali.

Ma started a Gujarati *Stree Mandal* (ladies' association) in Bhowanipur and later a *bal mandir* or nursery school for children. Both my parents were co-opted into the Managing Committee of the Anglo-Gujarati School in North Calcutta, Ma being the first woman ever having got into it and there was considerable opposition from the men regarding her appointment. She started adult literacy classes for women there, in both English and Gujarati and herself taught there. In 1941, she organised a *khadi* and village industries exhibition under the auspices of these classes, which was opened by Prof. Priyaranjan Sen, a member of the Harijan Sevak Sangh Board. But her activities were not confined to just Gujaratis. She started a *Shishu Mangal Bhavan*, a centre for Harijan children, which is running even today. She was active in the All India Women's Conference and attended its annual session in Lucknow in 1933 where her mother, Lady Vidyagauri Nilkanth presided. Ma read a paper at this conference on birth control. She opened a birth control clinic in Calcutta and was in correspondence with Margaret Sanger, the American feminist, who had started a birth control clinic in Brooklyn in 1923 and encouraged the opening of such clinics elsewhere. Ma had the full support of Bapu in all these activities and his letters to his brothers and father reveal that he was indeed very proud of her social work.

Bapu was not particularly happy with his job as the Manager of the Scindia office in Calcutta. He wrote to Batuk Kaka and this is one of several letters in the same vein, "I am unable to settle down to my present work and can't find any interest in it." He found the work boring and uncongenial. To divert his mind, he started writing a thesis on the 'Social Philosophy of Bertrand Russell' and submitted it to Bombay University for an

M.A degree. Dr. S. Radhakrishnan was one of his examiners and he was awarded a First Class. He was now keen on being an academic and applied to Benares Hindu University for a lecturership. He was interviewed and selected and was sorely tempted to join but Ma was not too keen. The salary was only Rs. 250 per month, whereas he was getting Rs. 500 every month in Scindias. In those days this was a princely salary comparable to the salary of an ICS officer of the same age. Moreover, a friend who was teaching in BHU informed him that salaries were often paid after six months! Ma felt that it would be very difficult to manage as they had no savings and did not want to borrow from his father. Both Lallubhai and Batuk Kaka were also against Bapu going to Benares and so after a great deal of family discussion and debate, the idea was given up. Ma often felt a little guilty in later years that she had dissuaded her husband from a career he had wanted to take up.

Bapu tried to diversify his interests. Having started as a journalist, his interest in journalism continued unabated. *Statesman*, the English language daily, represented the views of the government and the British business interests in Calcutta. There were, however, a number of daily newspapers, weeklies and other magazines owned and edited by Indians, published in English, representing the nationalist point of view. He was a frequent contributor of both serious and humorous articles and book reviews to many of these such as *Capital* (a financial and commercial weekly started in 1888), *Forward*, *Hindustan Standard*, *Advance*, *Indian Affairs* and *Modern Review*. But most of all to *Amrit Bazar Patrika*[1] of which he was a sort of honorary writer of editorials. *Amrit Bazar Patrika* was originally a bilingual daily published in English and Bengali. When Lord Lytton's Vernacular Press Act of 1878 muzzled the Indian language newspapers, *Patrika*, to evade the rigours of the Act, became a full fledged English daily. He wrote for *Vanguard*, a magazine started by the Congress Socialist leaders, Yusuf Meherally and

Upendra Desai. *Indian Finance* was started at almost the same time as when Bapu moved to Calcutta. He had known its editor, C.S. Rangaswamy, for over ten years and now became a regular contributor of humorous skits on economic and political subjects, under the initials G.L.M.,to this weekly. Dr. Bidhan Chandra Roy, (later Chief Minister of Bengal), once said that he subscribed to *Indian Finance* only for the articles of GLM which he found "witty but entirely free of malice." Bapu wrote an article entitled 'Why the Congress is always Wrong' and on reading it, Sir John Anderson, then Governor of Bengal, remarked that this was "one of the most brilliant pieces of light writings he had come across." He wrote on a wide variety of subjects. He reviewed several books of Bertrand Russell, Pyarelal's *The Epic Fast*, K. Sanataṇam's *Indian Road to Socialism*, Laski's *Where Do We Go From Here*, *An Essay in Interpretation*, etc. In 1938, British Prime Minister Neville Chamberlain's appeasement diplomacy averted war over German aggression in the Czech Sudetanland. Hitler's occupation of this area was acceded to by the British government at Munich. After the Munich Pact, Bapu wrote an article in the *Hindustan Times* 'Peace Prize for Hitler' : "Opinion is being canvassed in England for the award of the Nobel Peace Prize to Mr. Neville Chamberlain[2]. Undoubtedly he deserves it. It is he who more than anyone else peacefully arranged for Hitler's annexation of somebody else's territories, which Hitler would not have otherwise obtained without war. This is no small contribution to peace. Without however, disparaging in the slightest degree the immense contribution of Mr. Chamberlain to the cause of international peace, the fact remains that such peace could not have been promoted or even preserved but for Herr Hitler. In fact his claims for the Nobel Peace Prize far outweigh those of any other European statesman since Napoleon tried to establish peace all over Europe and the world. But then there was no peace prize at that time."

A collection of these humorous skits was published in a book entitled *From Wrong Angles* in 1933. Walchand Hirachand sent a copy of this book to Sir Samuel Findlater Stewart, a Member of the Secretary of State's Council in London. "It presents", he wrote, "in a sarcastic and humorous vein the view point and feelings of the educated Indian young men towards the political and economic problems of the day and I have no doubt you will appreciate these studies all the more because they depict men and things from a new angle." Sir Samuel found the book "most entertaining to read,"despite the fact that most of the skits made fun of British policies in India. In 1942 he published another collection of his humorous articles entitled *Perversities.* A reviewer wrote, "the author exhibits a blend of talent which runs coursing between Stephen Leacock and A.P. Herbert." The skits relate largely to political events between 1935 and 1942, but there are a few which are specimens of such wit and humour that they are not dated– such as the 'Interpretation of the Honours List', 'Report on Mishandling a Case' and 'The Other Fellow'– these have an appeal even today.

He wrote an editorial in the *Amrit Bazar Patrika* entitled "His and Her" in which he said that with the growing strength of feminism in the West, there were protests against using the male pronoun to refer to women also. Does 'he' include 'she', 'him', 'her'? Words such as chairman may have to be changed. His nationalist sympathies were evident in all that he wrote. In an editorial "Malice in Wonderland", he wrote, "The King's government must be carried on if not by the King's representatives than by his puppets. The job-hunters and the careerists do not ask so many questions. They simply take jobs when offered. Question: Was it not said in *Alice in Wonderland* that when the bone was taken from the dog what remained was the dog's temper? Answer: Yes. And when offices with power are denied to the representatives of the people, the spirit of the people is still there!" This referred to the constitutional reforms introduced under the Government of India Act of 1935 wherein only certain powers and offices were given to Indians who had been elected and others were reserved for the British Governor appointed by the Viceroy.

My parents were both fond of reading and writing. They started to learn Bengali from a friend and read Tagore's poems and short stories and Sarat Chandra Chatterjee's novels in Bengali. They adapted some of Rabindranath's poems and short stories into Gujarati. Bapu started a Gujarati Literary Association which met every Sunday morning where well known literary men were invited and discussions were held on various literary, and cultural subjects. An exhibition of Gujarati books and paintings was organised by it which was opened by Dr. Shyama Prasad Mukherjee, son of Sir Asutosh Mukherjee, one of the founders of the Jan Sangh and a cabinet minister under Nehru. The Gujarati Literary Association also published a Gujarati monthly journal, *Navchetan*.

Bapu soon became a popular speaker as he prepared his speeches with great care, his delivery was excellent and he always entertained the audience with some jokes and humorous anecdotes. He was invited to colleges, the Rotary Club and other places to deliver lectures. His speech on 'Economic Foundations of Politics' at St. Paul's College in August, 1935, was reported in full in the *Amrit Bazar Patrika, Statesman* and *Forward.*

From the start of his life in Calcutta, Bapu was immersed in the commercial politics of the city. At that time, the Bengal Chamber of Commerce represented European business interests and the Bengal National Chamber consisted mainly of Bengalis. After First World War, Calcutta became the country's chief battleground between British and Indian business interests. The former combined to form the Associated Chamber of Commerce in 1921 to meet the growing Indian challenge. The Indians replied by forming the Federation of Indian Chamber of Commerce and Industries organised in Calcutta at the initiative of G.D. Birla and some leaders of the Indian business community. In the same year, G.D. Birla[3], Sir Purshottamdas Thakurdas, Lallubhai Samaldas and a few others met in Calcutta and decided to start the Indian Chamber of Commerce with G.D. Birla as its first President. Thus there began in Calcutta under G.D. Birla's leadership, an offensive against British economic power. By this time, the Indian business classes were becoming more conscious of their distinct identity and there was a growing clash of interests between them and the British business classes. The 1920s saw a clear polarisation between the two groups – the Associated Chamber of Commerce, a coalition of all European trade organisations and the Federation of Indian Chambers of Commerce and Industries (FICCI), of Indian business houses.

Bapu was very active in the Indian Chamber and was soon on several of its committees. He was elected its President in 1939. "Apart from office work", he wrote to his brother, "the burden of the Chamber is on my shoulders... This keeps me engaged till late in the evenings, particularly as we are having a busy time with railway, general budgets, rise in bank rate, shortage of railway wagons, etc. On some days I get home at 8 p.m." He represented the Chamber on a number of committees including the Bengal Board of Apprentice Training, the Port Commissioner's Pilot Advisory Committee, Light House Advisory Committee, Commission for the Port Trust and the Bengal Board of Economic Enquiry. "I am put on every *ad hoc* committee of the Chamber", he wrote. His grasp of problems as well as his command of the English language and drafting were excellent and so he was made to write representations from the Chamber. One such representation on the Grand Trunk Canal Project, a scheme of waterways, created quite a stir in the local press. *Statesman* gave a full column and a half to the representation and the *Englishman* published it in full double column. He was intimately associated with the Chamber for twenty years till he left Calcutta in 1947. "Indian Chamber provided me a training ground for public work and a forum for expression of opinion on important questions," he wrote.

In Calcutta, Bapu came to know Sir C.V. Raman. In fact, as mentioned earlier, both of them had stayed in the same boarding house in London, 22, Oxford Road, Putney, one of the few places at the time which catered to vegetarians. From London, he had written to his father to help Raman financially, if required, on his return to India and had urged Brelvi to publish Raman's articles in the *Bombay Chronicle*. To his father he wrote, "Raman is unassuming and modest to the point of shyness that he will not approach anybody though he needs money for his laboratory. Poor man he is almost without money now having spent it on some rare apparatus. He is unknown in our country and will not be known until Europe recognises him." He heard Raman deliver two lectures in Rangoon in 1927 but it was in Calcutta that he came to know him better. Sir Asutosh Mukherjee, as Vice Chancellor of Calcutta University, tried to draw talent from different parts of the country and appointed Raman as the Palit Professor of Physics. Raman's wife, Loka Sundari Ammal, became Ma's friend. Raman had chosen his own bride when he was eighteen and married her just before he left for Calcutta. She was educated and was an accomplished *vina* player. Raman received the Nobel Prize in 1930 and in 1933, he left Calcutta to become the Director of the Indian Institute of Science, Bangalore. Raman came to Calcutta in 1944 and Bapu helped him to collect money for his Institute. When Bapu visited the Institute of Science, Raman had shown him round. Later, they were both associated with the Nuffield Scholarship Committee in the 1950s

A much closer friend of Bapu's was Dilip Kumar Roy whom he had first met him in London and subsequently they travelled on the same boat on their return journey to India. Before returning to Calcutta, Roy stayed for a few days in Lallubhai's

Andheri house and Bapu had lent him some money, taken him to a cultural conference in Bombay and arranged for a concert of his in Ahmedabad. Writing about Roy, Bapu said, "When I was posted to Calcutta, in January, 1928, I was overjoyed at the idea of being in the same city as Dilip Kumar Roy and looked forward to the opportunity of frequently meeting him...". This was a friendship which lasted till the end despite the fact that Roy moved to Pondicherry and later to Poona.

Roy introduced Bapu to Subhas Chandra Bose[4] when the latter came to Bombay for an All India Congress Committee meeting in May 1923. Bapu recalled, "This is my first recollection of an AICC session....I was then working for the *Bombay Chronicle*. I attended the session mainly to meet Subhas Bose who was to come there and a common friend, Dilip Kumar Roy, whom I had come to know on the steamer coming back from Europe had asked me to see him. That is where I first heard Rajaji speak. He was defending the use of *khadi* and I remember those short, crisp sentences, which he still uses. 'It is not a question of dress', he said, 'It is a question of ethics'. Subhas Bose had a striking personality. He came with me and we met at a friend's office in Meadow Street; it was the office of B. Das, later a Member of Parliament from Orissa. I had a long talk with Subhas Bose for about an hour and he told me that the idea of 'no change' was fundamentally wrong. We must change our policies and tactics. If entering the legislature was wrong, we would have to find some other method..."Bapu continued to meet him occasionally in Calcutta. Though he admired Bose's courage and patriotism, he did not approve of his methods, his militarism and his looking to Hitler and later Japan for support to fight British imperialism in India. Bapu totally disapproved of Hitler's Nazi policies and of totalitarianism in any form. My parents went and met Bose at his Elgin Road house, a few days before he disappeared in disguise for Germany. They were also frequent visitors to the Woodburn Park Road house of Sarat Chandra Bose[5], particularly when Gandhiji came and stayed there. They came to know Satish Chandra Das Gupta of the Khadi Pratishthan Ashram at Shodepur where also Gandhiji frequently stayed. Bapu knew the 'Big Five' of Bengal politics – Nalini Ranjan Sarkar[6], a businessman; Bidhan Chandra Roy[7], an eminent physican; Sarat Chandra Bose, brother of Subhas; Nirmal Chunder Chandra, a wealthy solicitor; and Tulsi Charan Goswami, a zamindar with rich interests in jute. Whenever Sarojini Naidu[8] came to Calcutta and stayed with Dr. Bidhan Roy, she would telephone Ma and ask her to cook one of her favourite Gujarati dishes and take it to Dr. Roy's house. Sometimes, we children were also taken. When any member of the family was seriously ill, Dr. Roy was consulted and he never charged any fees. In 1943 Brelvi was in Calcutta for the All India Newspaper Editors' Conference, of which that year he was the President. He was staying with us in our house, 11 Rawdon Street, when he had a massive heart attack and Dr. Roy used to visit him almost daily.

We visited Shantiniketan when Rabindranath was still alive and met the poet in his house *Uttarayan.* We also went to Tagore's house in Jorasanko in Calcutta. Ma had studied in school and college in Ahmedabad with Shrimati Hutheesingh who went on to learn dancing in Shantiniketan and married the Poet's nephew, Soumendranath Tagore. I remember one occasion when we went to Jorasanko where Shrimatiben was dancing while Rabindranath recited his poem *Natir Puja* . My sister, Uma recalls another occasion in Jorasanko when we heard Rabindranath sing *Hriday amar ajike nachere* (my heart today dances with joy).

Among my parents' other close personal friends in Calcutta were Dr. H. Ghosh of the Standard Pharmaceutical Works and his Polish wife Neuta; Kiran Shankar Roy of Bengal Lamps and his American wife, Anna, Dr. A.H. Pandya, the first Indian Principal of the Shibpur Engineering College and his wife Lily, and Muluk Singh Bedi, a Sikh businessman who was very fond of music, was extremely generous and lived in a palatial house near the Dhakuria Lakes (now Rabindra Sarovar) in South Calcutta.

By the 1930s Ma and Bapu knew a large number of people in Calcutta from different walks of life. In the 1940s, they established a close relationship with the Friends Service Unit group, specially with Horace Alexander[9], Hallam Tennyson, Stuart Nelson and others. Another friendship they made was with Mary Tweedy, the representative of *Time magazine* and her husband. Mrs. Tweedy recalled that Bapu arranged for her to meet Nehru after his release from prison in 1945. Several young Americans who were in Calcutta during the War came to our house, among them was Robert Crane, who later became a Professor of Indian History at Syracuse University, USA, and a friend of the family. Lin Yutang, the well-known Chinese author, came for tea and my father and he had a long talk on the Indian political situation and Bapu found him "very interesting, bright, very pleasant and charming." I remember listening quietly to their conversation. He later questioned me and signed in my autograph book.

Most of India's external trade in the pre-Independence period was in British hands, including the most lucrative trades in opium, jute, tea and later coal. There was little challenge to the British monopoly in shipping; therefore, these were easily beaten off by companies, which had much vaster financial resources than their challengers and enjoyed patronage from public authorities and from powerful firms. The European shipping companies plying along the coast and across the oceans enjoyed mail subventions from the Governments of UK and India. During the First World War, the British Government subsidised British shipping companies in other ways. Jamshedji Tata's efforts to break the monopoly of European lines in carrying the trade between India and China failed due to drastic rate cutting by P&O and its associates. The Indian shipping interest represented mainly by the Scindia Steam Navigation Company tried to pressurise the government to protect Indian shipping against unfair competition but failed. Scindias fought for reservation of Indian coastal trade to Indian vessels, for Indianisation of marine and port services, for appropriate facilities for training Indian cadets, for equality and decent treatment of Indian seamen and for safeguarding the national character of indigenous shipping. All the top managers of Scindias, Walchand Hirachand, M.A. Master[10] and my father were nationalists. Walchand kept the flag of Indian shipping flying under the most trying conditions against formidable British shipping firms such as P&O. When the very existence of Indian shipping was in danger, Walchand turned down Lord Inchcape's tempting offer to purchase Scindia Steamship Company without a second thought. Year after year, he carried on tirades against the government and forced concessions from unwilling hands. Sir Samuel Findlater Stewart wrote about Walchand, "I have never met an Indian who is so frankly utterly anti-British." The first national newsagency, the Free Press of India was established in 1927. Among its sponsors were Annie Besant, M.R. Jayakar and Walchand Hirachand.

The Coastal Shipping Bill occupied quite a bit of Bapu's time and he was constantly going to Delhi and Simla. As a result of the resolution of Sir Sivaswamy Iyer in the Central Legislative Assembly, the Indian Mercantile Marine Committee was appointed by the government in 1923 which recommended practically unanimously that India's coastal trade should be reserved for shipping companies, the controlling interests of which were predominantly Indian. As the government did not take any action on this recommendation, non-official members of the Legislative Assembly like K.C. Neogy and S.N. Haji introduced bills to reserve Indian coastal trade to Indian owned and Indian managed vessels. Bapu carried on a vigorous campaign for Haji's Bill and wrote a series of articles on coastal reservation in the *Bombay Chronicle*. The Scindia Company put in unremitting effort to canvass support for the Bill. Pandit Motilal Nehru, Lala Lajpat Rai and other nationalist leaders supported the Bill in the Assembly. It also received Gandhiji's blessings.

Haji's Bill passed the first reading in the Assembly by a large majority in 1928 and was referred to a select committee. When its report came before the Assembly in 1929, its further progress was stopped by convening a shipping conference by Lord Irwin and also by the boycott of the Assembly by the Swarajists.

In February 1938, a private bill on coastal shipping was once again tabled by Dr. Ziauddin Ahmed[11] and secured the first place in the list of opposition bills. Bapu went to Delhi, stayed in the house of Mathuradas Vasanji, (senior partner of Vasanji Sons & Co., chairman-founder of Globe Insurance Co. Ltd. who did all kinds of insurance business and was elected to the Legislative Assembly by the Indian Merchants Chamber in 1935), at 34, Ferozeshah Road, lobbying for the bill. He found several members supporting the bill, including N.M. Joshi. But he wrote to Batuk Kaka, "the great leader of the opposition [Bhulabhai Desai] who considers himself greater than Motilal, Gokhale and Das doesn't approve of it. Although he is a far better speaker than Motilal, in fact the best speaker in the House now – his manners are very obnoxious and his conceit has displeased many people. The Indian deputation from Burma was bitterly complaining about the treatment they received at his hands. Bhulabhai has, of course, created a very favourable impression on the government who are full of praise for his moderation and sweet reasonableness. I am afraid he will soon go the way of Jayakar[12] if he and the Congress Party and the great cabinet are not careful. ...Satyamurti[13] is a very fine speaker, in fact a more experienced Parliamentarian than any other Congressman in the Assembly. Govind Vallabh Pant[14] is an extremely fine type of man: a very good student, capable and sincere. It was a real pleasure to make his acquaintance. His speech on the JPC Report was one of the best in the debate."

Apart from the shipping bill, with his interest in politics, Bapu keenly followed the Assembly debates on the Joint Parliamentary Committee (JPC) Report. He wrote to his brother, "Many backbenchers are dissatisfied by the last minute whip of Bhulabhai[15] to vote for Jinnah's motion which is more moderate than the original. It is exactly what Muslim diehards like Iqbal wanted, viz. immediate and full provincial autonomy with responsibility at the centre delayed. Jinnah is, of course, proud as a peacock and when Shah and I congratulated him, he said 'Congratulate the country, my dear fellow' with his inimitable gestures. ...The only good speaker on the government side is Bhore[16]...On the whole it is a very poor Assembly. The first and second with Patel, Motilal, P.T., Birla, Kunzru[17], Neogy, Jayakar, Lajpatrai, Malaviya[18], Goswami, etc. can't be matched. Joshi's independence and spirit command respect."

Indian businessmen and industrialists had been drawn to Gandhi by his stress on truth, non-violence, peace and self-reliance. He symbolised the general urge among Indians for self-rule. His determination not to deviate from peaceful means under any circumstances fitted in admirably with the businessmen's abhorrence of violence and conflict. Gandhi's charisma, his precepts and his personal life style served to politicise the Indian business classes beyond measure.

Bapu had not been much impressed by Gandhi when he heard him first speak at the Congress session in Bombay in 1915 or at the Gujarat Provincial Conference at Godhra in 1917. However, as noted above, as a student in London, he had closely followed the non co-operation movement and became a great admirer of Gandhi. He attended the historic session of the Congress held in Calcutta in December 1928 where Motilal Nehru presided and Subhas Bose was the leader of the volunteers. He recalled, "The 1928 session, I attended almost throughout. Perhaps for the first time in the history of the Congress, nearly 50,000 workers from neighbouring mills and peasants independently marched to the site of the session in an orderly fushion 'to assert their rights' under the Congress banner. They saluted the national flag hoisted in the Congress grounds. The Congress session had to be adjourned for an hour and Jawaharlal Nehru, Subhas Bose and Gandhiji had to address the gathering.....Bose organised a para military parade of his volunteers with himself on horseback as General Officer Commanding....There was a tremendous tussle as to whether the Congress should have Dominion status or Independence as its goal." He once again went to the 1931 Congress session at Karachi where Sardar Patel presided. Bapu wrote an article on that session in a Gujarati journal called *Prasthan*. He remembered it as "a remarkable session over which Gandhiji dominated. The execution of Bhagat Singh[19] cast its shadow over the session but Gandhiji stood his ground....When the session was about to end, there were some noises from the back of the hall. Some thought it sounded like 'God save the King'. Jawaharlal got indignant and shouted 'stop that nonsense!' Actually it was not 'God save the King' but something else. That was my first glimpse of Jawaharlal Nehru. Later I went and saw him in connection with the question of the hold of foreign capital in the economy of the country. In the course of the conversation, I told him that I had been a student of Laski. He asked, 'You mean Harold Laski?' Did you know him well? He talked to me very pleasantly that day and was quite friendly."

At Karachi, Bapu also met Gandhi in a deputation of businessmen and industrialists who waited on him in connection with commercial safeguards. Jamshed Mehta of Karachi led the deputation. Bapu later recalled: "I did not participate in the discussion. Subsequently a report had to be drawn up about what Gandhiji said in the meeting and what was said in the meeting and what was said to him.. I drew up a brief report and before sending it to the press, I went to Mahadev Desai and said to him 'You please see this because there might be some inaccuracies in a report like this.' He asked me 'Who prepared this?' When I said, 'I did', he said, 'All right, just send it."

Bapu attended AICC meetings when they were held in Calcutta. Whenever Gandhiji came to Calcutta, Mahadevbhai would telephone him and my parents would go and meet Gandhiji in Sarat Bose's house or in Satish Chandra Das Gupta's Khadi Pratishthan Ashram in Shodepur. Mahadevbhai sometimes would come to our house for a meal. His son, Narayan, also used to come and borrow books and my parents were very fond of him. When Mahadevbhai died, soon after Gandhiji's arrest in 1942 in Aga Khan Palace, Poona, Bapu wrote to Batuk Kaka, "I was simply dumbfounded when I got a phone call from *Hindustan Times* about Mahadevbahi." In 1933, Bapu published a book *Conscience of a Nation* or *Studies in Gandhism,* which received very good reviews. He received many congratulatory letters including one from Acharya Prafulla Chandra Ray[20] who wrote, "You have so thoroughly entered into the spirit of Mahatmaji, that full justice has been done to the great saviour of India." His deep admiration, almost reverence for the Mahatma continued till the end, though he did not accept the Mahatma's economic policies – his stress on self sufficient villages and village industries and his distrust of almost everything modern.

In 1939, soon after the outbreak of World War II, the Congress Working Committee had adopted a resolution drafted by Nehru, asking for 'the right of the Indian people of framing their constitution through a constituent assembly' and sharing of power. If this was granted, they would contribute to the war effort. The Viceroy, Lord Linlithgow, invited over fifty Indian leaders of all shades of opinion for an interview. At the end of it, he issued a statement that dominion status was the goal of

British policy in India and at the end of the war the Act of 1935 could be reviewed. The Congress Working Committee promptly rejected the statement and by 15th November 1939, all the Congress provincial ministries resigned. Bapu felt that this was not the right decision as it left the field free for the Muslim League. He was also a bit uneasy about Gandhiji launching the Quit India movement in 1942 at a time when Britain was at war with Hitler whom he regarded as a greater danger than British rule. Speaking on the occasion of Gandhiji's birth centenary at the Indian Merchants Chamber, Bombay. Bapu said, "Though I was not a follower, disciple or an associate of Gandhiji, during the last ten years of his life, I came frequently in contact with him when I was privileged to enjoy his affection." In 1944, Vallabhbahi wrote a very affectionate letter to Bapu in which he said that Gandhiji thought very highly of him which naturally pleased Bapu and moved him deeply. No foreign clothes or goods were used in our house. We never even went to the fashionable stores in Calcutta like Whiteways and Laidlaws or Army and Navy which sold British goods but shopped in a store called Kamalalaya which sold only *swadeshi* products. The life style at our home was very simple. As in the house of our grandparents, we sat for our meals on wooden stools on the floor. A dining table and chairs were purchased only in 1946. The food was strictly Gujarati vegetarian.

In the summer of 1944, my parents rented a shack in the estate of Shanti Kumar Morarji on Juhu Beach in Bombay, where Gandhiji was recouping after his release from Aga Khan Palace. Mrs. Naidu and Mrs. Vijaya Lakshmi Pandit, Nehru's sister, were also there. This gave us an opportunity of daily attending Gandhiji's evening prayer meetings and occasionally having the privilege of walking with him on the beach. On one occasion, when my sister Uma was ill, Gandhiji came to our hut with Dr. Sushila Nayar, his personal physician and follower, to see her.

My parents were keen on joining the Civil Disobedience

movement in 1930, which began slowly in Calcutta thanks to the factional squabbles within the Bengal Provincial Congress Committee and the preoccupation of provincial leaders with Calcutta Corporation politics. Later, however, the movement gained momentum with Jawaharlal's arrest on April 15 and Gandhiji's imprisonment in early May, which brought the Calcutta crowds on the streets. Bapu wrote to Batuk Kaka, "I have been much disturbed in mind and soul (if any) about Mahatmaji's movement. I feel it is just now everybody's duty to help him as much as one can and I am certainly inclined to join the movement. Unfortunately, here again as in the case of BHU our circumstances are in the way. I don't mind the loss of salary but if the Bank of Baroda business had been out of the way and over, I would really have plunged into it. For the present, I am restraining myself with great difficulty." He went to two salt manufacturing centres in Bengal where volunteers had been assaulted and contraband salt was being collected. Batuk Kaka returned his Kaiser-i-Hind gold medal at this time. Ma was also very keen on joining the movement. She did some picketing in Calcutta, trying to stop football matches being held so that attention should not be diverted from the movement. At least two Calcutta soccer clubs, Mohan Bagan and the Aryans cancelled some fixtures. She wrote to Brelvi that she was very unhappy that she could not participate more and go to jail because of two small children and she was expecting a third baby. Ma did a great deal of work in the Harijan Sevak Sangh and became President of the Bengal Harijan Sevak Sangh.

In October 1936, my grandfather, Lallubhai Samaldas passed away. It was a blow from which my father found it hard to recover. He told us how he sat in the cremation ground with tears rolling down his cheeks feeling as if the world had come to an end. Lallubhai had been an unusually affectionate father and the bond between father and son had been very close.

The following year, Bapu attended the XXIII session of

the ILO Conference in Geneva. The Indian Employers' Delegate was Sir Hormusji (Homi) P. Mody and Bapu, who was then Vice-President of the Indian Chamber of Commerce, Calcutta and member of the Committee of FICCI, was the Adviser. Bapu spoke on Article 6 of the ILO Convention relating to India and the minimum age of employment in industry and his nationalist sympathies and desire for India's industrialisation were all too evident. He said, "nationalism is not merely a political policy but an economic policy as well. ...Like the Irish people, our people are also engaged in a difficult political struggle for autonomy," and he made an appeal for "a national economic policy". He did not want industrialisation to be stifled or hampered by regulations which have been devised for entirely different conditions and by countries "some of which are our competitors and some of which have not adopted the Conventions. He emphasised that India was still struggling to establish industries. "Social progress has no meaning or significance unless the East in its efforts to industrialise can learn from the errors and mistakes of the West and can achieve economic progress along with individual harmony and social justice". He was also a delegate to the International Chamber of Commerce session in Berlin where he and Ma, who accompanied him on this trip to Europe, saw Hitler. They went to Prague and met Prof. Vincene Lesny, an Indologist at Charles University in Prague who had taught himself Bengali and had read Tagore's work in the original and translated them. In the 1920s, he had spent some time in Shantiniketan. Prof. Lesny had written a biography of Tagore entitled *Rabindranath Tagore: His Personality and Work*. My parents went to meet Romain Rolland, who was a friend of Dilip Kumar Roy. Of this visit, Bapu wrote, "In a villa at Villeneuve about 60 miles from Geneva, we met the distinguished French savant through the kindness of Madame Horup, a Danish lady residing in Geneva who was deeply interested in Indian affairs and was active in the 'Friends of India' group. Villeneuve is a beautiful quiet Swiss village on the shore of Lac Leman. Rolland lived there with his Russian wife. Author of *Jean Christophe* and other French classics, he is a great pacifist and socialist. Madame Horup acted as the interpreter. We discussed the Spanish Civil War and whether socialism could be brought about without violence."

Bapu was keen to see a modern industrialised India. In 1941, the government appointed him a member of the Board of Industrial and Scientific Research. Bapu was elected Vice-President of the Federation of Indian Chamber of Commerce and Industries. A few months after the First World War began in 1914, a commercial Congress was convened in Bombay with Sir Fazalbhoy Currimbhoy as president. Sir Fazalbhoy in his presidential address stressed the paramount need for a Federation of Chambers of Commerce. It was not, however, till 1926 that the Indian Industrial and Commercial Congress meeting at Delhi under the Presidentship of Lala Harkishen Lal proposed to set up an Indian Associated Chamber of Commerce. This was renamed the Federation of Indian Chambers of Commerce and Industry (FICCI) two years later. Among its leaders were G.D. Birla, Sir Purshottamdas Thakurdas and Sir Shri Ram. In 1941, Bapu was elected Vice-President of FICCI. At its annual session in New Delhi in March 1942, he moved a resolution asking government to expand key industries and "deplored the absence of any initiative or planned effort on the part of the Government of India towards the establishment of any important defence or heavy industries." The resolution demanded the establishment and expansion of defence industries such as manufacture of aircraft, automobiles, ships, tanks, munitions as well as heavy and key industries such as locomotives, machine tools, heavy chemicals, etc. While moving the resolution, he emphasised that the development of heavy and defence industries was essential not only from India's own standpoint but also from that of the British Commonwealth, "that indeed was the spirit in which the self governing dominions were developing their resources and building up their industries." He quoted the statements of Field Marshal Smuts[21] and Mr. Curtis[22] and said that "these recognised the supreme national necessity of self sufficiency and contained no sermon against too rapid a pace of industrialisation such as had been heard in India. Australia and Canada had made enormous strides since the War began." Bapu was elected President of FICCI and presided over its 16th session held in New Delhi on 22-23 March 1943. Among those present when he delivered his Presidential address were C.Rajagopalachari; Tushar Kanti Ghosh, editor of *Amrit Bazar Patrika*; Sir Jeremy Raisman, Finance Member of the Viceroy's Executive Council; Sir Edward Benthall, Member for War Transport and Railways; Sir Jogendra Singh, Member, Viceroy's Executive Council; Sir J.P. Srivastava, Food Member; Dr. Ambedkar; Mr. C.E. Jones, ICS, Secretary to the Government of India, Finance Department; Mr. N.R.Pillai, ICS, Additional Secretary, Commerce Department; Mr. T.S. Pillai, ICS, Joint Secretary, Commerce Department; and Sir Theodore Gregory, ICS, Economic Advisor to the Government of India.

In his Presidential Address Bapu observed that "Industrial expansion must be broad based on the consuming capacity of the people and at the root of economic discontent are dire poverty, gross disparity in wealth and income, absence of security and the want of equality of opportunity." He dealt with several important economic, financial and commercial questions, which had been under consideration by the Federation and by the Indian commercial world during the year and said that there was need to have a national government at the centre backed by public opinion. Referring to the Cripp's Mission, he said that the principal reason for the deadlock was the reluctance of the British Government to transfer effective power to Indian hands. He criticised the appointment of a representative of the non-official British community as a member of the Viceroy's Council as being tantamount to recognition of the British community in India as a minority entitled to a separate seat. He dealt with persistent efforts being made by British commercial interests in India and England to reverse the principals enunciated by Sir Stafford Cripps that there would be no special protection for British capital or commercial interests in India. "Powerful countries adopt the creed of economic internationalism when it suits their interests but resort to nationalism when convenient. The irony of it is that while preaching virtues of internationalism to backward countries and inducing or compelling them to adopt it, they themselves practice nationalism." He pleaded for India's vital interests to be safeguarded. His speech was widely appreciated and 500 more copies had to be printed. All the Viceroy's Executive Council members present congratulated him including Jeremy Raisman and Edward Benthall. He wrote to his brother, "Jones, the Finance Secretary told Padampat Singhania that my English was wonderful. Gregory congratulated me but told some common friends that I was overemphasising nationalism, whereupon S.N. Ray (a friend of mine whose wife is now an M.L.A.) said 'Gaganvihari got all his economic ideas from the wrong people', whereupon Gregory said, 'But he quotes Keynes all the time!' Raisman told Ghaznavi[23] that if the speech has been a little less political, it would have been one of the finest speeches he had read or listened to! Srivastava wrote that it was an excellent speech. Dr. V.K.R.V. Rao and Dr. Lokenathan congratulated me. For two days Delhi talked a lot about the speech. Kunzru came forward after the speech and like a Bhownagree Nagarsheth said 'I thank you for the speech, (the gentleman referred to said when Tagore got the Nobel Prize that 'we must thank Tagore for this!). Chinese representatives and American correspondents warmly congratulated me on the speech, which they said was the best comprehensive review of the Indian situation they had seen. Waterfield of Reuters, specially came to a party given to me by

Dalmia (!!) to congratulate me. It has been extensively cabled out to Britain and America."

Three resolutions from the Chair were passed at this session. The first expressed grave concern with the political situation and reiterated the Federation's demand for the immediate and effective transfer of political power to a national government. The second urged the Government of India to desist from entering into any agreement on behalf of India, which involved acceptance of financial, fiscal or economic principles or policies as basis for post-war reconstruction. It demanded that in international conferences, Indian commercial community delegates must be included. The third resolution strongly disapproved of the policy pursued by the Government of India in selling accumulated stocks of Indian silver in the London market at a low price and urged that such sale must be stopped.

Bapu's Presidential address and his term as President of FICCI gave him an all India image and exposure. From 1942-43 onwards he was constantly travelling back and forth between Calcutta and Delhi on Federation work or to attend some meeting. In February 1942, he called on Gandhiji and Mahadev Desai at Birla House in Calcutta and also met there Marshall and Madame Chiang-kai Shek and Jawaharlal. Chiang-kai-Shek (1887-1975), the Kuomintang leader and China's then head of state, visited India from 8 to 25 February 1942. He supported the Indian Freedom movement and warned both the British and U.S. governments about the danger of not solving the Indian problem. An All Parties Conference was convened in Allahabad in December, 1942 by Sir Tej Bahadur Sapru[24] to discuss the political situation. Bapu attended this as the President of FICCI. C. Rajagopalachari was one of the leading figures at this conference and my father met him for the first time at one of the informal meetings and wrote, "While I had heard Rajaji and read his speeches, this contact was invigorating. I was immediately impressed by his colourful personality, his sharp intellect, quick grasp of the essence of the problem and his closely reasoned argument." They became good friends after this.

In August 1942, Gandhiji launched the Quit India movement and was interned in the Aga Khan Palace in Poona. Nehru, Patel, Azad and other Congress leaders were also imprisoned. As a protest, violence broke out in different parts of the country. Gandhiji went on a twenty-one days fast in February 1943 as the Viceroy, Lord Linlithgow had questioned his *bona fide* and even his faith in non-violence. There was an emotional upheaval in the country, and as the doctors' bulletins grew gloomier, three members of the Viceroy's Executive Council, Sir Homy Modi, Madhav Aney and Nalini Ranjan Sarkar decided that they preferred patriotism to position and resigned. About two hundred leaders – Hindus, Muslims, Christians, Parsis and Sikhs–from all parts of the country attended an All Parties Conference in New Delhi on 19th February, 1943 to give expression, as Rajaji in his address of welcome said, "to the feeling in the country that Mahatma Gandhi should be enabled to end his fast." Among those present were J.R.D. Tata, Sir Ardeshar Dalal[25], M.S. Aney[26], Bhulabhai Desai, Shyama Prasad Mukherjee[27], K.M. Munshi[28], M.R. Jayakar, Master Tara Singh[29], A.H. Ghaznavi, N.M. Joshi, H.N. Kunzru, Tej Bahadur Sapru, Sarala Devi Chaudhurani and Walchand Hirachand. Bapu was also invited and attended this conference which passed a resolution asking for the Mahatma's unconditional release in the interests of the future of India and of international goodwill. As President of FICCI, Bapu supported the resolution and in his speech referring to the British Prime Minister, Winston Churchill's remark that the commercial community in India was behind the Congress, said, "We are proud to be a part of the national movement. In 1930 when Gandhiji launched the Civil Disobedience movement, FICCI backed the Mahatma to the full. We are convinced that Gandhiji is a force working for social justice and social harmony. That is why some of the biggest commercial magnates are present at this Conference."

In October, 1943, Bapu was appointed to two post-war Reconstruction Committees of the Government of India, the General Policy Committee and the Ports and Civil Aviation Committee. In the latter, apart from him, there were three other non official members – J.R.D. Tata, G.D. Birla and Mr. Cambridge of Indian National Airway. Bapu was nominated a member of the Central Advisory Board of Education, which had Sir John Sargent as its Chairman. For this, he had to travel frequently to Delhi and elsewhere. After one of the meetings in Lucknow, a fellow member wrote to him, "I was struck with the literary finish of your impromptu speeches on various matters at the meetings of the Board. But now I see that you have not only literary skills but also a keen sense of humour, without which, as you say, ' life is apt to become unbearable.' But how you have kept your soul fresh and buoyant, even though immersed in a sea of business, is a marvel and must be an example to us all." In 1944, CABE presented its scheme on 'Post War Educational Development in India' which came popularly to be known as the Sargent Report on Education.

From 1943 onwards he went to Delhi very frequently to attend the meetings of these various committees. He never attended a meeting without reading the agenda and preparing himself fully. During these visits he met several members of the Viceroy's Executive Council, politicians, bureaucrats and journalists. He met old friends and made new ones. Among the latter was Tarlok Singh, ICS, "the more I meet him, the more I like him," he wrote to his brother. He always paid his respects after 1946 to Sardar Patel, Rajaji and Sir Shri Ram[30] with whom he often stayed. Once on a train journey back to Calcutta, "I travelled in the same AC coach as Dr. B.C. Roy, Nirmal Chandra Chunder, and Nalini Ranjan Sarkar and we discussed politics and gossiped all the way", he wrote to his brother.

Amidst all his multifarious public activities he kept his literary interests alive. He published in 1942, a collection of humorous skits entitled *Perversities*, which received many favourable reviews. He continued contributing articles to various newspapers and journals. He was always requesting Batuk Kaka to send him books not available in Calcutta such as Lin Yutang's *A Leaf in the Storm*. Brailsford's *Subject India*, G.D.H. Cole's *Fabian Socialism*, books by Hayek and Lionel Fielden and the complete works of Tennyson, Pope, Addison and Milton from their father's library. *New Statesman* and *Punch* were regularly sent to us in Calcutta after Batuk Kaka finished reading them in Bombay.

The Government offered him several posts during these years, none of which he accepted on the ground that he did not want to serve an alien government. He was asked to be Industrial Planning Officer. He was twice offered the post of Industrial Advisor to the Government of India, once by Sir Azizul Haq and the second time by Sir Ardeshir Dalal. He wrote to his brother that Sir Azizul Haq and Sir Ramaswamy Mudaliar[31] were both disappointed when he declined this offer. Mr. H.M. Patel, ICS, then Secretary Government of India, Department of Supply, told him that both he and Sir Akbar Hydari[32] were unhappy that he did not join. He, however, accepted the membership of the Shipping Policy Committee, the Lighthouse Committee as well as of the Committee for Technological Institutes and the Chairmanship of a Panel for machine tool industries. The Government wanted him to be a member of the Pay Commission but as Walchand Hirachand, Shanti Kumar Morarji and M.A. Master, his bosses in Scindia, were not in favour, he refused, as he did not want to offend them, without whose support, he felt, he could not have achieved whatever he had.

During the great Bengal Famine of 1943, which took away over one million lives in one year, there were hundreds of starving, men, women and children pouring into the streets of Calcutta from the countryside. The sight of the hungry people begging and crying for food, searching for vegetable skins and rotten fruit in the streets and in the garbage dumps was heart rending. Bapu collected money from Gujaratis and Marwaris from Calcutta and Bombay to organise free kitchens and cheap grain shops in the slums. He persuaded the Scindia Steam Navigation Company to donate Rs. 30,000 for famine relief and also bring free grain supplies from Bombay to Calcutta by their ships. Bapu helped Horace Alexander to collect money for famine relief. The Governor of Bengal set up a Central Relief Committee and Bapu was asked to be a member of this committee. Bapu was himself Chairman of another Famine Relief Committee for which he worked round the clock collecting money. He was issuing appeals and receiving cheques from all over the country. Ma also started doing relief work and opened a milk kitchen in her Harijan Bal Mandir. Vijayalakshmi Pandit, who had been released from jail because of her husband's death, wanted to see for herself the famine situation and came and stayed with us. So did Urmila Mehta, President that year, of the All India Women's Conference and Amtus Salam, a Gandhian worker.

In 1944, Bapu went to the United States of America in a business delegation to attend the Industrial Business Conference at Rye. He met Louis Fischer through J.J. Singh and the three of them lunched at the Rockefeller Plaza. Fischer asked him to carry a copy of his latest book, *Empire* that was banned in India, for Gandhij . Bapu took it in his overcoat pocket and personally delivered it to Gandhiji at Sewagram in January 1945.

In June, 1945, Churchill permitted Lord Wavell, the Viceroy, to start negotiations with Indian leader to resolve the political deadlock. Wavell ordered the release of all Congress Working Committee members who had been in jail since August, 1942, and proposed talks to set up a new Viceroy's Executive Council which would be entirely Indian, except for the Viceroy himself and the Commander-in-Chief. The Conference began in Simla on 25 June and lasted till 14 July. At the Simla Conference, the Indian National Congress submitted to the Viceroy, Lord Wavell, a list of 15 names from which the new Executive Council may be chosen. The names were: Maulana Azad, Jawaharlal Nehru, Vallabhbhai Patel, Rajendra Prasad, Jinnah, Mohammad Ismail Khan, Asaf Ali, Liaquat Ali, Amrit Kaur, Shyama Prasad Mukherjee, Muniswami Pillai, G.L. Mehta, Radhanath Das, Ardeshir Dalal and Master Tara Singh.The Conference failed because of Jinnah's intransigent demands that the Muslim League had the absolute right to choose all the Muslim members and that there should be a communal veto in the Executive Council, with decisions opposed by Muslims needing a two-thirds majority. Jinnah's claim that he was the sole spokesman of the Indian Muslims was unacceptable to the Congress whose Simla delegation was headed by its then President, Maulana Abul Kalam Azad, a Muslim. Moreover, the British had no desire of sacrificing the Unionist Party that still controlled the Punjab government and had been consistently loyal.

A number of Congress socialists, men and women, had organised an effective 'underground' group during the 'Quit India' movement in 1942. The government had issued warrants for their arrest. Among them was Aruna Asaf Ali, who was one of its leaders. She, who was still 'underground' in Calcutta under an assumed name and in fact, had hidden in our house for a few days. My father arranged for her to hide in the homes of some friends and also in Park Nursing Home under the name of Mrs. Mehta! M.L. Bhattacharya, Central Intelligence Officer, Calcutta wrote to J.W. Purdy. I.P., Spl. Supdt. of Police, Intelligence Branch, Central Intelligence Department, Calcutta, a confidential letter dated 4.9.1943 (F.28/Cong/42-A-111) stating that, "Gaganbehari Lal Mehta of the Federation of Indian Chamber of Commerce and Industry has been in close touch with Mrs. Aruna Asaf Ali in Delhi and Bombay. In December last G.L. Mehta is reported to have met Mrs. Aruna Asaf Ali at Bombay and brought her the new AICC directions purporting to be the fresh line of action for the second phase of the Congress movement. The leaflet was entitled The Freedom Struggle Front...G.L. Mehta was establishing contacts with the underground Congress Socialist Party rebels.... I would therefore submit that instead of concentrating on the Kabirs [i.e. Humayun Kabir] alone, we had better spread the net a bit wide. Past experience has shown that bigger circles and houses of prominent men afford better and safer sanctuary for absconders." Jawaharlal wanted to meet Aruna Asaf Ali during a visit to Calcutta in January 1946 and so a private dinner was arranged in our house.

After the departure of the Cabinet Mission in 1946, and its failure to resolve the political deadlock, relations between the Congress and the Muslim League deteriorated further. At this critical juncture, Lord Wavell invited Nehru to form an interim government. Jinnah was furious; 'We have forged a pistol and are in a position to use it', he said. The Muslim League declared 16th August 1946 as 'Direct Action Day'. The Muslim League government of Bengal declared the day a public holiday, and their cavalier attitude ensured that no police were in sight. On that day and for the next three days the streets of Calcutta ran with blood, leaving thousands dead, injured and homeless. Bapu wrote, " this was a deliberate and well laid plot of the Muslim League and a traumatic experience." Bapu had gone to Bombay and on arriving at Howrah railway station in Calcutta, found no car to receive him as his message had not reached us. In any case, even if it had, we could not have received him as there was a total breakdown of law and order. Looting, arson and stabbing were rampant. For 24 hours no army was called and police took no action under the orders of the Chief Minister, H.S. Suhrawardy. Large scale Muslim attacks on Hindus and Sikhs were followed by the latter attacking the Muslims. Fortunately, the driver of one of the lorries sent by the Birlas to rescue stranded passengers from Howrah railway station, recognised Bapu and asked him to hide in a crowded truck which brought him home. The driver asked him to remove his Gandhi cap. When he rang the door bell we were afraid to open the door and peeped through the key hole to see who it was! Our house was next to that of H.S Suhrawardy, but that was no guarantee of safety or security. Our downstairs neighbours, Mr. M.G. Bhagat, a Sikh, and his sons kept vigil throughout the night with kirpans and revolvers. Our Gurkha chowkidar also helped in guarding the house. Malik Bazaar, half a mile from our house was gutted, a temple was destroyed and the priest and his family brutally murdered. Our Hindu servant was stabbed as he was going to fetch milk in the early morning and died in front of our house. Muslim members of the Indian Merchants Chamber resigned because a message of congratulations had been sent to the Interim Government that had been formed at the Centre on September 2 , 1946, headed by Nehru. The Muslim League had initially refused to join it. A friend of my father's, Mr. Rehman, who did not support Jinnah and the demand for Pakistan was being continually harassed, black flags were put on his house that was stoned.

Meanwhile the orgy of communal violence, terror and slaughter spread to eastern Bengal, first to Dacca and then to remote districts of Noakhali and Tipperah, resulting in mass killing of Hindus. Deeply distressed, Gandhiji decided to go to Noakhali to 'bury' himself there till Hindus and Muslims learned to live together in peace and harmony. On the way he spent a few days in Calcutta. He stayed in a deserted house belonging to some Muslims in Beliaghata, an area where there had been looting and murder. When Suhrawardy urged Gandhi to stay on to restore communal peace, Gandhi said that he would do so only if Suhrawardy would stay with him, which he did.

Gradually peace was restored and the Muslims of the area one by one started surrendering their arms to him. I remember going with my mother to meet Gandhiji in that Beliaghata house. Ma had to take Gandhiji to a women's meeting. Suhrawardy wanted Gandhiji to go in his car. Gandhiji made a compromise by saying that as he had promised Ma, he would go in her car but Suhrawardy could drive the car! Ma wrote to Batuk Kaka that Gandhiji was in a very cordial mood and asked her to continue with her Harijan Sevak Sangh work.

An Asian Relations Conference was held in Delhi in March 1946. The Conference opened on 23 March in Purana Quila, New Delhi. It was an impressive gathering symbolising the renaissance of Asia. Arabs and Jews from the Middle East, Uzbeks and Kazaks from Central Asia, Burmese, Indonesians, Chinese and Koreans from East Asia, more than a score of nations, cultures and languages gathered together. Bapu was invited to be a delegate. He wrote to his brother that he walked in the inaugural procession led by Sarojini Naidu and Sir Shri Ram, with Jawaharlal Nehru at the rear.

In 1946, he was being pressurised to stand for elections to the Bengal Legislative Assembly from the Indian Merchants' Chamber but he refused. The Congress was also keen for him to contest the elections but he declined. Dr. Prafulla Ghosh, the first Chief Minister of West Bengal, wanted Bapu to be Finance Minister in his cabinet. Bapu recalled, "He telephoned me from Calcutta at midnight on 13th August, 1947, when I was in Delhi to attend the transfer of power ceremony, staying in Constitution House, and said that 'this is not an offer, it is an order. Dr. Ghosh said that he had consulted Sardar Patel, Rajendra Prasad and Acharya Kripalani[33] and they all wanted me to accept this offer." Despite his keen interest in politics and constitutional developments, he was averse to participating in active politics. Its narrowness, intrigues and compromises repelled him. He had keenly observed Bengal politics for twenty years and could not see himself as a participant in it. He also knew that the Birlas did not support the Ghosh ministry and wanted B.C. Roy as Chief Minister. "I consulted Vallabhbhai next morning but he advised me not to go in and I also had a talk with my office people and Mr. Pandya (a senior director of Scindias) told me that we should follow Sardar's advice. Dr. Ghosh and Acharya Kripalani also spoke to Gandhiji and requested him to intervene... Gandhiji said, 'If Vallabhbhai says no then the answer must be no. I don't interfere in these things but people like you should keep away from all these intrigues'...Dr. Ghosh has fortunately not misunderstood me and that is all I want," he wrote to his brother. It is possible that he told Shanti Kumar Morarji to tell Sardar Patel that he could not release him and so Shanti Kumar sent a telegram to Vallabhbhai saying that while they saw no difficulty in his going to the Constituent Assembly, releasing him for the Finance Ministership would be difficult as the Chairman of Scindia was out of the country. Shanti Kumar requested Vallabhbhai not to press my father to accept the Ministership and Prafulla Ghosh to make other arrangements. Sardar immediately replied that if Scindia could not relieve him, he would not press. And so Bapu did not become the Finance Minister of West Bengal though the fact that he had been offered the post, showed the reputation, he, a non-Bengali, had built up in Calcutta. Had he accepted the offer, two brothers would have been Finance Ministers, one in Bombay and one in Bengal.

He was requested by Balwantrai Mehta[34] to be President of the Saurashtra Praja Parishad and in November, 1951, Balwantrai offered him a seat for the Lok Sabha from Bhavnagar for the first General Elections in 1951-52 but he refused on the ground that he knew nothing of the politics of princely states. Bapu, however agreed to become a member of the Constituent Assembly, at the request of Sardar Patel, representing Bhavnagar on behalf of the States Peoples' Conference. He made his maiden speech on the Union Powers Committee Report on centre-state relations for which he was congratulated by 50 or 60 members including Sir Gopalaswamy Iyenger[35], B.L. Mitter[36] and Dewan Chamanlal. At that time his name was frequently mentioned in the press as a likely cabinet minister. It was rumoured that Sardar had suggested his name as Industries and Supply Minister and Sir Chintamani Deshmukh supported the idea but obviously some one opposed it. He met Gandhiji and told him that he had neither political ambitions nor flare for finance. In 1948, Nehru asked him to go as India's High Commissioner to Canada but he declined. Nehru appreciated his modesty and told him "Because you know certain things, you know your limitations. A politician never knows his limitations. Since he can talk on any subject, he thinks he knows every subject!" This reminded Bapu of the conversation between Andrew Undershaft and his son Stephen in George Bernard Shaw's *Major Barbara*, one of his favourite plays. The father asks the son whether he had a turn for literature, art, philosophy or whether he would like to go to the army, navy, Church or the Bar. But the son says that that he was not interested in any of these. The exasperated mother asks Andrew as to what their son should do. Andrew replies ' He knows nothing; and he thinks he knows everything. That clearly points to a political career."

In March, 1947, at the annual conference of FICCI, Bapu moved a resolution on civil aviation. He had been connected from the start with the post-war aviation policy committee. In May 1945, Sir Mohammad Usman, Member of the Viceroy's Council in charge of Posts and Air had declared that the policy of the Government of India was to promote the development and operation of air transport services internally and externally by a limited number of sound and reliable economical organisations. The question of nationalisation of civil aviation had been raised and Bapu wanted the government to clarify its stand and have a definite policy.

In May 1947, Bapu went to Geneva to address the Plenary Meeting of the Inland Transport Committee of ILO. He also spoke at the Plenary Session of the Congress of the International Chamber of Commerce at Montraux on 5th June 1947.

Sometime towards the latter part of 1947, Sir Shanmukham Chetty[37], Minister for Industries, asked Bapu whether he would consider becoming the President of the Tariff Board, then located in Bombay. My father agreed. He had come to Calcutta as an unknown young officer of Scindia Steam Navigation Company at the age of 28; he left it twenty years later as a well-known and respected figure not only in Calcutta but also in the commercial and political world of India. By then, their eldest daughter, Nilanjana had graduated from Calcutta University with English Honours and was studying in Cornell University, Ithaca, and USA. Their second daughter had graduated with Philosophy Honours from Calcutta University obtaining a First Class, and their youngest daughter, Aparna, was still in school. Not only was Bapu well known in Calcutta,but Ma also had established a reputation for her social work both among the Gujaratis of Calcutta as well as with the All India Women's Conference of whose Calcutta Branch she was elected President and with the Harijan Sewak Sangh, Bengal of which she was also the President.

REFERENCES

1. *Amrit Bazar Patrika*, founded in 1868 by Motilal Ghosh (1847-1922), journalist and nationalist and his brother. Ghosh edited it alone till his death in 1911. It was a bilingual daily, originally published in Bengali and English. When Lord Lytton's Vernacular Press Act of 1878 muzzled the Indian language newspapers, the *Patrika*, to evade the rigours of the law became a full fledged English daily. Its editor, Tushar Kanti Ghosh was a friend of Bapu.
2. Neville Chamberlain (1869-1940). British statesman, Conservative M.P. who became Prime Minister in 1937.He advocated a policy of appeasement towards Hitler.

3. G.D. Birla, (1894-1983). Leading businessman and industrialist. Close associate of Gandhiji.
4. Subhas Chandra Bose (1896-1945), Netaji. A leading nationalist, freedom fighter. Founded Indian National Army to fight the British during World War II.
5. Sarat Chandra Bose, brother of Subhas Bose, took prominent part in the Non-co-operation and Civil Disobedience movements of 1921, 1930 and 1932; imprisoned several times; a leading politician of Bengal in the 1930s and 1940s.
6. Nalini Ranjan Sarkar, Mayor of Calcutta, 1934-35; President FICCI 1935; Finance Minister, Govt. of Bengal. Member, Executive Council of Governor-General for Education, Health and Lands and later for Commerce, resigned in 1943 when British Govt. refused to release Gandhiji when the latter went on a fast.
7. Bidhan Chandra Roy (1882-1962), MRCP, FRCS. One of India's foremost physicians and Congress politician. Chief Minister, West Bengal, 1948-62.
8. Sarojini Naidu (Chattopadhyaya) (1879-1949); Politician and poet. She became President of the Indian National Congress in 1925.
9. Horace Alexander, Member Society of Friends. Friend of Mahatma Gandhi. Visited India in 1927-28, 1932, 1942-43, 1946. Author of *The Indian Ferment, India Since Cripps.*
10. M.A. Master, (b. 1884). General Manager of Scindia Steam Navigation Co. Ltd. since 1919. Director, Bombay Steam Navigation Co. Ltd. Government of India representative at the Geneva meeting of the Joint Maritime Commission, 1947.
11. Sir Ziauddin Ahmed, C.I.E., Vice-Chancellor, Aligarh Muslim University, 1935-38. Member, Calcutta University Commission.
12. Dr. Mukund Ramrao Jayakar, (1873-1959). Barrister. Judge Federal Court of India, 1937. Member of Judicial Committee of Privy Council in London. Resigned in 1942. President of Social Conference, 1917. Leader of Swaraj Party in Bombay Legislative Council. Elected to Central Legislative Assembly, Dy. Leader of the National Party (1926-30). Represented India at three Round Table Conferences.
13. S. Satyamurti (1887-1943); Lawyer, active politician, freedom fighter, member, Indian National Congress. Joined Swaraj Party. Member, Madras Legislative Assembly, 1923-30. Member, Central Legislative Assembly, 1935-42..
14. Govind Vallabh Pant, (b. 1886). Elected to U.P. Legislative Council, 1923. Leader of Swaraj Party in U.P. Member, Working Committee of the Indian National Congress. Elected to the Central Legislative

Assembly, 1934. Deputy leader of the Congress Party in the Assembly. Chief Minister of U.P., 1937-39 and 1947-50. Home Minister, Govt. of India.

15. Bhulabhai Desai (1877-1946), lawyer, Bombay High Court. Congress Party leader in the Central Legislative Assembly and leader of the Opposition in the Assembly in the 1930s.
16. Sir Joseph Bhore, Secretary to the Govt. of India in the Department of Education and later Member of the Viceroy's Executive Council in charge of Commerce and Railways.
17. Hridaynath Kunzru (1887-1978). President, Servants of India Society. In politics he was a moderate liberal. Member of the Congress till it adopted the technique of non-co-operation in 1920. Formed the National Liberal Federation. Member, Indian Legislative Assembly, 1927-30 and again in 1937. Member. Constituent Assembly and Provisional Parliament, 1946-52. Member, Rajya Sabha, 1952-62. Member, UGC, 1955-66.
18. Pandit Madan Mohan Malaviya (1861-1946), President of Indian National Congress in 1909, 1918, 1932, 1933. Founded Hindu Mahasabha in 1906. Elected to Imperial Legislative Council in 1909. Member Central Legislative Assembly, 1924-30. Founder, Benares Hindu University.
19. Bhagat Singh (1909-1931). Joined the revolutionary movement in 1924. Founded the Hindustan Socialist Republican Army along with other revolutionaries. Exploded a bomb in the Central Legislative Assembly on April 18, 1929. He was tried and along with Sukhdev and Shivram Rajguru sentenced to death. The news of the execution of these three cast a gloom over the Congress session. The Congress resolution while disassociating itself from it, disapproving of political violence in any shape or form, placed on record its admiration of the bravery and sacrifice of the three.
20. Prafulla Chandra Ray, Acharya. Professor of Chemistry, Calcutta University. Founder of Bengal Chemicals Ltd.
21. Jan Christian Smuts (1870-1950). Prime Minister of South Africa, 1919-24; 1939-48.
22. Lionel Curtis (1872-1955). Public servant; joined constitutional discussions in India, 1916-17; published *Dyarchy* 1920; Adviser to Colonial Office on Irish Affairs, 1921-24.
23. Abdul Hamid Ghaznavi, landlord and merchant. Member, Indian Legislative Assembly. Delegate to all three Round Table Conferences.
24. Tej Bahadur Sapru (1875-1949) Member, Imperial Legislative Council, 1916-20; Member, Southborough Franchise Committee, 1917-19;

President, Liberal League; Law Member, Viceroy's Executive Council.

25. Ardeshir Dalal, Director, Messrs. Tata Sons Ltd. Member, Viceroy's Executive Council, Planning and Development, 1944-46.
26. M.S.Aney (1880-1968). Organised Berar wing of the Swaraj Party and represented it in the Central Legislative Assembly, 1924-26. Secretary, National Party under leadership of Lala Lajpat Rai. Acting President, Indian National Congress, 1933.
27. Shyama Prasad Mukherji. Son of Sir Asutosh Mukherji, founder of Jan Sangh Party.
28. K.M. Munshi, Lawyer; Joint Editor, *Young India*, 1915. Secretary, Bombay Home Rule League, 1919-1920. Participated in Bardoli and salt satyagrahas. Member, Central Legislative Assembly representing Bombay University. Home Minister, Bombay, 1937-39. Minister for Food in the Union cabinet in 1950s. President and founder of Bharatiya Vidya Bhavan.
29. Master Tara Singh. Akali Sikh leader; President Akali Shiromani Gurudwara Prabandhak Committee; supported creation of separate Punjabi speaking state.
30. Sir Shri Ram. Industrialist, founder of Delhi Cloth Mills; founded Shri Ram College of Commerce, Lady Shri Ram College, etc.
31. Sir Ramaswamy Mudaliar, Member, for Commerce, Viceroy's Executive Council, 1939-42, Member, Madras Legislative Council, 1920-26. Member, Council of State, 1930. Member, Indian Legislative Assembly, 1931-34. India's representative on the Preparatory Commission to the U.N.O., 1945.
32. Sir Akbar Hydari, President of Nizam's Executive Council, Hyderabad. Member, Viceroy's Executive Council.
33. Acharya J.B. Kripalani, Principal, Gujarat Vidyapith, 1920-27. President, Indian National Congress, 1946.
34. Balwantrai Mehta, Dy. Chief Minister, Govt. of United States of Saurashtra. Took active part in establishing All India States Peoples' Conference in 1927 in Bhavnagar. Chief Minister of Gujarat, 1963-65.
35. Sir Gopalaswamy Iyengar (1882-1953). Member, Indian Legislative Assembly, 1927 and Council of States, 1944-46. Diwan of Kashmir. Cabinet Minister in 1947 as Minister without Portfolio. Later, Minister of Railways; temporary Minister for States and Defence, 1952.
36. Sir Binod L. Mitter, Barrister, Calcutta. Member, Council of States, 1921. Advocate General, Bengal. President, National Liberal League. Member, Moderate Deputation to England, 1919.
37. Sir Shanmukham Chetty. Diwan of Cochin State. Elected to first Legislative Council on Justice Party ticket, 1920. Minister, Central Cabinet, Govt. of India, 1947.

5

Foundations of Planning 1947-52

It was only after the Montague-Chelmsford Reforms were introduced in 1921 that it was possible for India to have any kind of fiscal autonomy, to have its own fiscal policy, not dictated from Whitehall. The acceptance of the 'Fiscal Autonomy Convention' was followed by the appointment in March 1921 of the first Indian Fiscal Commission, which through its majority report, recommended what came to be known as the policy of 'Discriminating Protection' which formed the basis of the country's fiscal policy for nearly three decades till 1949-50 when the Second Fiscal Commission was appointed and suggested a different approach.

The Fiscal Commission of 1921 had recommended the constitution of a permanent Tariff Board in order that there might be consistency and continuity of policy. But the Government of India adopted the practice of constituting *ad hoc* Tariff Boards for each individual industry or industries, which, in the opinion of the government had established a *prima facie* case for protection. Up to 1939, only nine industries were protected, namely, steel, cotton textile, sericulture, paper, sugar, silver thread and wire, magnesium chloride, heavy chemicals and matches. Fiscal protection did help some of these not only to survive foreign competition but even to expand, when industries all over the world went through a depression.

The Second World War led to a re-thinking on a protectionist policy which had been followed so far. Wartime restrictions on imports and Allied demand for Indian products had stimulated the growth of Indian industries. A number of new industries had come into existence and there had been diversification and expansion of old industries. The conclusion of the War, however, released the restrictions on imports and allied wartime demands also ceased to exist. There was the danger of industries set up during the War collapsing and there was need to let at least the better and more efficient ones amongst them survive. The need for tariff protection was thus revived. A Tariff Board was appointed, on a continuing basis, to investigate the claims of those industries that had already applied or might later apply for protection. As India was approaching independence, the Indian middle classes desired that the tariff policy should be directed towards helping the rapid industrialisation of the country. This had been a demand of Indian nationalists since a long time. Thus the Tariff Board was reconstituted in November 1947 with some additional responsibilities. Sir Shanmukham Chetty, the Industries Minister in the first cabinet of independent India, asked Bapu to become the Chairman of this and he agreed. Among the many offices Sir Shanmukham had held in pre-independent India, was that of President of the Tariff Board in 1945. The Tariff Board was located in Bombay and so at the end of 1947 we shifted to Bombay from Calcutta. For my parents this was the close of a period of two decades of their life in Calcutta. While they were sad to leave, my father had always wanted to serve free India in some way.

In Bombay, they began a new life. The Tariff Board allotted a flat on the third floor of 'Gulistan', a building on New Cuffe Parade, Colaba, to Bapu. Colaba was then a very peaceful and quiet locality, unlike the concrete jungle it now is. In the same building, the Reserve Bank of India had a flat for one of its Deputy Governors. Durga Khote, a famous actress, and the then equally famous actor Sohrab Modi and his wife, Mehtab also lived in 'Gulistan' The sea was right in front of us and we went for daily walks on the sea front. My sisters were by then studying in the United States and I joined Elphinstone College.

My father immersed himself in his new job full of ideas and enthusiasm. The main functions of the Tariff Board were (1) to investigate the claims of protection or assistance from pre-war, war-time and post-war industries; (2) maintain a continuous watch over the progress of protected industries and advise the government regarding the necessity or otherwise of modifying or terminating the protection or assistance granted, and (3) determine the fair prices of controlled commodities. After its reconstitution in 1947, the Board completed 90 inquiries on tariff protection or continuance of protection (of which 46 were new cases and the rest related to the continuance or modification of protection) and five on price control (cotton textiles, pig iron, steel, paper and super-phosphates). Besides, the Board discharged its other ancillary duties such as maintaining a continuous watch over the progress of protected industries, looking into complaints about higher prices charged in respect of protected commodities, tariff valuation, etc. Out of the ninety cases of tariff inquiry, the Board recommended the grant of protection in as many as sixty cases. In the remaining cases, the Board rejected the claims, as in its view, they were not sustainable. Bapu had always been deeply interested in the industrial growth of India and this new job gave him an opportunity both to learn and evolve new policies. At the same time a need was felt to relate protection to an overall strategy of economic development so as to avoid an unequal distribution of burden and uncoordinated growth of industries. The Second Fiscal Commission appointed in 1949 recommended the establishment of a permanent, statutory Tariff Commission, with wider powers than enjoyed by its predecessor bodies. The Tariff Commission Act, spelling out in detail the Commission's composition, powers and functions and procedures in its working, was passed in 1951. The Commission came into being in 1952 and Bapu who had moved to Delhi as Member, Planning Commission moved back to Bombay as Chairman of the Tariff Commission. He never liked the bureaucratic atmosphere of Delhi and much preferred living in Bombay which he regarded as his own city.

" In January, 1950, when I was President of the Tariff Board in Bombay," wrote Bapu, " I received a telephone call from Mr. K.C. Neogy, who was then Commerce Minister, asking me to come to Delhi as the Prime Minister wanted to see me. He did not disclose the reason on the phone. Upon arriving in Delhi, I met Mr. Neogy and Mr. S. Ranganathan, ICS, Secretary, Ministry of Commerce. They told me that the Prime Minister wanted me to join the Planning Commission. That night I dined with Mr. Nehru along with Mr. Neogy. After dinner, he took us to another room and told us about his scheme for the Planning Commission. I told the Prime Minister that I was quite happy with the work I was doing in the Tariff Board. He replied that he knew that I was doing good work on the Tariff Board but planning for the whole nation was a much bigger task and it would be of considerable value. Subsequently, I consulted Sardar Patel who approved of the idea of my joining the Planning Commission, though at heart, I think he was not in favour of the Planning Commission and felt that it was a fifth wheel in a coach. Rajaji also was of the view that Nehru was creating too many new bodies and was not in favour of setting up a Planning Commission. Neither, I believe, was Dr. John Matthai, though as Finance Minister he moved the motion in Parliament for setting up the Commission. Later, when he resigned as Finance Minister, this was one of the issues he cited for his resignation. And so I moved to Delhi. We lived on 30 Prithviraj Road, the

Jawaharlal Nehru and G.L. Mehta

house allotted to me by the government.

"I had been interested in planning for some years. In 1938, a National Planning Committee had been set up by the Indian National Congress with Jawaharlal Nehru as chairman. Subhas Bose was then President of the Congress. I was offered the post of one of the Joint Honorary Secretaries but Walchand Hirachand, chairman of Scindia Steam Navigation Company, whose employee I was, was unwilling to lend my services. The setting up of this Committee was an important event in the direction of economic planning." It was a non-official body with a large number of distinguished Indians from different walks of life on it. It formed about 29 sub-committees, which made a broad survey of the needs and resources of the country. The Second World War however interrupted its work.

"In 1944, a group of leading industrialists, including G.D. Birla, J.R.D. Tata, Kasturbhai Lalbhai, Sir Shri Ram and others formulated a plan for the economic development of India which was popularly called the 'Bombay Plan'. Other plans like the 'People's Plan' and a 'Gandhian Plan' were also put forward.

"Even before independence the Government realised the importance of evolving a plan for meeting both the short term problems of post-war reconstruction and long term problems of economic development. A Planning and Development Department was set up under Sir Ardeshir Dalal in 1944 and various provincial governments started working on post-war schemes of development. Some Princely states such as Mysore and Baroda had also done some work on planning. The Planning and Development Department set up a number of industrial panels to survey the problems of major industries. About 30 panels were constituted for different industries that investigated their conditions and problems and had fixed targets of production and consumption and surveyed the position regarding raw materials and markets along with technical problems. Each panel worked for 6 to 8 months along with industrial and technical experts. They made recommendations regarding the scope of development in these industries and the lines along which such development should take place. Sir Ardeshir Dalal had asked me to serve as Industrial Advisor in this Department but I refused, as I did not want to serve an alien government.

"In November, 1946, during the time of the Interim Government, the Government of India appointed an Advisory Planning Board under the Chairmanship of Mr. K.C. Neogy, who afterwards became Commerce Minister, to review the various plans and suggest the appropriate machinery for the formulation and implementation of plans. I was appointed a member of this Board. We undertook a rapid survey of the planning work done previously and also made some interesting recommendations regarding a planning organisation and suggested a Planning Commission of three to five members who were to be experts in their fields .We said that these experts should be non -political appointments and that there should be no Ministers on the Commission. We presented our Report in January 1947. In my judgement, it was a very good Report. With the Partition of the country, however, everything changed.

"In July, 1947, I delivered a lecture on the 'Machinery of Planning' on the occasion of the Silver Jubilee of the Bombay School of Economics where I advocated the setting up of a Planning Board not dissimilar from the Planning Commission that was set up in 1950.

"The Government of India's statement on Industrial Policy issued on 6th April, 1948, mentioned the need for a planned economy and the desirability of setting up a Planning Commission.

"The Planning Commission was officially announced by the Finance Minister, Dr. John Matthai, in his budget speech on the eve of 1st March, 1950. Its principal function was to co-ordinate the existing development plans of the central and state governments and determine priorities and formulate a plan for the most effective and balanced utilisation of resources. The chairmanship of the Commission was first offered to Rajaji who had just relinquished his post as governor-general. When he declined, Gopalaswamy Iyengar was considered but ultimately the Prime Minister himself became the chairman. Gulzarilal Nanda, who was Labour Minister in Bombay, and was a well-known Trade Union leader, was to be deputy chairman. As such he was in overall charge of the Commission but was also concerned with labour and social welfare. The other members were R.K. Patil, I.C.S., who was Food Commissioner, Government of India, who was responsible for agriculture, and Sir V.T. Krishnamachari, an experienced administrator, who before independence, had been dewan of Baroda for seventeen years, was in charge of natural resources and scientific matters. I was in charge of industry, commerce and transport. Sir Raghavan Pillai, I.C.S., Cabinet Secretary was Member-Secretary and Dr. Tarlok Singh, I.C.S. was Deputy Secretary.

"The first informal meeting of the Commission was held on 15 March, 1950 and the Commission began to function regularly from the beginning of April. I remember the considerable zeal and élan that informed our work, feelings that had spilled over from the achievement of independence and feelings that were borne out of a sense of mission and desire to improve the lot of the people. Full meetings of the Commission were held almost daily and in the beginning the Prime Minister attended them regularly. The personal relations between the members were most cordial and the atmosphere was harmonious. Members of the Planning Commission had Cabinet status and we attended most of the meetings of the Economic Committee of the Cabinet which was presided over by Rajaji who had returned to Delhi in May-June 1950 at the special request of the Prime Minister and functioned as Minister without Portfolio and subsequently became Home Minister. After the

Meeting of first Planning Commission - J. Nehru (Clockwise) - V.T. Krishanamachari, R.K. Patil, N.R. Pillai, Tarlok Singh (not known) - G.L. Mehta, C.D. Deshmukh, Gulzarilal Nanda

General Elections of 1951-52 and the departure of Rajaji, C.D. Deshmukh presided over the meetings of the Economic Committee of the Cabinet. On one or two occasions I also attended full cabinet meetings to which I was invited.

"As I said earlier, I was Member in charge of industry, commerce and transport. The Chief of the Industry Division was Dr. Nagraj Rao and the Assistant Chief was Mr.Vyaslu. From March/April 1950 to April, 1951, i.e. for a year, we consulted representatives of industry, commerce and economists and set up a number of committees dealing with specific industries such as paper, chemicals, engineering, etc. whose meetings were convened to determine targets of production, review capacity and go into specific questions both technical and financial. These meetings proved useful and its results can be seen in the Report published by Penderal Moon in the First Five Year Plan.

"Valuable experience was gained during the First Plan, although on a small scale, in constructing industrial plants and in producing capital goods. Important state owned factories for ammonium sulphate fertiliser (Sindri), locomotives (Chittaranjan), telecommunication equipment (Bangalore), coaches, cables and penicillin were set up during and just before the First Plan. During the First Plan all preparatory work for the new steel plants which included detailed planning and negotiations for financial and technical assistance were completed. Our broad objectives were: (i) meeting the demands of industrial products on account of schemes for agricultural development and expansion of irrigation and power; (ii) fuller utilisation of existing capacity of producer goods industries like cotton textiles and sugar; (iii) expansion of industries like pig iron, steel, heavy chemicals which are basically important for the general economic development of the country; (iv) completion of industrial units on which a part of the capital expenditure has been incurred; and (v) removing lacunae and drawbacks in the existing industries. The Commission worked out targets of production and consumption for several industries. A survey of 18 industries was made and their targets laid down in the Plan. These targets were determined after discussion with representatives of industries, Central Ministries and other technical opinion and were fixed taking into account the position of raw material, market, capital as well as capital goods. The target for the textile industry was fixed, for instance, after consultation with the Ministry of Commerce and Industries. A Textile Development Committee was set up where various problems relating to this industry were discussed. This Committee consisted of representatives of the employers as well as the principal labour unions in the textile industry and certain technical experts. It was after consultation with this Committee that the target was fixed by the Commission.

"The same procedure was followed for other industries. All this meant hard work and sometimes we were in office till mid-night. The person who worked almost around the clock with utmost dedication and diligence was Dr. Tarlok Singh."

Delivering the G.L. Mehta Memorial Lecture at the Institute for Financial Management and Research in Madras on 7 January, 1987, Dr. Tarlok Singh observed, "Shri G.L. Mehta helped to lay the foundations of planning in India. His presence brought prestige and goodwill to the Planning Commission, in its earlier years and he set the pattern of planning for the private sector. Shri G.L. Mehta's warmth, sense of humour and generous temperament, added to his deep insight into the problems of Indian industry and personal acquaintance with the leaders of industry and trade, were greatly valued by all his colleagues. He helped the Planning Commission to break new ground. He was missed greatly when he left for Washington after two years and five months as a Member of the Commission. However, the Planning Commission remained in touch with him, and he was a signatory to the First Five-Year Plan. In a nation's life, whatever the limitations, its First Five Year Plan may often come closest to its aspirations as it seeks to blend a fresh vision of the future with the reality of the present and considers no obstacle too difficult to overcome

"The First Plan to which Shri G.L. Mehta made a vital contribution, was the product of a singular unity of approach and unusual team-work. There was complete agreement among all concerned about the relationship between the public sector and the private sector in the Indian economy. The distinction, it was felt, related to the mode of operation rather than to the ultimate objective. Private enterprise should have a public purpose. The private and public sector must function as parts of a single organism. It was in this spirit that Shri G.L. Mehta arranged for the first time a series of consultations with representatives of industry on the five-year programmes for all industries, a mode of functioning which continued for many years to the advantage both of national planning and of industry. The keynote was co-operation and thinking together for the common good, and a planned economy involving increasing coordination between the two sectors."

Mr. R. Venkataraman, former President of India, who in 1950 had just been elected as a Member of Parliament, recalls "I came to the Provisional Parliament in 1950. Shri G.L. Mehta, after a distinguished career in the Private Sector, joined as a Member of the Planning Commission. At that time, there was a raging controversy whether India should have a planned economy or only priorities selected for implementation. Dr. John Matthai who was the Finance Minister, strongly supported the latter point of view. Among the Gandhians there was a genuine apprehension that planning will lead to regimentation, rigid controls and re-enactment of the rigours of the Soviet system. Prime Minister Nehru was sold out on a planned economy and was nervous of an opposition building up against planning. I was a fairly vocal member of the Provisional Parliament, which then consisted of a single Chamber with 250 members. Youngsters had plenty of opportunity to speak in the House. I was a Member of the Standing Finance Committee which in those days, used to approve proposals for expenditure and, therefore, well acquainted with Dr. Matthai, the Finance Minister. At the same time, I was a strong supporter of Nehru's social legislation, the Special Marriage Act, the Hindu Code Bill and one of the vociferous shouters of ' Hindi-Chini Bhai Bhai'.

"In those days, the Members and the Finance Minister used to have dinner on the nights of the Standing Finance Committee and Dr. Matthai spoke to me about his objection to total planning. I was in a fix. I supported the idea of a planned economy. I mildly remonstrated that having missed the Industrial Revolution, we had to accelerate development. Some other Members, intervening at this stage cut a meaningful dialogue short. Soon after this, Dr. Matthai dissenting from the proposal of a planned economy resigned from the Cabinet. Nehru, the true democrat that he was, immediately organised an informal meeting in the Parliament House between the Planning Commission and Members interested in the subject. I met Dr. Deshmukh, G.L. Mehta and others. These two created a deep impression in my mind. G.L. Mehta had a dignified presence, with a suppressed smile all the time on his face with easy and fluent expression, enlivened by soft humour. The Gandhians voiced their familiar views that priority should be given to cottage and rural industries, village development programmes and their objection to large scale industries. It was G.L. Mehta's turn to take up these issues. Though coming from the large industrial sector, Mehta did not take a confrontationist line but soothingly agreed with the Gandhians saying that all these will be taken care of in the Plan and added that the large scale sector was necessary in areas which were beyond the capacity of the rural sector. He said we all want railways for transport of rural products but engines could not be made in the rural sector. He quoted Gandhiji's own statement regarding railway engines. This is a sample of the manner in which he handled even irate opponents. When it came to my turn, I said we should have a composite industrial policy where large, small and cottage industries should have their appropriate place. This established a rapport between me and G.L. Mehta which ripened to mutual respect and friendship.

By April 1951, a draft report was prepared which was signed on July 7, 1951 and released for study and criticism. The final version of the First Five-Year Plan was published in December 1952 but by then Bapu was in Washington.

Although the First Five-Year Plan (1951-56) was modest in scope and cautious in approach on fiscal policy, there was a discernible change in tone and approach to industrial development. Compared to the Draft Outline, the First Plan raised the allocation to industry from Rs. 101 crores to Rs. 173 crores, or from 6.1 percent to 8.4 percent of total outlay. The bulk of the increase went toward expansion of basic industries, including mineral development, heavy electrical equipment, and a new iron and steel complex. The Plan was an amalgam of specific projects drafted by the pre-independence Planning Department and its successor, the Advisory Board on Planning. The First Plan integrated them into a rational framework, established priorities, allocated additional funds where necessary and provided further guidance for their speedy implementation. The Plan reflected Nehru's new authority over national questions of economic and social policy. The broad outlines of an indirect attack on the prerogatives and position of private enterprise were beginning to emerge. The planners announced their intention to increase central supervision and control over the private sector They also gave notice of a much larger role for the public sector in basic industries in future plans.

6

Challanges of Diplomacy : 1952-58

We were living at Gulistan on Cuffe Parade when my father came back to Bombay for his second stint in the Tariff Commission. He had hardly been in his new assignment for two or three months when in June, 1952, Bapu received a phone call from the Prime Minister's office that the Jawaharlal Nehru wanted to see him and that he should come to Delhi immediately. He had no idea why he was being summoned and upon his arrival in Delhi, met Nehru who told him that he would like him to go to Washington as India's Ambassador to the United States of America. It was his performance in the Planning Commission, which had impressed the Prime Minister and the Finance Minister, Sir Chintamani Deshmukh. They felt that someone who had an understanding of India's economy, business and industry should represent India in the United States. Since independence, India had been represented by Mr. Asaf Ali, a politician and then by Mrs. Vijayalakshmi Pandit, Nehru's sister.

On 2 September 1952, Ma, Bapu, my sister Uma and I left for Washington from Bombay by Air India Super Constellation. A large number of relatives and friends and former colleagues of Bapu's came to Santa Cruz airport to see us off. Our first halt was London where we stayed for about a week at the Ritz Hotel on Piccadilly Circus. Mr. B.G. Kher, who had formerly been Chief Minister of Bombay and hence a colleague of Batuk Kaka, was then India's High Commissioner to the UK. He arranged a private lunch for my father at 9 Kensington Palace Gardens, the High Commissioner's residence, where he invited the American Ambassador to the Court of St. James. Bapu also met Sir Edwin Plowden, Chief of the Planning Staff of the Treasury. Bapu had been a life long reader of the *New Statesman* and *Nation* and it was, therefore, with great pleasure that he met and had a long discussion with its editor, Kingsley Martin, who had been a long time supporter of Nehru and India's struggle for freedom. We saw two plays, 'Love of Four Colonels' and 'Waters of the Moon'. Prof. Robbins invited us for lunch at the London School of Economics. We drove to Cambridge where I had got admission at Newnham College and on the way saw George Bernard Shaw's house. Uma's boss in Bombay, Mr. Brower of the British Council took us to Marlow on Thames and we lunched at a delightful pub by the river called the 'Compleat Angler'. Shelley was a favourite poet of my parents and they were excited to know that he had lived in Marlow and we saw the house where he and Mary Shelley had lived.

On 10th September we left London by boat train to Southampton and sailed for New York by 'Queen Elizabeth' arriving in New York on 15th September. London, in 1952 was still recovering from the severe bombing of World War II. In comparison, the, sky scrapers, shops and glitter of New York were dazzling. After a day's stay at 'Essex House' hotel in New York, we proceeded to Washington by train. On our arrival in Washington, we were received at the station by almost the entire staff of the Indian Embassy and their spouses, several Ambassadors of Commonwealth countries and the Chief of Protocol of the US government, Mr. Simmons. The Georgian mansion on 2700 Macomb Street, NW, overlooking Rock Creek Park, was then as now the residence of the Indian Ambassador. The property had been very wisely purchased by Sir Girja

Shanker Bajpai when he was posted as India's Agent General in Washington, attached to the British Embassy, during the Second World War.

Bapu was not a career diplomat and this was an entirely new experience for him. "When my appointment was made as Ambassador", he wrote, "a none-to-friendly critic wondered how I could be a successful ambassador when I did not eat meat or drink whisky." But his gift for conversation and ready sparkling wit made him a much sought after guest at diplomatic parties. "The cocktail party", he said, "was a remarkable modern device for wasting time. Yet I had to go, since while one's presence may not always be noticed, absence at important functions becomes conspicuous....In Washington I heard the saying that it does not matter whether Ambassadors are weak in their heads, they have to be strong on their feet!"

Soon after his arrival, Bapu paid a courtesy call on the Secretary of State, Dean Acheson, and presented his credential to President Truman on 25th September. The President showed him a small statuette of Gandhiji on his table that had been presented to him by an Indian film delegation. Truman told him that he was deeply interested in the economic advancement of underdeveloped countries and desired that such aid as was possible should be given by the United States. Bapu replied that India welcomed such aid as was necessary and this should make the receiving country steadily independent and not perpetually dependent on foreign aid. The President entirely agreed.

> When a person is accredited as Ambassador to any country, one of his first tasks is to improve further the relations between the two countries. Indo-U.S. relations were not at their best in 1952. The big issue for India during this period was U.S. military aid to Pakistan. For the U.S.A., communism was the supreme danger in the world and containing it had the highest priority in its programme. The American

approach to Asia was military based on the traditional balance of power concept. Military alliances, military aid, military bases were tools of an effort to balance communist strength. It underestimated the strength of nationalism. When Chiang-kai-Shek fled from Mainland China, the West looked hopefully, next, to Nehru and India. Nehru adopted a policy of non-alignment and was quick to rebuff overtures for Indo-American military collaboration during his first visit to Washington in October 1949. India's refusal to align itself with the Western grouping of states which it had automatically been a member of until 1946-47, had a special meaning for Indo-American relationship. India's independence in world affairs had to be achieved by disentangling itself from Western foreign policy objectives. When India refused to align with the Western powers, the United States turned to Pakistan. The pro-Pakistan policy gained momentum after the Korean War started in June 1950. Nehru's instinctive horror of open aggression and the sanction of the UN Charter initially overcame his suspicion of the USA giving armed protection to an Asian state. India supported the early Security Council resolutions on Korea. But as the UN's Korean objectives became inextricably mixed up with American policy of containing China, India's efforts to befriend China and its opposition to Western military presence in Asia overcame the earlier stand on UN-US action in Korea. As a result, Indo-American differences sharpened. As the Korean War dragged on, India's vocal role in championing the admission of China to the UN intensified. India's view was that admitting Communist China into the UN could help solve the problem of the Korean War. USA did not agree. America was deeply suspicious of China and was not prepared to give any credit to the Chinese sincerity of purpose. While American policy was to prevent the emergence of China as a dominant Asian power, India was seeking close ties with the People's Republic of China. The pro-Chiang-kai-Shek lobby was against US aid to India. American impatience with Nehru and New Delhi emboldened advocates of US-Pakistan military alliance. The anti neutralist accent of the nascent Dulles diplomacy and the interest of the new Secretary of State in a possible 'northern tier defence pact' created a favourable climate for the idea of a military alliance with Pakistan. John Foster Dulles[1], who had taken over from Dean Acheson as Secretary of State, had a general aversion to neutralism. He perceived the struggle between communism and democracy as a struggle between good and evil where no neutral attitude was possible. For him, non-alignment was immoral and 'those who are not for us are against us.' Secondly, he believed that communism could be defeated only by some kind of collective security. He shrugged off the warning by Nehru, the American Ambassador to India, Chester Bowles, and others such as Paul Hoffman, that Pakistan was building her military strength as a bargain counter against India rather than as a defence against other communist countries including the Soviet Union or China. Nehru told Dulles that the military assistance the United States was giving to Pakistan was sought by the latter not really to defend itself against a possible aggression from the North, instigated by the Soviet Union, but rather, to get strength to use it against India. He said that Pakistan's militant people are of martial disposition; they are fanatical because they are a religious state and they could work themselves upto a point where they would attack India. Bapu also felt strongly that the decision to give military aid to Pakistan was taken "without taking into account the very serious risk that was run not only of antagonising India, but bringing about a costly arms race between the two countries..." "Mr. Dulles told me, I remember, that they had taken a calculated risk. Similar military aid was offered to India at the time by President Eisenhower but Nehru rejected it..." "Mr. Dulles told me two things. Once, while discussing SEATO, he said that it provides only that America will come to aid only if there is communist aggression– not in internecine quarrels. He said that this had not been sufficiently noticed in India. He also said in case Pakistan attacked India and India asked for military aid, we shall be on the side of India". "Now", he told me, "that did not make me popular in Pakistan." I told Dulles that "whatever your motives and objectives, Pakistan has only one enemy and that is India and they want to use your arms against us..." And that is what happened." The United States in these years was obsessed with the danger of communism at home and abroad. There was a difference in outlook and policy between the United States and India regarding how peace in Asia could be ensured. USA wanted to build up centres of military strength in various parts of the world while India's view was that this would only increase tension. All this naturally estranged Indo-American relations. The proceedings of the United States Congress House and Senate Committees on Foreign Affairs reveal the anger of many Congressmen and Senators at India's unsympathetic attitude to USA. On January 26, 1951, Senator Connally, Chairman of the Senate Foreign Relations Committee said, " Our relations with India are not very good are they? Nehru is giving us hell all the time, working against us and voting against us." Senator Henry Cabot Lodge said, "The record of India in co-operating with us has been extremely disappointing." The Indian press in these years was hostile towards and critical of the United States. Once when Secretary of State Dulles came for dinner to the Indian Embassy, he said, "You know, today, Mr. Ambassador, I was asked at the Senate Foreign Relations

Left to Right : President Eisenhower ; Secretary of State, Mr. John Foster Dulles; Mr. V.K. Krishna Menon and Ambassador G.L. Mehta.

Committee -- 'Why should we assist India, when on every key issue, it sides with the Soviet Union?' " Bapu told him that "freedom accepts diversity. Freedom involves diversity. It is because we are a free people that we can disagree and yet co-operate for common purposes." After Dulles' first visit to India in May 1953, Bapu met him at a party at the British Embassy on the occasion of the Queen's birthday. Bapu recorded, "It was the first time I found him effusive and rather cordial. He took me aside and told me that of all the countries he visited, it was in India with Prime Minister Nehru that he was able to have discussion on some of the fundamentals of foreign policy and the situation in Asia." "And", he said, "I was really very glad to have the talk." Bapu conveyed this to Nehru at Burgestenstock in Switzerland when there was a conference of heads of Indian missions in Europe in June 1953, where Bapu was specially invited, and Nehru was very pleased to hear it and said, "Yes, I felt that he had some kind of prejudice. I've no reason at all to be anti-American. Why should I be anti-American?"

Bapu tried his best to present India's case and counteract misrepresentation. He met State Department officials, journalists, Senators and Congressmen, spoke in universities, Chambers of Commerce, American Academy of Political and Social Science, etc., got articles written in newspapers and magazines explaining India's foreign policy and her economic development.

It was not an easy job under these circumstances to be India's ambassador to the United States. V.K. Krishna Menon was during this period Nehru's closest foreign policy advisor and India's spokesman at the United Nations. His frequent visits to USA, as leader of the Indian delegation to the United Nations did not make matters easier. He took

Mr. G.L. Mehta and Mrs. Mehta, Madame Pandit in Conversation with U.S. Senator John Cabot Lodge at a reception in honour of Madame Vijaya Lakshmi Pandit on Saturday, December 13, 1952

every possible opportunity of rubbing the U.S government on the wrong side. Menon was a lone operator who carried on secret negotiations with the United States government without keeping the Indian Ambassador informed. He asked for appointments with the President and Secretary of State without keeping the Indian Ambassador in Washington informed. Dulles, wrote to President Eisenhower that Krishna Menon has been "pushing very hard for the appointment using the name of Nehru and also having mutual friends call me up at the State Department. He is as you probably know, a very adroit and unscrupulous maneuverer who likes to have his finger in every pie." Even Mrs. Vijayalakshmi Pandit, Nehru's sister and then President of the UN General Assembly was kept in the dark by Menon. She wrote to Bapu, "I am sorry I could not send you a copy of our resolution on Korea before it was tabled at the UN. Krishna Menon only showed it to me a few hours before and even then he would not give me a copy. He has worked alone and secretly on this issue and had it not been for the fact that I know the Heads of Delegations personally, I would have had no inkling of what was going on. The whole proceeding was extraordinary and the delegates of the Asian-Arab groups as well as our people are feeling aggrieved. I confess I have not understood the necessity of so much secrecy."

The American Consul General in Bombay reported to the State Department that Frank Moraes, a distinguished journalist and Editor of *Times of India*, after a visit to the United States in 1956 told Morarji Desai, then Minister for Commerce and Industries, that Menon had done "almost irreperable damage to United States-India relations." Desai is said to have replied that "I know Americans are allergic to Krishna Menon but the Prime Minister is allergic to criticism of Krishna Menon." Moraes told Desai that Menon's approach in the United Nations was doing more than alienate Americans. He was alienating Canadians and would in the end disrupt the Afro-Asian bloc through "viciousness and bad manners." During Nehru's visit to Washington, according to a report published in *Swarajya* by an Indian correspondent in New York, P.G. Krishnayya, "In diplomatic language Eisenhower complained that the grand standing diplomat Krishna Menon seemed to be more a spokesman for Moscow at the United Nations than for India, Nehru did not reply directly." Dr. Clifford Manshardt, Deputy Chief Public Affairs Officer in the American Embassy in New Delhi met the Vice President, Dr. S. Radhakrishnan on 7.2.1957 and wrote to the State Department on the following day that the Vice President was "extremely bitter against Krishna Menon". Dr. Radhakrishnan urged Nehru to recall Krishna Menon from New York but Nehru said that he was "entirely satisfied with Krishna Menon." "How can a representative be satisfactory" queried the Vice President, "who antagonises his hearers every time he speaks? We can no longer tell whether other nations are voting against India or against Menon."

On at least two occasions, Bapu gave in his resignation. He was asked by the Ministry of External Affairs to lead the Indian delegation to the San Francisco meeting of the United Nations in May 1955. Suddenly, Menon's name was announced as leader by the Indian Government without even informing Bapu who was naturally very upset. He said so to Nehru, who replied, "I am sorry my message to you about Krishna Menon's appointment as our principal representative for San Francisco upset your arrangements. I did NOT know how far matters had proceeded in this matter. No discourtesy at all was intended to you. I wish to assure you that there is no question at all of our having lack of confidence in you. Your work as Ambassador in the United States has been very good." Nehru added that Menon was the only person fully conversant with Formosa and Indo China and with Chou En Lai. As such, Menon's presence in San Francisco was essential. "I should very much like you to accompany Krishna Menon to the San Francisco Conference. In fact Krishna Menon himself is anxious that you should go with him...Please be rest assured that we have greatly appreciated your work..." Bapu did not go to San Francisco. In May, 1955, he wrote to Nehru, "His (Menon's) desire to carry on negotiations without taking the Head of the Mission into confidence and to see and talk with the Head of the State or the Foreign Secretary by himself puts one in my position in a very embarrassing situation. For instance, even to this day, I do not know what transpired between Dulles and Mr. Menon during his interview here...this is not a personal question at all but a matter of propriety and proçedure whoever may be the representative here and whoever may be the special envoy. Similarly, Mrs. Pandit also arranged interviews directly with the White House and with the State Department without advising us. It is, therefore, necessary in the interest of the government and fair to myself that a person in whom there is complete confidence is at the head here so that the Mission is not bypassed and is kept fully advised about developments. This is essential for the efficient working of the Mission as well as its prestige. There is also complete lack of co-ordination between the Indian delegation at the UN in New York and the Embassy in Washington..." Nehru in his reply agreed that there should be "close and continuous liaison between our work at the UN and more especially to the General Assembly Sessions of the Security

Council meetings and our Embassy. Indeed we have laid stress on this repeatedly."

In December 1955, Bapu again wrote to Nehru that he would like to return home by mid 1956. The Scindia Steam Navigation Company wanted him to come back as Chairman. Mr. Dharamsey Khatau[2] wrote, "There is only one name which has the approval of all and that name is yours." Sir Chunilal B. Mehta[3] and Shanti Kumar Morarji also urged him to accept the Chairmanship of Scindias. But the Prime Minister urged him to stay on. The Foreign Secretary, Sir Raghavan Pillai wrote, "P.M. considers that it would be in public interest if you could make it convenient to stay on in Washington for some months beyond July next." On each occasion that Bapu wrote that he wanted to resign, the Prime Minister assured him that he was very satisfied with his performance and did not want him to resign. "It is not our intention", wrote Nehru, "that Krishna Menon should act against established procedure or bypass you in any way...I can assure you that there is no lack of confidence in you. I think you have done very good work in Washington and the United States." Nehru also agreed that "some of Krishna Menon's statements to the press, etc. were very unfortunate. The facts he stated were correct but there was no reason for him to say that there".

One of Menon's chief tasks was to ensure that the Security Council did not force a plebiscite on Kashmir and for this he needed Soviet support, if necessary, in the form of a veto. This meant that he had to support Soviet policy in the Cold War era which naturally antagonised the Americans. As it is, Menon's political sympathies were left wing and more towards the USSR than the U.S.A. Moreover, in the US Presidential elections of 1952, India had supported the Democratic candidate, Adlai Stevenson, in the belief that both the Democratic Party and Stevenson were more liberal and pro-India. The new Republican administration under President Eisenhower was, therefore, naturally not very well disposed towards India.

It was not easy for Bapu to explain India's foreign policy, counteract misrepresentation, and win friends for his country in such an atmosphere. His great achievement was the friendship he established, despite this unfriendly atmosphere, with State Department officials, Senators and Congressmen belonging to both the Democratic and Republican parties, with Supreme Court judges, journalists, academics, bankers, businessmen and labour leaders. He was in close touch with Chester Bowles and developed good relations with Stassen, Secretary of State for Commerce, General Bedell Smith, Under Secretary of State for Foreign Affairs and Byroad, Assistant Secretary of State in charge of Asia. He felt that public opinion in the United States was formulated by universities, commercial bodies, literary societies and so he travelled widely, speaking to audiences across the United States trying to interpret India, to make India better known to wide sections of the American public. He wrote later, "A diplomat has also to explain and interpret and defend the policy of his own government; and in the United States he has to do this to the public at large in various forums and through mass media of communication like the radio and T.V. The traditional concept of the diplomat was a representative of one government to another. But that concept has changed to contact with the people." The School of Advanced International Studies, Johns Hopkins University arranged a two days conference in Washington in which several business firms interested in India discussed India's economic and industrial problems. The American Academy of Political and Social Science at Philadelphia held a 'New India Conference'. At Rochester University an audience of 600 students and faculty members gave him a standing ovation. At these conferences and elsewhere, Bapu tried to explain India's domestic and foreign policy and argued for a better appreciation by the United States and India of the motives and objectives of each other's policies and of tolerance for each other's devotion to common good. He urged against the tendency to oversimplify the attitude of other countries and indulge in superficial and somewhat hasty generalisations. He went on pleading for a sympathetic understanding of India's neutrality on historical and psychological grounds. He tried to explain that Pakistan was seeking arms for use against India rather that against communist powers. SEATO was created in September 1954 to provide for the region's security and to deter further communist expansion in the area. Pakistan joined SEATO, India did not. Through the 1950s, India eschewed formal alliances, pursued a neutralist course in foreign relations, often attacked the intransigent anti-Communist position of the United States and professed to be on friendly terms with both the Soviet Union and China. Despite the intense debate and criticism between the two countries and their failure to reach any beneficial political accords, the decade of the 1950's in Indo-American relations laid a firm, though by no means deep, foundation for future collaboration chiefly because the governments and informed public opinion came to respect each other's interests, to be realistic in their expectations about each other's policies, and to develop some familiarity with each other's domestic life. Bapu in the USA and the US Ambassadors in India during those years, Ellsworth Bunker and John Sherman Cooper played a key role in this.

Bapu built up excellent relations with the successive Presidents of the World Bank– Eugene Black and George Woods as well as with other officials in the Bank and the IMF. He worked hard for the continuance of U.S. and World Bank economic and technical aid to India. In late 1957 India faced a serious economic crisis and U.S. loan was crucial. Maurice Zinkin, an ex-ICS and member of the Board of Directors of Hindustan Levers, who according to William Turner, the U.S. Consul General in Bombay, was one of the most competent Western observers of Indian affairs, commented that refusal of U.S. loan would put not so much the careers of T.T. Krishnamacahari or Krishna Menon at stake as the career of the Prime Minister himself. T.T. Krishnamachari, the Finance Minister, in fact requested Bapu to stay on in Washington to finalise the loan negotiations and Bapu worked very hard for securing this loan. He always prepared the ground carefully through informal discussions before making any formal request for assistance. Later, writing about foreign aid, Bapu recalled, "In the U.S. during my term of office as India's Ambassador, I was closely associated with various discussions and negotiations regarding aid from 1952 to 1958. I might mention that it was on January 11, 1958, that Mr. Douglas Dillon, then Under Secretary of State for Economic Affairs, phoned me from Washington when I was in New York and told me that the U.S. government had decided to give India $150 million loan from the Export Import Bank and $ 75 million from the Development Loan Fund which is now called the Agency for International Development (A.I.D.) Since my return to India, in my association with a premier development bank, I have also had close contacts with the World Bank and the A.I.D. as well as the Kreditanstelt fur Wiederaufbau of the Federal Republic of Germany and the Ministry of Overseas Development of the U.K." He held that "foreign aid could be a stimulus for national development, not a substitute for self help. It could be a springboard, not a sofa. Foreign aid could supplement not supplant national effort."

As an Ambassador, his second task was to report fully and honestly to his government about American opinion and sentiment not only with regard to India's policies but also with regard to international relations. In this, he believed that the Ambassador "must be precise and honest and resist the temptation of telling his government what pleases it or what it would like to hear. The reluctance or inability of heads of mission to convey to their home governments what is taking place in the country or conveying frankly the views of the government to which he is accredited has often caused grave misunderstanding. If an Ambassador performs this function faithfully, he might be able to influence, to some extent at any rate, the judgement and consequently the policy of his own government." He wrote detailed letters, almost every week to the Prime Minister, reporting his meetings and discussions with officials in the State Department, other Ambassadors, journalists, etc. He also wrote about reactions in the American press and trends of opinion in the United States about India, China and other international events. Nehru wrote that he found these letters most interesting.

The press in the United States has always been very powerful. Having been a journalist, Bapu could establish a ready rapport with journalists. He had excellent relations with Philip and Martha Graham, proprietors of *Washington Post*, Robert Estabrook, its editor, as well as with Alfred Friendly, Ferdinand Kuhn and J.R. Wiggins of the *Post.* He was in touch with distinguished columnists such as Walter Lippman, Roscoe Drummond, Joseph Harch, Michael Straight and Marquis Childs. Selig Harrison of the *New Republic* and Norman Cousins of the *Saturday Review* were his specially good friends, so also Stringer, the head of the Washington Bureau of the *Christian Science Monitor* and the *Baltimore Sun* correspondent in Washington. Whenever he went to New York, he made it a point to meet Arthur Sulzberger and other members of the *New York Times.* James Reston, the Washington representative of the *Times* was also a friend. Bapu frequently lunched and dined with these journalists and invited them to the Indian Embassy parties. In April 1954, Bapu had been irked by a remark made in an editorial in the *Washington Post* that India's decision to refuse American planes to carry French troops across India was "a manifestation of the spite Mr. Nehru had been showing since the military aid agreement with Pakistan." He explained India's viewpoint on

Indo-China and the ban on airlift freely and frankly at a meeting of the editorial board of *Washington Post.* Edward Murrow who succeeded George V.Allen as Director of the United States Information Agency in the Kennedy era was also a good friend. Bapu took special pains to cultivate the press and appraise them of India's policy and stand on various international issues. He recalled how "of his own accord, Walter Lippman came to me at the Indian Embassy in August 1957 on the eve of the visit by Mr. T.T. Krishnamachari, then Finance Minister of the Union Government, to ask me whether he could be helpful in putting across our views in regard to aid programmes. He told me that he had many important contacts in the State Department, which could be useful. I arranged a cordial and constructive meeting with the Finance Minister."

Among the diplomatic corps he had very cordial relations with several Commonwealth Ambassadors, including Sir Oliver Franks and his successor Sir Roger Makins of Great Britain. With Sir Oliver, who was very close to the Secretary of State, Dean Acheson and highly regarded in the State Department and by the press and public in the USA, Bapu discussed often and in complete confidence various international problems. He frequently met Ambassador Barrington of Burma, and Ambassador Gunawardane of Sri Lanka. He also developed friendly relations with Ambassador Notowidigdo of Indonesia and Sir Percy Spender, the Australian Ambassador who later became a judge of the International Court of Justice. Mr. Lester Pearson, then Foreign Minister of Canada, was also friend. He kept in touch with Ambassador Zaroubin of USSR.

His built up over the years excellent relations with officials in the State Department despite the fact that many of them failed to sufficiently appreciate India's stand on many international issues. In June 1954 he met the Secretary of State to discuss Indo-China relations. He frequently met officials to convey India's views regarding military aid to Pakistan and the

Kashmir question. On December 1, 1955, he called at the Department of State to ascertain U.S. reactions to the visit to India of the Soviet leaders– Khrushchev and Bulganin. George Allen told him that the U.S. government did not care for the fact that the Soviet leaders had used public platforms while official guests of the Indian government to attack the United States. He discussed with George Allen and William L.S. Williams the U.S.-India Air agreement and co-operation on peaceful uses of atomic energy. During the Suez crisis in August 1956 he met Secretary of State Dulles three times to discuss the British invasion of Suez Canal and Egypt which both the United States and India opposed.

At the same time as the Suez crisis there was a national uprising in Hungary which was brutally crushed by the Soviet army. The request of the United States, the United Kingdom and France to consider the Hungarian situation in the Security Council was vetoed by the Soviet Union. In the United Nations General Assembly a resolution was moved condemning the Soviet Union. Fifty countries voted in favour of the US Resolution asking the USSR to stop repression and withdraw its troops from Hungary, eight voted against, and fifteen abstained. India abstained, as it did not want to offend the Soviet Union on whose support it depended for the Kashmir issue in the UN. Krishna Menon voted against the Italian resolution that among other things called for U.N. supervised free elections in Hungary. Many Americans felt that Nehru's government was not sincerely committed to human rights and freedom and was instead anxious to cultivate close relations with the Communist states. Bapu who supported Nehru's policy of non-alignment and tried to explain to Americans India's foreign policy vis-a-vis great power disputes, however, found it difficult to defend India's hesitation to condemn Soviet armed intervention in Budapest. He was personally also deeply disturbed by this episode and wrote so to Nehru.

William T. Turner, American Consul General in Bombay wrote to the Secretary of State (22.11.1956) that for the first time there was outspoken criticism in the press and among the public of Nehru's handling of the Hungarian crisis. Jayaprakash Narayan issued a statement criticising Nehru and so did C. Rajagopalachari. Nehru had to bow to public opinion and make a statement in parliament going back on his earlier position.

Bapu developed a close relationship with the outstanding judge of the Supreme Court at that time, Justice Felix Frankfurter, a remarkable man in many ways. Frankfurter was a disciple of Justice Holmes. The common link between my father and Frankfurter was Harold Laski. Another judge, who became a close friend, was Justice William O. Douglas and his wife Mercedes. They met at parties and were frequent visitors to the Indian Embassy.

Bapu met George F. Kennan, who in 1947 had become the head of the State Department's first Policy Planning Staff which became a primary influence in the formation of post-World War II foreign policy. Kennan was appointed US Ambassador to Moscow in 1952 and was a renowned foreign policy expert who impressed Bapu immensely and he wrote to Nehru, "He is one of the ablest men I have met in this country during the last seven months. Justice Frankfurter told me that if he was Secretary of State, he would keep Kennan in an adjoining room for close consultation and advice."

His equation with President Eisenhower was also good. He held that Eisenhower was a brake on some of the hot heads in the Pentagon and the Congress and exercised a moderating influence. The President and Mrs. Eisenhower attended the showing of a film on Mahatma Gandhi in Washington D.C. which had been produced by the Academy of Asian Studies in San Francisco. This was the first such function they attended after he became President. Dr. I.G. Patel, former Finance Scretary, Government of India and former Governor of the

Ambassador G.L. Mehta presents volumes of the Biography of Mahatma Gandhi to President Eisenhower in June 1954.

Ambassador B.K. Nehru, Mr. George Woods, President, World Bank and Ambassador G.L. Mehta signing ICICI loan

Reserve Bank of India, recalls an incident when he accompanied Mr. T.T. Krishnamachari, who was then India's Finance Minister, on a visit to Washington for the World Bank, IMF annual meeting. Mr. Krishnamachari wished to meet President Eisenhower. This was not easy as hundreds of Finance Minister's crowd Washington for this annual Bank, Fund meeting. Bapu, however, was able to arrange the interview through Nelson Rockefeller and despite a heavy storm and disruption of air services, the President and the Finance Minister had a very cordial meeting in September 1957.

During Bapu's tenure numerous distinguished Indians visited Washington, including Vice President Radhakrishnan whom he received in New York and accompanied him during his meetings with President Eisenhower and General Bedell Smith, Acting Secretary of State. He sent detailed notes of these meetings to Nehru. Raj Kumari Amrit Kaur, then Union Minister of Health also came and was immensely pleased by her visit and so was Durgabai Deshmukh who was then Member of the Planning Commission and Chairperson of the newly constituted Central Social Welfare Board. General Shrinagesh, Chief of Army Staff , also had a very successful visit.

There was considerable exchange of correspondence about Nehru's visit to the U.S.A. The first time it was fixed, it had to be postponed because President Eisenhower fell ill and also because of the possibility of Krishna Menon accompanying Nehru. Secretary of State Dulles told Adams that this "would louse it up terribly". George Allen told the Minister in the Indian Embassy in Washington, Mr. Hareshwar Dayal that the addition of Menon would "complicate the visit." Bapu agreed that the circumstances were not propitious for a visit and cabled Nehru recommending postponement. Prior to the Prime Minister's visit, Bapu met officials of the State Department to indicate his hope that there would be no fixed agenda thus permitting the President and the Prime Minister to engage in talks on a "man to man basis." In December 1956, Jawaharlal Nehru and Indira Gandhi came to Washington and had a very successful visit. The Prime Minister was most impressed with Bapu's work and reputation. In a memorandum of a conversation between Dulles and Nehru at Blair House in Washington on 16 December 1956, the Secretary of State noted, "in this connection I said I was sorry to learn that Ambassador Mehta might be leaving. He was a very fine Ambassador and we had developed good understanding with him." Raghavan Pillai, the Foreign Secretary, told Bapu that he should stay longer in Washington. Apparently President Eisenhower, Secretary of State Dulles, Justice Frankfurter, Justice Douglas and several others spoke very highly of him to Nehru and urged him not to remove him. Both M.O. Mathai, Nehru's Private Secretary and Pillai requested him to stay on.

The Indian Ambassador to the United States was also accredited to Mexico and so Bapu went in October 1952 to present his credentials to the Mexican President. He initiated the move for the exchange of scholars between Mexico and India. Satish Gujral then a young artist, who had gone to Mexico to study murals and other types of paintings had a scholarship, which was not adequate. He came to meet Bapu who helped him to put up an exhibition and to extend his stay by a year. At his request the Mexican government also increased the amount of Gujral's scholarship.

Bapu had written to Nehru that Mexico was sufficiently important to have an independent Embassy. Nehru replied that he entirely agreed, "I consider Mexico important. In some ways more important than the South American countries. It is unfortunate that we have not got an office there. We should have it. We are looking into this matter."

In August 1955, Bapu and his Private Secretary Rajagopalan had to change planes in Houston, Texas. At that time there were separate restaurants on the airport for 'whites' and 'coloured' people. Not aware of this, Bapu and Rajagoplalan entered the one reserved for 'whites only'. They were asked to leave. When the manager realised who Bapu was, he personally came and was deeply apologetic. He requested Bapu to return but Bapu refused. This was the only occasion on which he faced discrimination on racial grounds. While American and Indian newspapers made a great fuss over this incident, Bapu ignored it.

Bapu's Washington years were, despite his occasional irritations with the Ministry of External Affairs and his unhappiness over Krishna Menon's behaviour, some of the happiest years of his life. He made friends with a large number of people from different walks of life. He met among others, the distinguished writers, Aldous Huxley, Christopher Isherwood, the foreign policy expert, Owen Lattimore, Sir Edmund Hillary and Sir John Hunt, who had climbed Mount Everest. He developed great regard for Barbara Castle[4]. Among his most memorable meetings was that with Albert Einstein. He wrote, "4th April, 1953 was a memorable day in my life when I went to meet Albert Einstein to invite him to the Indian Science Congress on behalf of Prime Minister Jawaharlal Nehru. My daughter Aparna and I drove down from New York to Princeton. Miss Helen Daks who had looked after Einstein for 25 years welcomed us. He was waiting for us on the top of the stairs. His daughter was with him. He showed great regard for Gandhiji and about half of the time we spent with him, he spoke of Gandhiji. He showed us a book on Gandhiji by some American author, whose name he did not reveal, of which he had been asked to write the introduction." When Bapu mentioned to him that I had been nervous and hesitant in coming to meet such a distinguished scientist, Einstein asked me whether I had met Gandhi and when I replied in the affirmative he said if so, why was I afraid since Gandhi was a much greater human being than he was.

Left to Right: Dr. S. Radhakrishnan, Chief Justice Earl Warren, Ambassador G.L. Mehta

Fortunately for Bapu, Nehru repeatedly expressed full confidence in him and appreciated his work. So did the successive Foreign Secretaries, Subimal Dutt, ICS and Sir Raghavan Pillai, ICS whom he had known for many years and who respected him. He travelled extensively in the United States, lectured at universities, business meetings and at economic forums, established good contacts not only with the Secretary of State's Office, Senators and Congressmen but with a whole range of people – Supreme Court judges, journalists, businessmen, academics and trade union leaders. I was fortunate in going with him to the Democratic Party Convention in Chicago in August 1956 where Adlai Stevenson was re-nominated as the Democratic Party Presidential candidate and to the Republican Party Convention in San Francisco where President Eisenhower was re-nominated as the candidate. There was tremendous excitement at both places and I learnt a great deal about actual American politics about which until then I knew only from textbooks.

The testimonial dinner given in his honour by the National Committee in the Terrace Room of the Shoreham Hotel in Washington D.C. on April 30, 1958 on the eve of his leaving Washington was a unique tribute and an evidence of his popularity. Mrs. Eleanor Roosevelt, H. Rowan Gaither Jr., Chairman, Ford Foundation, George Woods, Paul Hoffman, Senators Hubert Humphrey and John Kennedy were some of the members of the Committee, which hosted the dinner. George Allen, U.S. Ambassador to India told the correspondent of *Hindu* that after the departure of the British Ambassador, Sir Oliver Franks in 1952 no Ambassador's departure had caused so much sadness. More than 500 leaders in public life, government, education, labour movement, business and industry gathered to honour him. Tributes were paid to his services in improving Indo-American relations by Senator John Sherman Cooper (former U.S. Ambassador to India), Mr. John D.

Rockefeller (Chairman of the Board of Rockefeller Foundation and President of Asia Society), Mr. Justice William O. Douglas (of the Supreme Court), Mr. Walter P. Reuther (Vice President of the American Federation of Labour and Congress of Industrial Organisations) and Dr. M.W. Johnson (President of Howard University). Dr. Johnson read out the following citation:

"To His Excellency Gaganvihari Lalubai Mehta, Ambassador Extraordinary and Plenipotentiary from the Republic of India, who came to us not as a stranger in September, 1952, and departs in May 1958, a firm, warm friend; who has ably represented India to the American people, and sincerely reported America to the people of India; who has sustained the interests of his own loved country and high regard for the concerns of other peoples; who has united dignity of office with charm of person; this parting tribute of esteem, of admiration and gratitude is tendered, in token of enduring amity and concord between the peoples of India and the United States, by his colleagues, his associates, his friends in the city of Washington, D.C., this thirtieth day of April, nineteen hundred and fifty eight."

Dr. Johnson went on to say, "From September 1952 to May 1958, Ambassador G.L. Mehta has served the people of India and the United States. During this period his official position has been that of Ambassador to the United States from the Republic of India, a responsibility he has met with high purpose, skill and distinction. But he assigned to himself an ever wider and more demanding task; to interpret creatively the culture, history, and aspirations of one people to another. In so doing, he brought to his post a capacity for inspired friendship and the kind of intellectual excitement that widened the understanding by both peoples of their common needs and purposes. He was a rallying point for men of good will who were profoundly aware of the extent to which a strong and healthy relationship between India and the United States could contribute to meaningful peace in our time.

"The brightest episodes in the history of America's connections with the rest of the world have invariably been associated with a few individuals who became personal symbols of friendship between their nations and the United States. G.L. Mehta has joined that company. His knowledge of the cultural diversity represented by each people; his gift of creative expression in writing or speaking; his ability to see beyond temporary differences to the community of hope that binds nations together; his inspiring patience and good humour – all these have gone into the success of his mission and entitle him to the recognition and gratitude of all those who would speak of the adventure of a truly creative peace."

Mr. Norman Cousins, editor of *Saturday Review* served as toastmaster. Among those present on the occasion were Ambassadors, Senators, Congressmen, the Assistant Secretary of State, the Director of the U.S. Information Service, bankers, journalists, Managing Director of IMF, academics, etc. In his speech Bapu said "What is essential is not identity of views but community of aims; not conformity and acquiescence but comprehension, patience and tolerance."

He was literally overwhelmed by the letters he received on the eve of his departure. Dr. Arthur H. Crompton of Washington University, St. Louis Missouri wrote, "I cannot help but feel a personal loss in your departure from the United States. I share with you, however, a deep sense of pride in your outstanding record of accomplishments in furthering understanding between our two countries during your period of residence here..."

Dr. Robert Burgess Stewart, Dean of the Fletcher School of Diplomacy wrote, "Your departure from Washington marks the end of an era in the history of relations between the United States and India. The foundations of happy and fruitful diplomacy which you have built will serve our two countries well in the years ahead and will make easier the task of those who follow you. We see you go with great sorrow but with grateful hearts for your great services and achievements and for the quality of your friendship which will remain one of our cherished possessions."

H. Rowan Gaither Jr., Chairman of the Ford Foundation wrote, "It was a great privilege to be among the many friends who honoured you at the dinner. Your service to your country and in the furtherance of Indo-American relations has made a permanent contribution to a better world and will long be remembered in the United States."

Prof. Philip C. Jessup of Columbia University wrote, "You must take great satisfaction in having discharged so ably your duties in this country. I am sure that all you have said and done and particularly what you are, have done much to promote good relations between India and the United States."

Francis O. Wilcox in the Secretary of State's office said, "As you depart our country, I want you to know what a splendid job you have done in the United States. You have represented your country with distinction and ability. The many friends you leave here attest to the fact that you have been eminently successful in your efforts to improve relations between our two countries. Your success in this important area of your work has been very fruitful and gratifying for us. It has been a real pleasure to know you and to work with you in an official capacity."

Chester Bowles, former U.S. Ambassador to India wrote: "We want to express our sorrow that you will soon be leaving and our gratitude to you as India's Ambassador to the United States for your contribution to closer understanding between our two countries and for your warm friendship for our country."

Several newspapers across the United States such as the *Washington Post, Christian Science Monitor, Pittsburgh Post Gazette, Milwaukee Journal, The Courier Journal*, and others. wrote editorials on the eve of his departure. *St. Louis Post Despatch* wrote (May,

2, 1958, 'A Distinguished Ambassador') "It is not often that an Ambassador to the United States leaves behind a record of accomplishments of the character and quality of that of G.L. Mehta who returns to India in the next few days. The testimonial of esteem and appreciation which is being paid to Ambassador Mehta in his final week in Washington is a measure of the good that he has achieved in the five and a half years since he came to the United States.

"In the first half of India's decade of independence, Ambassadors from New Delhi came and went like shadows in the night. There were four in hardly more than that many years. During much of that time relations between India and the United States were frayed if not strained. Washington did not understand Mr. Nehru. Officials in India often misread our intentions.

Ambassador Mehta did not try to represent the Indian policy, as being anything other than what it was – resolute independence. Nor did he try to cover up his country's dislike of our military pact with Pakistan and shipment of arms to Karachi or its amazement that Secretary of State Dulles could seemingly go out of his way to fracture relations with India with his support for Portuguese colonialism in Goa. That period also included the tensions over India's stand against Pakistan's claims over Kashmir.

"Mr. Mehta accepted these and other problems and handled them by explaining them not only in Washington, Cuba and Mexico to which he was likewise accredited, but also directly to the American people. Surely few Ambassadors have seen more of the United States and talked first hand to more diverse American groups."

Norman Cousins, editor of *Saturday Review*, wrote of "the spontaneous overflow of good feeling for you that is shared by many thousands of people in this country. It is true that not for many years has there been any farewell tribute to an Ambassador of these dimensions."

The editor of the *Reader's Digest*, D. Wallace, wrote of "the deep feeling of appreciation for the goodwill and friendliness which have been so much in evidence during your stay in Washington." Mr. K. Balaraman, Washington correspondent of *Hindu* wrote that it would take him time "to adjust to a Mehta-less Chancery."

Frank Moraes (Ariel) in his column 'Men, Matters and Memories' in the *Times of India* wrote, "As Ariel knows from what he saw and heard in the United States, G.L. rates highly in the regard and affection not only of State Department officials but of politicians, journalists, university deans and professors and students. He has traits which the American instinctively likes and which he does not always associate with Indians – a warm friendliness of approach, a willingness to listen and understand, and a profound disinclination to pontificate and preach. The absence, rather than the presence of these attributes, is what distinguishes some of our representatives at the UN."

Bapu gave a farewell reception at the Indian Embassy which was attended among others by the Assistant to the President, Mr. Sherman Adams and Mrs. Adams, Secretary to the Cabinet, Maxwell Rabb, Special Assistant to the President, Mr. Hague, Chief Justice Earl Warren, Justice Felix Frankfurter, Justice William O. Douglas, Senators Fulbright, Hubert Humphrey, Sherman Cooper, Jacob Javits, John Kennedy and his wife Jacqueline Kennedy, several members of the Cabinet and officials of the State Department. Among the journalists present were Philip Graham, Mr. And Mrs. Eugene Meyer, Alfred Friendly, and Frederick Kuhn of the *Washington Post*; Mr. and Mrs. Walter Lippman, Mr. and Mrs. Marquis Childs, Mr. and Mrs. Drew Pearson; Washington correspondents of *New York Times*, *Christian Science Monitor*, *Baltimore Sun*, *Newsweek*, etc. So also were correspondents of the American Broadcasting Corporation and the National Broadcasting Corporation. Among the guests were Presidents, Deans and Professors of universities, bankers, industrialists, businessmen and personal friends.

Bapu left Washington for New York *en route* to India on May 5, 1958. He was seen off at the Union Station by a gathering of about 150 people, which included the Ambassadors of the United Kingdom, Australia, Canada, Ghana, New Zealand and Laos; officers of the Indian Embassy, State Department, the International Bank for Reconstruction and Development and the International Monetary Fund. The Ambassador was garlanded on behalf of the Embassy and by many of the ladies present in traditional Indian manner.

After spending five years and seven and a half months as India's Ambassador, in his last letter from Washington to his brother, Vaikunthbhai, he wrote, "I have benefited a great deal by coming here. I have seen and learnt a great deal. Because of my position, I got an opportunity to work and show my worth and capacity. People are really sad at my leaving." Bapu was honoured on his return to India with the highest honour, next to Bharat Ratna, the award of Padma Vibhushan. The citation read as follows:

> "An experienced businessman and a man of wide public activities, Shri Gaganvihari Lallubhai Mehta has been India's Ambassador to the United States of America for six years. During this period he made ceaseless efforts for a better appreciation in the United States, of India's domestic and foreign policies. His persistent advocacy of the Indian cause and his keenness and sincerity not only won for him and for India, friends in U.S.A. but also helped in the creation of better understanding of .India's view points in that country.
>
> "Shri Mehta was President of the Indian Chamber of Commerce in 1939-40 and President of the Federation of the Indian Chamber of Commerce and Industry in 1942-43. He was a member of the Planning Commission before he took up his assignment as Ambassador in the United

States.

"Shri Mehta has represented India in a number of International Conferences. He was a member of the Constituent Assembly of India and of the governing body of the Council for Scientific and Industrial Research. He is now Chairman of the Hindustan Shipyard, Visakhapatnam."

After Bapu's passing away, Frederick Kuhn of the *Washington Post* wrote, "Mr. Mehta was without any doubt the finest Ambassador India ever sent to Washington". Norman Palmer, Professor of Political Science at Wharton School of Business echoed the sentiment, "He was an Ambassador in more than the formal sense. In fact, one might say that he was probably the best Ambassador of goodwill and understanding between our two countries, before and after as well as during his tenure of the post of Ambassador".

REFERENCES

1. John Foster Dulles (1888-1959) US politician, educated at Princeton University and Sorbonne. At the conference at Versailles he was adviser to President Wilson. In 1953 he became US Secretary of State, opening a vigorous diplomacy of personal conferences with statesmen in other countries. In 1954 he launched the concept of SEATO.
2. Dharamsey Khatau, Industrialist, Chairman, Khatau Mills, Chairman, Scindia Steam Navigation Co. Ltd.
3. Chunilal B. Mehta (1881) Director, Scindia Steam Navigation Co. Ltd., President, Bombay Shroffs' Association, Sheriff of Bombay, 1936, President, Indian Merchants' Chamber, Bombay.
4. Barbara Castle (1911-) English Labour politician. Minister for Overseas Development (1964-65), Minister of Transport (1965-68), Secretary of State for Employment and Productivity (1968-70), and Minister of Health and Social Security (1974).

7

Building a Financial Institution : ICICI, 1958-1971

The few months between Bapu's return from Washington and his joining the Industrial and Credit Corporation of India were an unsettled period. He was anxious to do something for the country, do some public service. Nehru wanted him to rejoin the Planning Commission but Bapu was not too keen as he felt that the Planning Commission was no longer fulfilling the role it was originally meant to, it had grown too vast and unwieldy. Morarji Desai, who was then Finance Minister, was keen that he should be taken into the Cabinet as Minister for Industry and Commerce but obviously could not persuade the Prime Minister who probably regarded him as too pro American and for the private sector. Meanwhile Bapu was under pressure from the World Bank to take up the chairmanship of ICICI whose foundations were laid when he was Ambassador in Washington. In February, 1954, Mr. Eugene Black, then President of the International Bank for Reconstruction and Development (popularly known as the World Bank) sent a small team of three persons headed by Mr. George Woods (then Chairman of the First Boston Corporation and later President of the World Bank), Mr. Robert Craft of the American Security Corporation and Mr. Rucinski of the World Bank to India to investigate the possibilities of setting up a development financial institution in co-operation with the World Bank to provide long term finance and foreign currency loans to industry and also help build up a capital market in India. Woods had discussed this proposal with Bapu in Washington. Bapu wrote: "Years later, in 1964, I asked George Woods whose idea it was to have such an institution...He told me that the idea was suggested to Mr. Eugene Black by Mr. Clifford Wilson who was head of the Technical Co-operation Administration, later known as the Agency for International Development (AID)...I first met George Woods when he came to Delhi in June 1952 as the World Bank's expert advising on the loan applications of the Tata Iron and Steel Company. I was then a Member of the Planning Commission. At a dinner given for Woods by the Prime Minister, I was sitting next to him and told him of my appointment as India's Ambassador to Washington, which had not yet been officially announced. Over the years we became close friends." The Woods team met industrialists and bankers in Bombay, Calcutta and Madras and held discussions with the Finance Minister, C.D. Deshmukh who was responsive and helpful. The Indian business group set up a small steering committee consisting of Sir Ramaswamy Mudaliar, Mr. G.D. Birla and Mr. A.D. Shroff to work out a scheme and see it through.

Eugene Black and George Woods between them persuaded four American parties – the Bank of America, Olin Matheson, Westinghouse and Rockefeller Brothers to put in a quarter million dollars each. The British parties then came in with some banks, insurance companies and the Commonwealth Development Finance Company participating in the scheme. The Government of India gave an interest free loan of Rs.seven and a half crores while the World Bank extended a line of credit of U.S. $ 10 million. The capital of the Corporation was Rs. 5 crore.

In the early autumn of 1954, Mr. Ramaswamy Mudaliar

and Mr. A.D. Shroff went to Washington to finalise the scheme. Bapu writes: "They discussed the project at the Embassy after a lunch I had given although I did not participate in the discussion. Later in October, when the scheme materialised, there was a lunch at the World Bank to which I was invited... Speaking on the occasion, and little dreaming that I would be connected with this institution one day, I recollect that I said that this Corporation might serve as a catalytic agent for mobilising capital and for industrial development...I also said that it was a tripartite arrangement in more than one sense: three parties, namely Indian capital, the Indian government and the World Bank were participating in it as also Indian private capital along with British and American capital. I signed the Guarantee Agreement for the first line of credit of U.S.$ 10 million from the World Bank on March 14, 1955."

ICICI was formally set up on January 5, 1955 when Bapu was India's Ambassador in Washington. A year was taken in formulating basic guidelines in policy and in getting the institution moulded, in establishing relationships with the Reserve Bank of India and other financial institutions, particularly the Industrial and Financial Corporation of India and in organisational matters. ICICI's Board of Directors was then a high powered one, comprising persons like Sir Ramaswami Mudaliar as Chairman and A.D. Shroff[1], G.D. Birla and Kasturbhai Lalbhai[2] as members. The first General Manager was Mr.P.S. Beale, an Englishman, who had been Chief Cashier of the Bank of England. This was in accordance with the World Bank's initial philosophy that the G.M. should be a non-Indian in order to insulate the institution from government and local pressure. The first three years of ICICI were years of mixed achievements. The institution had been set up and began its operations but it had done nothing in making foreign currency loans available and increasingly organisational problems were coming to the fore. The World Bank as well as the Indian members of the Board were unhappy with the way the Corporation was functioning. In 1956-57, ICICI was nearly wound up partly due to personality factors. There were conflicts between Beale and some of the industrialists who were Directors of the Board. The conflicts were rooted partly in personalities, partly in differences over policy. A major factor was the difference in perception of the role that ICICI was expected to play. Beale, an expatriate, whose professional roots were in a regulatory monetary authority, could not have shared the 'development perspective' of the Indians on the Board. Beale was expected to 'safeguard' expatriate 'shareholder' interests - Americans as well as British, and therefore, perhaps, insisted on certain procedures while sanctioning assistance. Indian industrialists did not want to be evaluated or appraised and found ICICI's assistance too little too late. A major conflict was on the question of exchange risk on IBRD credit. Beale actually wrote to the World Bank to close down ICICI.

Bapu writes: "In June 1957 Eugene Black invited me to lunch at the World Bank and said that he had heard that I intended to relinquish my post after the Finance Minister, Mr. T.T. Krishnamachari's visit and asked me what I proposed to do on my return. I told him that it was true that I was leaving but that I had not made up my mind as to what I would do thereafter. I also told him that Prime Minister Nehru and the Deputy Chairman of the Planning Commission, Sir V.T. Krishnamachari wanted me to join the Planning Commission with which I had been connected before I came to Washington. Mr. Eugene Black thereupon said that if it was not inappropriate he wanted to know whether I would be interested in ICICI as they in the World Bank felt that it had not been running satisfactorily. He even went to the extent of telling me that if it continued in the manner it was doing the World Bank might even consider withdrawing from it.

"I thanked him for his suggestion and said that I would

consider the proposal although I did not know anything about the Corporation or its working. I also told him that I had no first-hand experience in banking except that I had been on the Local Committee of the Bank of India in Calcutta from 1937 to 1947.

"When I went to New York after a few days, Mr. George Woods raised the same question and asked me to consider the proposal. I understood from Mr. T.T. Krishnamachari , then Finance Minister that both Mr. Black and Mr. Woods had spoken to him. He gave me to understand that he told them that our Government might have some other ideas of utilising my services in New Delhi but he wanted me to continue in Washington for some more time in view of the fact that the question of aid was very important and that I had built up good contacts which might be useful to the Government.

" I agreed to continue in Washington on condition that as soon as the first instalment of aid was communicated to us by the U.S. authorities I should be free to return home. When in January 1958, Mr. Douglas Dillon, then Under Secretary of State (Economic Affairs) who was subsequently Secretary to the Treasury, phoned me when I was in New York and advised me about the first quantum of aid of U.S.$225 million, I wrote to the Ministry of External Affairs that I would like to relinquish my charge in early May.

"Immediately this was known, both Mr. Eugene Black and Mr. George Woods again approached me and asked me to consider the proposition regarding ICICI. My informal discussions with Mr. George Woods in this connection continued until I relinquished charge in May 1958. I told him that I could not make any commitment until I looked round in India and had consulted the Prime Minister and Mr. Morarji Desai who was then Finance Minister. I gave him to understand, however, that I would give this proposition the first preference although it might have to be on a part- time basis as I might stay outside Bombay and commute, if necessary. We agreed to remain in touch with each other in this matter.

"After my return to India when I went to Delhi, I discussed this question with the Prime Minister, Mr. Morarji Desai and Sir V.T. Krishnamachari, the Deputy Chairman of the Planning Commission who was very keen that I should rejoin the Planning Commission and take charge of the Industries Division with which I had been connected before I went to Washington. Mr. Morarji Desai also asked me to consider this proposal favourably although he left the decision entirely to me.

"I told Prime Minister Nehru that while I was not competent to express an opinion on the working of the Planning Commission, I felt that I could not make any useful contribution to it in the set up and conditions of the time. I also told him that rather than being useless in a large sphere, I preferred to be useful in a small sphere.

"In the meanwhile, Mr. P.S. Beale had retired in April 1958, and the post of General Manager of ICICI was vacant. The World Bank was in search of a substitute from abroad. It had selected a Netherlands banker who, after accepting the offer changed his mind... Then an Italian was selected but the British shareholders were not happy with him; finally a Canadian banker was selected but his parent bank was unable to spare his services. I was kept advised about these negotiations but I thought there was no reason to have a foreigner for this post.

"For all I had heard about Mr. H.T. Parekh who was Deputy General Manager at the time, I felt that he would fit the bill very well. Some industrialists as well as senior Government officials in Delhi had spoken highly about him to me. I thereupon suggested to Mr. George Woods not to look for any non-Indian and conveyed to him that if the Board was reorganised and Mr. Parekh was appointed General Manager I was prepared to accept Chairmanship provided the Board of Directors, the shareholders and the Government of India agreed.

"Mr. Eugene Black and Mr. George Woods came to Delhi for the World Bank and Fund Meetings in October, 1958, and had discussions with some of the Directors of ICICI as well as with the Finance Minister, the Governor of the Reserve Bank and the Finance Secretary in this connection. It was agreed that some of the senior Directors might retire and younger men might be taken in their place while a few might remain for the sake of continuity.

"This arrangement, however, was not relished by one or two Directors who thought that the World Bank was "pressurising" the Board and not leaving the choice to the Corporation. However, Dr. Ramaswami Mudaliar who was then Chairman, appreciated the need for a change as did Mr. G.D. Birla and Mr. Kasturbhai Lalbhai. Both at the Board Meeting and at the Meeting of the Shareholders, Dr. Ramaswamy Mudaliar was most gracious in proposing my name as Chairman.

"I had the privilege of knowing him since the early forties when he was Supply Member and Commerce Member of the Viceroy's Executive Council and I was with Scindias and had the good fortune of enjoying his goodwill and confidence."

On September 8, 1958, George Woods sent Bapu a cable that U.K. and U.S.A. shareholders and IBRD all agreed that he should be the Chairman of ICICI. Eugene Black wrote to him, "I need hardly say how delighted I have been to learn the definite confirmation of your willingness to serve as Chairman of ICICI under its new regime..." A month later, on October 8, Ramaswamy Mudaliar, Chairman ICICI met two members of the Board, G.D. Birla and A.D. Shroff and informed George Woods, Burke-Knapp and Rucinski of the World Bank that some changes were being made in the Board of ICICI. Sir Badridas Goenka was to resign from the Board to make room for Bapu. Ramaswamy Mudaliar was to resign as Chairman and the Board was to elect Bapu as Chairman and Chief Executive Officer. He joined ICICI in October 1958 and his appointment as

ICICI Board Meeting

Chairman was approved by shareholders at a special meeting on December 1, 1958.

"Some other changes in the Board were made and young people were brought in. I was very glad that I was able to persuade Mr. N.A. Palkhivala[3] to join the Board despite his heavy pre-occupations and give us the benefit of his legal knowledge and experience. Later, at my request Mr. N.M. Wagle, ex-ICS and Chairman of Greaves Cotton, also agreed to join the Board."

Bapu's appointment was widely welcomed in financial and commercial circles. *Commerce* wrote: "The choice of Mr. G.L. Mehta for the post of Chief Executive Officer of the Corporation is a happy one for more than one reason. The most important is the fact that Mr. Mehta enjoys the confidence of the Government of India and the business community in this country, on the one hand, and the American and British investment circles on the other. His popularity with American businessmen is phenomenal...As India's Ambassador to the United States for over five years, he has played an important part in securing several loans from the World Bank, including the one the Corporation obtained in 1955...He is thus known to the Bank intimately and held in high esteem...One of the functions of the Corporation is to act as a catalytic agent for attracting foreign private capital...Given a more positive investment climate, Mr. Mehta can, thanks to his wide contacts and knowledge of men and matters, enable the Corporation to play this role effectively...The Corporation now in its fourth year, has been fortunate in securing the services of Mr. Mehta...He has the enviable distinction of possessing the goodwill of the Government of India, the U.S. Government and the World Bank." The *Economic Weekly* also welcomed his appointment.

After taking over as Chairman, Bapu wrote to Eugene Black on 11 December 1958, "I can honestly tell you that I have accepted this post and agreed to work in the Corporation mainly at your instance and because of George Woods's insistence..."

Thus began Bapu's association with ICICI which was to end with his death and he often felt that his years with ICICI represented the most fruitful and rewarding period of his career. "I was new to this kind of work and I believe I presided over a Board Meeting for the first time in my life", he wrote, "but the Directors showed me courtesy and extended full co-operation. Throughout the last thirteen years, the Board has worked with complete harmony."

For being initiated in this new kind of work, he acknowledged that he depended almost entirely on Mr. H.T. Parekh. To Eugene Black, Bapu wrote, "I find Parekh a first class man in every respect and I am glad he has been confirmed as General Manager..." "Apart from having a grounding in economics in the Bombay University and the London School of Economics, Mr. Parekh had twenty years' experience on the Bombay Stock Exchange, having been connected with a well-known stock broker's firm. He, therefore, had an insight into the working of important joint stock companies and knew almost by heart their financial condition and problems, and had a feel for the ups and downs of the market. But I soon found that the mere monetary aspect did not distort his judgement and he sought to evaluate financial problems in a wider economic context." ICICI could not have asked for a better partnership. Mr. William Diamond who had been assigned by the World Bank to work with ICICI writes, "A crucial matter was the relationship between Parekh and G.L. Mehta, the new Chairman. I do not think they knew each other before Mehta became Chairman, though they certainly knew of each other. They were hardly equals in the public eye. Mehta was well-known in India as well as abroad (especially so in the United States). He had an excellent reputation with the business community, both as a journalist and as a businessman. He was much respected in the government as a former member of the Planning Commission, former Chairman of the Tariff Commission and, until mid 1958, Ambassador to Washington. Parekh also had an excellent reputation, but among a much smaller circle of businessmen. Moreover Mehta, though nominally a 'part-time' Director, had been given 'executive powers'. That grant made the Government nervous because it might be interpreted as a violation of the Companies Act, under which the General Manager had 'powers of management'. ICICI therefore had to give formal assurances that Mehta was only 'part-time' Chairman and that the 'executive powers' given him 'do not include any powers of management', which belonged to a 'full time' Managing Director. In this ambiguous situation, there was plenty of room for conflict.

"It was ICICI's good fortune that the conflict never developed, thanks to the personalities and intelligence of both Mehta and Parekh. They were deeply interested in the mission of ICICI and they had the wit to see quickly that they complemented each other. Mehta was out-going, vivacious, knew his way in both the political and bureaucratic power structures, and was first class in public relations. But he knew he lacked the deep company knowledge and financial expertise that Parekh had. Parekh was quiet and introverted, did little (I think) spontaneously. I took a photo of Mehta clowning in my flat in Bombay while wearing a fur hat that I had just made in preparation for visiting Russia. I cannot imagine Parekh evoking a laugh that way, let alone allowing it to be recorded.

"Mehta and Parekh recognised that they complemented each other, and they hit it off. Yet Mehta was clearly the 'Boss', so long as he was Chairman. While he was free to do what he wished and did in fact participate in all decision-making, he focused primarily on external matters (Board relations, the government, foreign leaders, the media and links with the business organisations) and links with the power structure. Parekh concentrated on managing ICICI on a day-to-day basis: investments, administration and the like. On all matters of policy and recruitment, each took initiatives, but all important decisions were taken by consensus, although as time went on Mehta spent more and more time in ICICI. Of course, it took a little while, but not long, to develop this happy and productive relationship".

Mr. Parekh, Hasmukhbhai as we called him and his wife Hirabhen became like members of our family. Hasmukhbhai was a gentle, reticent and modest person but extremely knowledgeable about the stock market, investments, etc. He was also a man of impeccable integrity. Bapu took him into confidence on all matters and trusted him fully and regarded him like a younger brother. Hasmukhbhai had great regard and respect towards Bapu. On his deathbed, a few hours before he passed away, Bapu asked for Parekh as he called him.

Mr. Parekh wrote in *Swayam*, the House journal of ICICI, in January 1995, "In 1958, Shri Gaganvihari Mehta became Chairman of ICICI and I became General Manager. ICICI's management techniques also changed. With the new management, we ushered in a new era in ICICI. In 1959, the Indian economy received a new impetus...ICICI's business was rising every year. At the same time, ICICI's staff strength increased fourfold. Along with this able and efficient staff, the entire group was well tuned like a perfect symphony.

"Under Gaganvihari Mehta's leadership, the prestige of the Corporation had increased. ICICI's role in the economic development of the country was important. The Corporation was recognised as the organisation for industrial financing as well as a development-banking organisation. This provided the staff happiness and satisfaction.... All of us together experienced this. Gaganviharibhai would often say that he had never experienced such peace, happiness and satisfaction elsewhere...In all these years, rarely have we experienced animosity towards others. Though we were firm in our opinions, we also respected and accepted the views of others. Such team spirit made ICICI's development possible." Soon after Bapu's death in an article in an issue of *Granth*, which was a memorial volume to him, Mr. Parekh wrote, "His last, and perhaps his fondest, love was ICICI, with which he was associated for the last 15 years of his life. He was never tired of saying that these were among the happiest years of his life. It was during these long years that I had the privilege of working with him in ICICI. Having to work closely with him day after day, we, in ICICI came under his spell. He captured the hearts of everyone, high and low, by his charm, his informality, his wit, his youthful spirit, his restlessness, his wide outlook, and his deep interest and by his leadership. If we all provided the sinews, he provided the spirit and inspiration for the building of ICICI."

Another colleague, Mr. James Raj, in the same journal, wrote: "It was however after coming back to India in 1959 that I came to know the full measure of the generosity of G.L. I had at that time considerable trouble getting myself back into the Secretariat hierarchy at New Delhi and was more or less exiled to Bombay as Additional Director of Stock Exchanges. This was a thankless task, the idea being to enforce the Securities (Contracts) Regulations Act of 1953 with a small office which could hardly keep New Delhi posted with the factual developments at the Bombay Stock Exchange. Nevertheless our office was expected to police the many regulations which poured in from North Block. It so happened that I called on G.L. once and mentioned to him the nature of my work. At that time he had taken over as Chairman of ICICI and had been in that position for nearly a year. All of a sudden he turned to me and said, "Why don't you stop being a policeman and start doing something useful? We have a post of Deputy General Manager in ICICI consequent on the promotion of Mr. H.T. Parekh. We can consider you for that post if you are interested..." I was taken aback because until that time I had not had even a nodding acquaintance with banking, let alone development banking. I said as much to G.L. but he pooh-poohed my objections and said, 'I am sure something can be worked out and you can do the job.' Something was worked out and to my amazement within four months I found myself as Deputy General Manager of ICICI.

"The three and a half years which followed were, I can say without hesitation, the happiest period of my life. There was the excitement of building up a new institution under the leadership of G.L. and H.T. Parekh, who made an admirable team, each of whom had human qualities, which endeared them to the entire staff. My years in ICICI appeared to me to be no work at all, such was the cheerful atmosphere and the excitement of learning new things. It was during these years that I came to know G.L. at his best. He was meticulous in his work as Chairman, and he would make it a point always to have the Board papers prepared in the clearest language possible. His knowledge of industry and finance was unrivalled. His leadership qualities were amazing and he had the ability to put everyone at ease and get the best out of him. In administrative matters he was extremely fair-minded and generous to a fault.

"Despite his suave manners and tactful behaviour, G.L. was one of the toughest negotiators I knew. I have never come across another man who could say 'no' with such pleasantness as he could. I had the privilege of accompanying him to Washington in 1963 to negotiate a World Bank loan for ICICI and I can never forget the manner in which he sailed with ease through the many shoals which had been fixed for him by the "Reception Committee" on the other side of the table. In fact if I remember rightly the final negotiations in which G.L. met the President of the World Bank, Mr. George Woods, were concluded in exactly 12 minutes."

Dr. Phiroze B. Medhora who was Joint Managing Director wrote, "Before I joined ICICI, I had heard of ICICI essentially as a frosty, U-class organisation: it was selective, formal and acted superior to its clients. When I joined ICICI in 1960, this

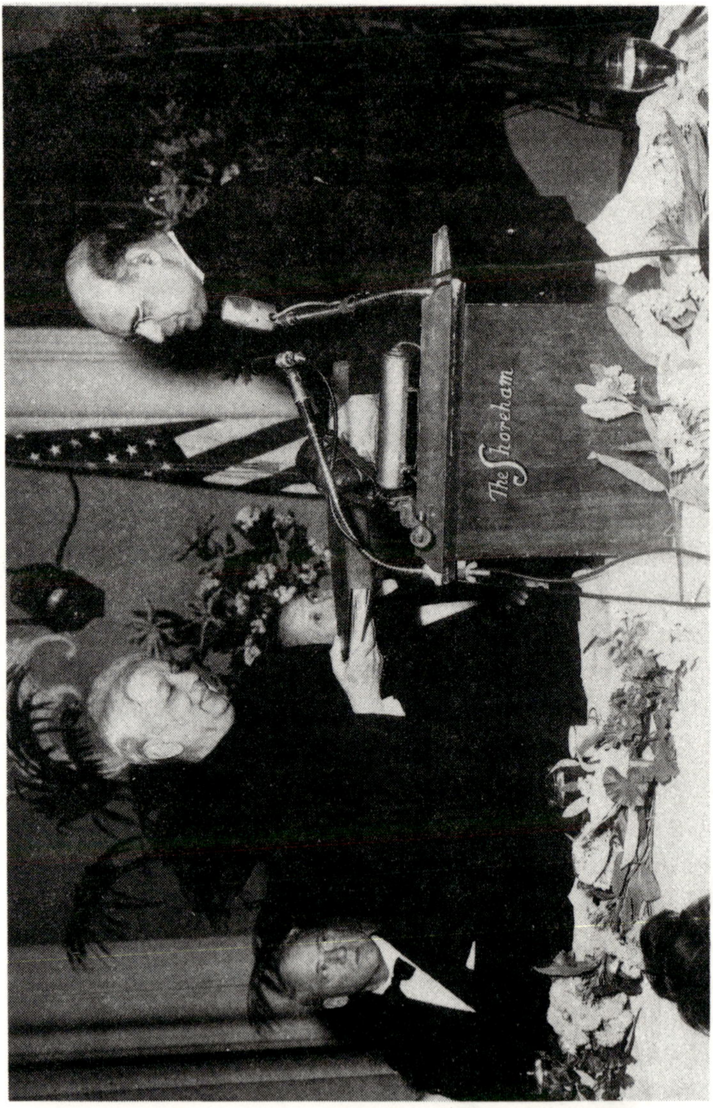

Testimonial Dinner: L to R:
Ambassador John Sherman Cooper, Ambassador G.L. Mehta and
Dr. M. Johnson, President Howard University

image of ICICI was confirmed as prevailing before 1958. However, by 1960 ICICI had been established as a humane, sympathetic development bank, willing to encourage new entrepreneurs to take risks. Credit is due to two persons – G.L. Mehta and H.T.Parekh – for bringing about this transformation.

"G.L. Mehta also brought to the organisation a degree of informality which it lacked in the earlier days. He believed in delegating jobs, and certainly believed in not doing things for which he had no capacity. Under him relationships among the staff became easy and relaxed.

"His direct association with ICICI began when he was 58. However, he brought to the task the zeal and drive of a much younger man. He took his duties seriously, and was fully conversant with what was happening in the organisation. More important he brought to his job an élan, a sense of mission. With him ICICI came out of its shell, became an outward looking organisation.

"My first image of him, perhaps derived from his attire, was that business and office work would not be his forte. Within a short time I realised the meticulousness with which he performed his duties. He read ICICI papers, corrected them, and asked questions where he thought elucidation was necessary. He discussed with us in depth the agenda of meetings he attended– whether these were an ICICI Board meetings or meetings convened by a Ministry or the Planning Commission; he spoke to the agenda, and laced his remarks with a reminiscence or a joke– again to the point...in a way he was detached in his outlook; I am not sure that his wit came from this detachment or the detachment came from the wit. Regarding one promoter who had applied to ICICI for a loan, he suggested that we impose a condition that he tie the knot of his tie properly: and we then seriously considered whether that would not be interpreted as attaching strings to our aid or interfering in his domestic affairs! Whether it was a meeting or lunch, it came alive with his presence."

P.H. Vaidya reminiscing about his days in ICICI writes, "G.L. Mehta was known for his humour. While talking about ICICI, he observed that the name ICICI contains two 'seas' and three 'eyes'. The two 'seas' reflect the connection between the Pacific Ocean (World Bank) and the Arabian Sea (India). While each person has two eyes, ICICI has three, the third could be opened, like Lord Shiva, when the client seriously defaulted."

P.R. Surve who was with ICICI for 26 years writes," I served under G.L. Mehta for four years. During that period, I worked directly under him. He looked like Prime Minister Nehru, his temper was mercurial; but he would calm down just as fast. He was very fond of reading and, I think, it was during his tenure that our library was established. It had 7000 books at that time. The only two individuals who used the Library at that time were G.L. Mehta and Dr. Phiroze Medhora."

Bapu started holding ICICI Board meetings in different parts of India to use these as an excuse for explaining the purposes, hopes and aspirations of ICICI. He kept George Woods fully appraised of developments in ICICI. After receiving some newspaper reports from India, Woods wrote to Burke-Knapp of the World Bank on 21.1.1959,... "They give me the impression that our friend Mehta is really doing very well..." And again he wrote in another letter "I am accumulating a most interesting file of correspondence with our friend Mehta...I have the feeling that he is very much on top of his job and more and more, I feel that we made a wise choice although it is of course too early to be certain" (26.1.1959) Burke Knapp replied "It is encouraging to see that he is getting around and getting this degree of attention for the ICICI". (29.1.1959)

On 19 March, 1959, "for the first time in the history of ICICI, a meeting was held with press representatives. It was not a press conference but simply a meeting for background briefing. The occasion was the issuance of the latest annual report and the Chairman's statement...Mr. Mehta did a very good job..." wrote William Diamond.

The major problem facing the country when Bapu joined the Corporation was the foreign currency crisis of 1957-58. Until 1957, ICICI had not sanctioned any amount out of the first foreign currency loan of U.S. $ 10 million sanctioned by the World Bank. Because of the foreign currency crisis, there was a growing demand for foreign currency loans. "It is at this point we took a safeguarding measure to conserve the Corporation's foreign currency resources and distribute them as widely as possible....The Board of ICICI therefore decided that it would restrict the grant of foreign currency loans to companies belonging to any one business group to a total of U.S. $ 1 million only. Out of this decision two other consequences followed.... First, when the first loan was fully utilised, we approached the World Bank for a further line of credit. We found the Bank responsive to India's requirements and appreciative of ICICI's new management and direction policy. This was my first experience of negotiating a line of credit with the World Bank....While we continued to support new entrepreneurs and new products and new processes with funds obtained from the World Bank, we also increased the limit set for companies belonging to one group, commensurate with our increasing foreign currency resources.

"In other words, a decision did not become a matter of routine to be changed only under pressure, but every policy decision was constantly being reviewed to meet the changing needs of the economy. It is this watchfulness and flexibility which have characterised all ICICI decisions and has enabled it to respond to the emerging needs of the economy," wrote Bapu.

"The period 1958-62 was marked by a tremendous upsurge in ICICI's foreign currency loan operations. But its rupee loans tended to have a secondary place. However, the Corporation did not withdraw from the rupee business but continued to take marginal interest in rupee operations...Performing its function as a provider of risk finance, the Corporation continued to take a small share in the equity of new companies financed by it. To some extent this was an expression of confidence in the projects financed by it. In this manner it began to build up a risk portfolio to enable it to keep its foot in the rupee market.

"Using the opportunity of a buoyant capital market, ICICI began to sell a part of its investment portfolio on the market. Thus the Corporation helped to broaden public shareholding in industry, in the process helping the growth of the capital market and replenishing its own rupee resources."

The period after 1962 marked a new phase in ICICI's operations. It is in this phase when there was a recession in industrial growth that ICICI's role as a development bank clearly emerged. Many companies were not able to meet their repayment commitments and some found themselves short of finance to complete their projects. ICICI perceived its role as a development bank to create and not to destroy, to take a long view and not be swayed by temporary difficulties. The Corporation rescheduled the repayment obligations and provided additional finance to companies as required.

"At that time, we underwrote public issues of many shares in the full knowledge that there was little difference between underwriting and taking up of shares, so little was the public response to public issue of shares. It was then that speaking at a meeting of the Central Advisory Council of Industries, I remarked that "underwriters had become undertakers" – a phrase which has become quite popular.... In fact, some shareholders at our annual meetings used to suggest that we should give loans and not underwrite issues because of adverse stock market conditions. We had to explain that it was precisely at such times that development banks had a function to perform in supporting the capital market.

"As one of the older development banks, ICICI also began to take an increasing interest in developing relations with other development banks in India and abroad. It organised a regional conference of development banks in Asia on March 29, 1962 – the first such conference to be organised....

"In 1965 ICICI instituted a scheme of inviting officers from two development banks in developing countries for training at ICICI at its own cost. Under this arrangement officers have come from Malaysia, Nigeria, Thailand, Ghana, Singapore, Mauritius, the Philippines, Ceylon, South Korea, Indonesia and Uganda...."

At the request of the World Bank and the International Finance Corporation, as well as some development banks in other countries, ICICI made available the services of some of its senior officers to assist development banks or in making economic surveys of other countries. Mr. James Raj when he was with the Corporation went to Afghanistan and Dr. P.B. Medhora went to Mauritius for advising on the establishment and organisation of development banks in these countries. ICICI's reputation as a leading development bank and the high quality of its staff was by now widely acknowledged. Mr. George Woods, then President of the World Bank, requested the Corporation for the services of Mr. J.S. Raj for the Development Bank in Nigeria.... Mr. R.K. Chari was deputed to the Malaysian Industrial Development Bank and Mr. M.C. Shetty to the Asian Development Bank. Thus ICICI offered facilities for training and deputed its own officers where assistance was sought and the Corporation could give it. During these years Mr. George Woods and Mr. McNamara both visited India and had discussions with ICICI.

ICICI took broad initiatives to cultivate better relations with its clients in various ways. In 1964 a conference of its clients was organised so that they could appreciate their problems better and discuss the various factors which guide ICICI's decisions on project financing. In 1967, a conference of clients, representatives of the Government and educational institutions regarding exports was organised. In December 1970, ICICI held a conference on Research and Development. It also provided finance to many companies like Associated Cement, Hindustan Lever and Camphor and Allied Products to set up research centres.

"The initials ICICI have been the subject of good humour, digs and puns", wrote Bapu. "Soon after the Corporation's inception, some wag in the Reserve Bank is said to have accused it of being egoistic (I see I see I – it sees only itself – rather poor English grammar but still). Prof. Galbraith when he was American Ambassador in New Delhi told me once that 'while your Corporation is doing good work, it reminds me of frozen credits (ice)' But the best remark I heard was from a banker in Philadelphia in 1966 who after welcoming me said, "You are Chairman of ICICI – please tell me when to stop." Which reminded me of the young boy who when asked to write 'banana' complained that he did not know when to stop.

ICICI's activities had contracted appreciably in 1958 to a level much below that of 1957 and far below reasonable expectations. In the Resolution passed by the Board of ICICI at a meeting held on May 9, 1974, "The Board recalled that Mr.G.L. Mehta joined ICICI at a time of crisis in its career. It was because of his able leadership, provided at that time and later, that ICICI was able to come out of the crisis and to develop itself as a major financial institution in the country. Within ICICI Mr. Mehta brought to its activities a sense of purpose and mission which helped to make ICICI a major institution providing finance and advice to its clients. Mr. Mehta also contributed to the growth of ICICI by building up its relationship with Government of India, the Reserve Bank and other financial institutions. As a result of Mr. Mehta's efforts and activities, ICICI built up a cordial understanding with the Government, which helped to establish a sound basis of working relationship with the concerned Ministries of Government. Mr. Mehta also helped restore the confidence of the World Bank in ICICI and its role in the Indian economy. As a result, ICICI obtained continuing support in the form of loans from the World Bank and, in addition, was able to establish a cordial relationship with the Bank and its officials. During Mr. Mehta's stewardship of ICICI, the Corporation grew not only in its operations but also in its functions, stature and its internal staff relationships. Under his leadership, the Corporation broadened the benefits provided to staff members. In addition, by his informality and easy accessibility, he helped to build up an environment, which enabled ICICI to obtain from its staff loyalty and co-operation.

" Mr. Mehta was more than a Chairman to this Corporation, and the standing and stature, which this Corporation enjoys today, are entirely due to his unbounded devotion to this Corporation in all its multifarious roles. His inspiring leadership, dedication to work, mature counsel and guidance resulted in an efficient administration of the affairs of the Corporation."

On his retirement as Chairman of ICICI, he wrote, "However, towards the end of my career – when 58 and when most people would retire or have to – it was a stroke of good fortune for me (through the good offices of Mr.George Woods and Mr. Black on one side and the courtesy of Dr. Ramaswamy Mudaliar on the other) to have joined this Corporation. It has been a creative and rewarding experience – seeing industries being established and expanding technical talents being developed, new products and processes coming into vogue. When I joined the Corporation, the number of projects assisted was about 62 and total gross sanctions about Rs. 18 crores; when I left, the total number of projects had come to 1339 and the total gross sanctions to Rs.405 crores. The discipline, integrity, enthusiasm and harmony with which all those associated with ICICI have worked these years have been a source of satisfaction.

"We have sought to combine the best of what private enterprise can offer – adaptability to changing conditions, promptness in decision making, flexibility in operations – with a spirit of service and an awareness of wider public interests. The efficiency with which the Corporation is run has evoked appreciation from the clientele as well as financial institutions abroad...Institutions are shaped by men and, finally depend on those who work in them. Yet they survive us and have a life of their own. As I laid down my office at the end of December 1971, I had the satisfaction of

'Something attempted
Something done
Earns a night's repose'"

He expressed a wish in his will that his funeral cortege should go past the ICICI office, then on 163, Backbay Reclamation.

Indian Investment Centre

The Indian Investment Centre was launched in 1960 with the support, encouragement and assistance from the Ministry of Finance when Morarji Desai was Finance Minister. The Ford Foundation in 1959 first suggested setting up such a centre. But the proposal remained in a state of suspended animation. There was abysmal ignorance about international financial markets and little knowledge of the real situation in the international capital markets. Besides, there was a strong antipathy to and fear of foreign private investment based on the experience of the East India Company, which had come to trade, and had conquered the country. India having escaped British rule was afraid of succumbing to the control of other creditors. "Among the ominous figures in history, Eugene Black is unlikely to rank with Robert Clive, Warren Hastings or even Curzon," said Bapu, "facts have a way of outstripping thinking; it is only with pain that nations achieve maturity." These fears and prejudices had to be removed. Bapu spoke for foreign investment when it was not popular.

The proposal for an Investment Centre was revived when the Technical Co-operation Mission of the U.S. Government began to take interest in it and promised financial assistance in terms of foreign currency for bringing out technicians, training of personnel and purchases of necessary equipment. The Government of India entered into two agreements with TCM under which $780,000 were made available for payment of contract services and commodities and Rs. 22 lakhs for local currency cost for two years. The IIC was registered as a society under the Societies' Registration Act on 30.11.1960. Its objectives were: (1) to bring together basic economic, legal and financial data needed by foreign investors, prepare market surveys and prospectuses concerning investment opportunities in India; (2) act as an intermediary between Indian and foreign entrepreneurs; (3) guide potential for foreign investors through the bureaucratic jungle of New Delhi. Bapu was appointed its first Chairman and remained so for the next 12 years. The Investment Centre made during these years some useful contribution towards promoting a better understanding of Indian plans, policies and procedures, in breaking down some psychological resistance on both sides and creating a more favourable atmosphere in the capital exporting countries. By constant endeavour and his gift for public relations, he was able to win international recognition and reputation for the Centre. He tried to remove the fear of foreign investment and argued that given the scarcity of capital, foreign capital was necessary for India's industrial development. Foreign private investment would bring foreign technical know-how, "safeguards and laws we shall need to make the inflow of capital suitable for our needs and conditions and consistent with our policies. But within these limits an open-door policy to foreign investment would be advantageous to us. We are part of the comity of nations and should not seek to close our doors to winds of knowledge and skills abroad." He believed that the private sector had a legitimate role to perform in a mixed and planned economy. He said that Indian industries had benefited by the policy of protection "which had been a blessing in disguise, because it has helped industries, it has provided a ready market, a sellers' market in many cases, but it has also been a disadvantage in that it has reduced initiative and efficiency of their production and increased costs to the consumer. After all, a sellers' market is negation of consumer sovereignty...If people believe in private enterprise, they should believe in competition. They should believe in efficiency."

The Indian Investment Centre opened offices in London, New York and Dusseldorf. It started publishing a monthly newsletter and also had several other publications to its credit. It played a useful though modest role in attracting foreign investment in India, assisted technical collaboration agreements and promoted joint ventures within the ambit of government plans and policies. It also rendered assistance in locating foreign collaboration for public sector undertakings including the Gujarat Mineral Development Corporation and the State Industrial and Investment Corporation, of Maharashtra, which utilised the services of the IIC.

A high-powered business delegation from Germany of industrialists and bankers visited Indian at the invitation of the Investment Centre. Dr. Hermann Abs, an outstanding economic statesman of the world, headed the delegation.

Under Bapu's chairmanship, the Investment Centre tried to create a better 'climate' for private foreign investment in India.

REFERENCES

1. A.D. Shroff (1899-1965), Industrialist, Director Tata Sons Limited.
2. Kasturbhai Lalbhai, Textile magnet of Ahmedabad. Member, Central Legislative Assembly as a representative of the Mill Owners' Association, 1923-26. President, FICCI, 1934-35.
3. N.A. Palkhiwala (1920—) Eminent Lawyer, Director Tata Sons Ltd., India's Ambassador to the USA.

8

A Many Splendoured Person

During the fifteen years in Bombay, while he was Chairman of ICICI, and in the last three years when he was Advisor, Bapu kept himself extremely busy widening his interests and activities and got increasingly involved with a number of voluntary organisations. One such group was the Consumer Guidance Society of India established in 1966 to protect and promote the rights and interests of consumers, provide them with information and counsel, take up their complaints with the offending party and/or the authorities and help them select goods and services which are a fair return for the money they spend. Dr. Mrs. Kamala Sohonie, then Chairman of the Managing Committee and some of her colleagues approached him and persuaded him to become the President of this Society at a time when he was relinquishing his public responsibilities on grounds of health. He had suffered a heart attack in 1962 and Ma was opposed to his taking on any further public responsibilities. But during his Ambassadorship in Washington, he had seen the powerful force of the consumer movement in the United States. He had also seen nearer home the beginning and end of a similar movement sponsored with government aid in Delhi. He agreed to be President because of his faith in the importance of voluntary organisations in the nation's socio-economic life and his belief that the rights of the consumer were important and had to be protected. After he became President, a large number of industrial houses enrolled as Associate Members that showed the high regard he enjoyed in the industrial world. Mrs. Leela Jog wrote in *Keemat, The Consumer's Voice* in April 1974, "Being considerate and punctilious, he found time to ring you up first thing in the morning should his office staff be unable to establish contact...In the death of Mr. Gaganvihari Mehta, the country has lost a distinguished son and the consumer movement in India a leader of unassailable credibility – a vital qualification for a people's movement when there is loss of credibility all around".

He was Chairman of the Indian Council of World Affairs (1966-1973) and was a keen participant in the meetings and debates organised by it. One occasion I recollect is a debate which was held on the subject of whether India should go in for a nuclear bomb. Mr. Nath Pai, a Member of Parliament, for whom Bapu had a great deal of affection and regard proposed the motion while Bapu opposed it on the ground that money spent on manufacturing atom bombs could be more fruitfully spent by a poor country like India on health and education. It was a most interesting debate and the house voted in favour of the motion.

Bapu was Chairman of the Board of Governors of the Indian Institute of Technology, Powai for two terms from 1965 to 1971. He was also founder President of the Friends of the London School of Economics. He was an honorary member of the Indian Merchants' Chamber and evinced great interest in its growth and development. He was associated with the Society for International Development, Indian Institute of Public Administration, the Harold Laski Institute, Ahmedabad, Amnesty International and with the Suruchi Chhapmala Trust, Bardoli, a training institute for adivasis (tribals) for which he obtained a printing press from Germany. He was President of the Indo-American Chamber of Commerce and also of the Indo-American Society. He severed his ties with the last in 1971 "in view of the most unconscionable and utterly unjustified stand of the U.S. government in the conflict between India and Pakistan. The American government's lack of sympathy for the democratic aspirations of the people of Bangladesh and their callous indifference to the enormous and terrible suffering they have experienced." He found the U.S. attitude "completely unjust and harmful." In June-July 1971, on a visit to Washington, he met a group of Senators from both the Democratic and Republican parties at a tea party given by Senator Sherman Cooper, former U.S. Ambassador to India. Among those present were Senators Church, Javits, Hartke, Mondale, Aiken and Case. He argued that arms supply to Pakistan should be banned. In a letter to the *New York Times* he wrote, "As one who has sincerely endeavoured to promote Indo-American goodwill and friendship for the last several years and who has appreciated all that the U.S. has done in assisting my country's economic development, I am not only deeply distressed but outraged by the attitude and policy of the U.S. administration in regard to arms supply to Pakistan." He said that he failed to understand the rationale of American policy in supporting directly and indirectly what is tantamount to genocide in East Pakistan... "When the United States administration gave military aid to Pakistan in the middle fifties, as a representative of the Indian government, I had warned that the arms supplied would be used only against India and not for any self-defence or against Soviet Russia or China. This was proved twice, in 1965 and now these arms, made available over the past two decades and valued at nearly $1 billion, have been turned with a vicious ferocity upon their own people." *The New York Times* not only prominently published the letter but also printed along with it a gruesome photograph of refugees from Bangladesh to emphasise the point. He wrote a similar letter to the *Washington Post* on August 18, 1971 questioning U.S. policy on Pakistan. He also wrote letters to various Indian newspapers expressing his deep anguish and anger at the "callous indifference to and silence about the unprecedented atrocities in Bangladesh" by the Nixon administration. When President Nixon said that U.S policy on Bangladesh was not anti-India but anti-war, Bapu sarcastically wrote, "This is very evident from what is happening in Vietnam, Cambodia and Laos where the prolonged love affair is being intensified by him." In a letter to the *Times of India* (19.4.1971), he suggested that Nixon be given the Ig-Nobel Prize for international hypocrisy. He was made President of a committee set up in Bombay to collect funds for Bangladesh refugees.

After the Bangladesh war, Jayaprakash Narain, J.J. Singh, Khushwant Singh and several others set up an Indo-Pakistan Conciliation Group. Bapu was a member of this group. A delegation from this group went to meet the Prime Minister, Indira Gandhi to urge her to release the 93,000 Pakistani prisoners of war who were being held by India. Mrs. Gandhi did not receive the delegation cordially and was rather dismissive of their suggestion. According to Mr. Inder Malhotra, she requested Bapu to stay on after other members of the delegation had left, and told him that he should at least understand her difficulties in releasing these prisoners. Bapu told her that it would gain her enormous international prestige and popularity if the next day's newspapers carry the news that India had agreed to release 93,000 Pakistani prisoners of war.

Bapu was President of the Bombay Social Service League for six and a half years during which period he worked for the development of the League's High School, gymnasium and the Mafatlal Gagalbhai Textile Technical Institute. He had particular affection for the League as both his father and brother, Vaikunthbhai had been connected with it and he used to visit the institution in his younger days with his father. He made personal efforts for raising substantial funds on the occasion of the silver jubilee of the Social Service League.

Bapu was a trustee of the Hindustan Welfare Trust set up by Shri K.K. Birla, and through it helped various organisations such as the Indian Cancer Society, Society for the Vocational Rehabilitation of the Retarded, the Cerebral Palsy Association, the Bhagini Samaj Sewa Mandir, the Tuberculosis Association of India, the Society for the Rehabilitation of Crippled Children, the Harijan Sewak Sangh and the Masina Hospital.

During these years, Bapu was much in demand as a speaker and broadcaster on All India Radio and addressed such diverse forums as the Rotary Club, Bankers' Training College, the Co-operative Society, Social Service League, National Defence College, Indian Merchants' Chamber, Indian Council of Foreign Trade, All India Manufacturers' Association, Commonwealth Parliamentary Association, etc. He spoke on a wide variety of subjects such as "UN Hope or Illusion", "Role of Elections in a Democracy", "Patterns of India's Mixed Economy, "Making of India's Foreign Policy", "Climate for Foreign Investment in India", "Relevance of Gandhiji Today", "Problems and Prospects of the Oil, Soap and Detergent Industries", and "A Century of Social Reform". He took considerable trouble in preparing these speeches and wrote them out himself, often several drafts, before he got them typed. He made copious notes from the books and articles he had read so that he could refer to them in his speeches and articles He gave the John F. Kennedy Memorial Lecture in Bombay in 1970 on "Foreign Aid Stimulus or Soporific?"

He never gave up writi[illegible]h and Gujarati, serious as well as humorc[illegible] he spent his weekends and holidays. He w[illegible]y, management, banking, foreign aid, entrepreneurship, etc. He contributed humorous and serious articles frequently to the *Illustrated Weekly of India, Times of India, Indian Express* and *Commerce.* He also wrote in Gujarati for *Sanskriti, Akhand Anand* and *Granth.* His writings and speeches reveal his deep commitment to Indian's industrial growth, to democracy, individual freedom and liberty. He was a great believer in individual freedom and against all totalitarian regimes. How to reconcile planning with individual freedom, economic growth with social justice was one of his central concerns. He had a deep sense of duty to society and a social conscience. In 1958, he was deeply disturbed when Soviet tanks and troops moving into Hungary to crush the rebellion there. Ten years later, when Soviet troops moved into Czechoslovakia, he wrote, "Once again twenty years after the Communist take over, the Czechs who were about to sing with the angels are being compelled by comradely artillery, tanks and planes to learn to howl with the wolves...The Czechs will arise again. In Byron's words,

> "Freedom's battle once begun
> Bequeathed from bleeding sire to son
> Though baffled oft
> Is ever won!"

A year before his death, Bapu, depressed about Bombay's deteriorating civic life, joined the 'Save Bombay Campaign' which he felt deserved the widespread and constructive support of all responsible citizens. "Bombay is not a city but a chaos", he wrote in the *Times of India* (7.2.1973). "Cinemas, luxury hotels and what you have rightly called 'vertical slums'... come up like mushrooms, while lakes of people live in disgraceful hovels and sleep on pavements. Familiarity has bred callousness and indifference. The first thing in planning one would have thought would have been the provision of an infrastructure – water, power, sewage, roads. And yet it has been greed and grab that have led to land speculation, a roaring black market in real estate, rocking prices, congested streets and buildings which are an eyesore...It is because of public apathy and inertia that the once beautiful city of Bombay is being vulgarised, defaced and ruined...After two decades of planning "our cities are most unplanned, our priorities are preposterous in the literal sense of the word...Whenever I see the glaring contrasts in the living

Shri S.K. Wankhede presenting a momento to Shri G.L. Mehta on his 70th birthday

conditions of the affluent and the poor, I am reminded of Disraeli's memorable observation that the rich and the poor are two nations between whom there is no intercourse and no sympathy, who are ignorant of each other's habit, thoughts and feelings, as if they were dwellers in different zones or inhabitants of different places... Bombay is a great heritage which we the transients of today have no right to squander...It is time we come together to deal with the problem of Bombay - not as lobbyists but as responsible citizens of a great metropolitan town ...It is time we bestir ourselves to stop the decay in the city's life."

Bombay citizens honoured him at a felicitation dinner on his 70th birthday. Shri S.K. Wankhede, then Finance Minister of Maharashtra, presided over the function held in Taj Mahal Hotel. Shri S.P. Godrej gave the Welcome Speech and the speakers were Shri D.C. Kothari, Shri N.A. Palkhiwala and Shri A.G. Noorani. The Committee of hosts included a large number of distinguished citizens of Bombay

Bapu was not only despondent about the deteriorating condition of Bombay but about the country as a whole, depressed when he thought about what they had dreamt and sought to achieve after independence and what had been actually been done. "What we find", he wrote, "is a land divided into two sections, the rich and the poor, where the ordinary people are ground down by private institutions and where merit and talent are subordinated to influence and nepotism...The economy is stagnant, with unutilised and wasted resources – physical, human and economic...Above all there is a crisis of national character which makes nonsense of brave promises. There never was such deterioration in ethical standards in social and economic relationships. This has led to degeneration not only in politics and business but also in education, scientific and technical pursuits and religion." But he never gave way to cynicism and continued to do what he considered to be right until the end.

9

Enduring Memories

On Sunday, the 28th of April 1974 at 3.15. p.m., when my father's voice stopped for ever, as I sat in his fifth floor bedroom in "Jeevan Jyot", overlooking the Indian Ocean, gazing at his beautiful, gentle face, one of the handsomest I have ever seen, knowing that I would never see it again, memories overwhelmed me. Life without Bapu seemed unimaginable. What do I remember most about my father? Not one thing but rather a number of inter-related traits. It is not easy for a daughter who was deeply attached to her father to write about him objectively, in a detached manner. In these last twenty-six years since his death, I have often asked myself, "what is my father's legacy to me, what have I learnt from him and his life?"

For Bapu, work was worship; to live was to function. I cannot ever picture him sitting idle doing nothing. He gave his best to whatever job he was doing whether it was as the Calcutta Manager of the Scindia Steam Navigation Company, Chairman of the Tariff Commission, Member of the Planning Commission, Ambassador to the United States or Chairman of ICICI. A month before he died, when he had recovered slightly from a heart attack, the doctor asked him what he now wanted. My father's only wish was that he should be permitted to go to the office for an hour or two every day. He shared Dag Hammarskjoeld's belief that 'in our era the road to holiness necessarily passes through the world of action'. And his world of action was confined to no narrow sphere. He had a deep dedication to public causes, a live interest in the country's problems, a concern for the promotion of democratic values and an eagerness to promote the highest standards in public life. His interests ranged over such varied spheres as journalism, shipping, industry, development banking, diplomacy, social service, literature and politics. He was raising funds for victims of the Bengal Famine of 1943, for the refugees from Bangladesh in 1971, for the physically handicapped and the mentally retarded; encouraging amateur theatrical groups; leading the consumer guidance movement; helping adivasis (tribals) of Bardoli to obtain a printing press; trying to save Bombay city. At home, he was always reading or writing or meeting people who came to him with all kinds of problems, recommendations for jobs, admission or scholarship for studying abroad, financial assistance and so on. He continued working till the last day since he held that one preventive against old age was to maintain keen and wide interests and have activities in which one could be useful without worrying about the fact that one was no longer young.

His wide range of activities and interests and his popularity were evident from the condolence letters and telegrams that poured in from all over the world from industrialists, bankers, journalists, academics, writers, poets, social workers, diplomats, ministers and administrators after his passing away. Condolence messages were received from the then President of India, Shri V.V. Giri, and the Prime Minister, Mrs. Indira Gandhi, from the Governors of Andhra Pradesh, Kerala, Maharashtra, Tamilnadu and the Lt. Governor of Goa. Homage was paid to him in the Indian Parliament on 29th April 1974, the very next day after his death. Everyone spoke of his unquestionable integrity and his eloquent advocacy of the humanitarianism, which he espoused.

Though deeply rooted in Gujarati culture, Bapu was not at all parochial. He was completely free from communal, caste or linguistic prejudices. We grew up in Calcutta but were never conscious that we belonged to another province. We were sent to a school where at the primary stage Bengali was the medium of instruction. Till I finished high school, I did not even know what caste I belonged to or what in fact was meant by caste.

Bapu never tried to impose his views or beliefs on us or dictate our lives in any fashion. He was not a domineering person at all. In fact, he was extremely tolerant and broad minded and held that no one could lay down the rules for another and that each person had to mould his or her own life and find his or her own path. He left it to us to choose what we wanted to study what vocation we wanted to follow, whom we wanted to marry and never interfered. This did not mean that he did not care or was indifferent. His family meant more to him than anything else and he was deeply interested in what we did, read, felt and thought. He was particularly fond of his grand-children and there was a special glow in his face and around him when he spoke of them. He would have been so proud of their subsequent academic and professional achievements.

Sanjay studied at London School of Economics and got his Ph.D. in Economics from Yale and is at present with the World Bank in Washington. Nandita graduated from Columbia University. Shalini studied at Oxford and Berlin and teaches Sociology at Berlin University. Mohit, with a Ph.D. in Physics from Cornell Univeristy and working at TIFR, Mumbai. Anuradha having obtained a doctorate from Cambridge University, U.K. and an MBA from IIM, teaches at Reading University, U.K. Priya got a B.A. and M.Sc. from Oxford and is with IMF, Washington.

Though extremely particular about his official and business correspondence, never failing to reply to a letter, in fact he dictated a reply to Mr. K.K. Birla the day before his death, he was very lazy about writing to us. Ma took care of that. His excuse was that his handwriting was becoming increasingly illegible. But he expected letters from us regularly and if we failed to write, he would worry endlessly. Since direct trunk dialling was introduced between Bombay and Delhi, he telephoned at least once a week and we would discuss family news, political gossip or some latest joke.

Bapu was extremely simple in dress and appearance. Despite this, one could not help noticing him when he entered a room. There was truly a charisma about him. He always wore a white *churidar*, *sherwani* and a 'Gandhi' cap, except when abroad. The offices he held and the honours he received did not change or affect him. He never forgot his old friends and colleagues or relatives – poor or unsuccessful though they might have been. He gave his time freely to all believing that there was something to learn from everyone if only we have curiosity and humility. Minoo Masani wrote "Gaganvihari was a very generous person and I do not mean it in the financial sense, but in a broader and more important aspect. He gave of himself freely... He always responded to appeals for one good cause or another".

Born into a wealthy family, Bapu never really cared for money. Born rich, he did not have to work his way up the hard way. He enriched himself during his lifetime but not materially. The enrichment he sought was intellectual. Moving in the world of businessmen and industrialists, he was not tainted by their values. We learnt from him that what mattered was integrity and intellectual honesty, that individuals should be judged, not by their position or worldly success but by their intellectual and moral worth. George Woods, President of the World Bank, wrote to Ma after Bapu's death, "I have always felt that Gagan was my oldest and closest Indian friend. My admiration for him grew as the years passed – through the tour of duty as Ambassador in Washington and through the trying but challenging years as Chairman of ICICI. His was the highest integrity. He had great intelligence and a superb ability to express his thoughts and viewpoints."

My father had an excellent ear for words and a remarkable vocabulary. He always scored full marks in the *Reader's Digest* 'How to increase your word power'. I learnt from him to write simply, to avoid jargon, clichés, unnecessary adjectives and words whose meaning I did not know. He loved jokes, cartoons and humorous articles. When we were young, he showed us cartoons from *Punch* and read to us amusing articles by A.P. Herbert and others. We read Stephen Leacock and the hilarious *"1066 And All That."* He enjoyed enormously a cartoon by Shankar in the *Hindustan Times* and later in the *Shanker's Weekly*, by David Low, R.K. Laxman in the *Times of India*, by Herbloc in the *Washington Post* or a piece by Art Buchwald, Russell Baker or 'Busy Bee'. I can still picture him laughing uproariously till sometimes tears came to his eyes. He had a ready wit and ability to pun and coin jokes and relate them with a delightful sense of humour which enabled him not to take himself too seriously and to see the ludicrous in life. Humbug, hypocrisy, pomposity and pretension he made fun of but he was never cynical or flippant. He felt that "without some sense of humour life was apt to become unbearable. Public life even more than private life needs the alchemy of humour to transmute the sorrows and pain and discomfort of life into laughter. Humour makes you see things upside down. In the ultimate analysis, humour is a form of criticism and an interpretation of life...It is only another name for a sense of proportion". Underlying all his gaiety and laughter was an awareness of the deep tragedy of life. Separation and death reminded him clearly from time to time that grief is terribly true. He was aware that anxiety and grief are the world's true realities. No one lives on, nothing survives. He was a deeply sensitive human being who was moved by scenes of natural beauty, poetry or a beautiful film or novel. After seeing Satyajit Ray's *Pather Panchali*, he wrote, " It was an indescribably beautiful film, something I will remember all my life. The story, the photography, acting, direction, it is difficult to say which should be praised more. I had constantly tears in my eyes seeing the sufferings of poverty and little Durga's tragic death." The last film I saw with him was Ray's '*Ashani Sanket*'. Many years ago, when I was introduced to Guy Wint at a party at Lord Kaldor's house, 2 Adams Road in Cambridge, he told me "I know your father, he is a poet". I replied that he was perhaps mistaking me for somebody, as my father did not write poetry. Mr. Wint said that he knew my father was not a poet but he had the sensitivity of a poet. He was extremely well read in English and Gujarati poetry and himself composed a few short poems in Gujarati.

Bapu always wanted to share all his experiences with us. He was extremely communicative by nature. From London, in 1921, he had written to Brelvi, " Like a child that I still am, we are all essentially children, I need to rely on someone, long for someone who would listen to me enthusiastically and affectionately". If he read anything worthwhile, he wanted us to read it and would send clippings from newspapers and magazines. We looked forward to his coming home from office or from a tour or some meeting or function for he would always vividly describe all that had happened, especially anything ludicrous or funny. He was a brilliant conversationalist. Through the years we all developed the habit of sharing our ideas and thoughts with him. If I read a good book or article, saw a good film or play or met someone interesting or came across a good joke, my instinctive reaction was "I must tell Bapu about this."

What endeared my father to everyone were his qualities of heart. As Mr. G.L. Chandavarkar said of him "He was a man in every sense great but in a greater sense good." Professor Lionel Robbins wrote, "In my range of experience, Gagan was not only one of most loveable but also one of the wisest men I have ever known and the memory of our nearly lifelong friendship is one of my most precious possessions." Full of love and compassion, refined and sensitive, there was nothing petty or mean about him. He taught us always to look for the good in human beings and not to be hyper critical. He was incredibly soft and gentle and suffering in any form moved him deeply. His favourite s*loka* from the *Upanishads* was:

> *Natvaham kamaye rajyam*
> *na svargam na punarbhavam*
> *kamaye dukhataptaham*
> *praninam arti-nashanam.*

(I do not desire any kingdom for myself, nor do I want heaven. Moksha also I do not ask for. I only wish that the sufferings of all living beings be destroyed)

Physically frail but full of intellectual vigour, pessimistic by nature but radiating joy and laughter, gentle but firm, impatient of social injustice but rejecting solutions of violence, a great believer in individual liberty, he pursued the path of duty as he saw it. Mr. H.V.R. Iyengar, ICS and Governor of the Reserve Bank remembered him as "a vital, cheerful and dynamic figure." He was never negative in outlook and disliked armchair critics that did nothing to improve things. Philip Talbot, President of the Asia Society, said that Bapu was "a man of great acumen and integrity but also of constructive spirit, a man who believed in finding and vigorously pursuing the most positive paths towards better understanding between peoples..." We learnt from him that instead of complaining about one's job or situation, we should do something about it. "We are for a brief moment in this world – beautiful yet sad", he wrote. "In this short time, we must make the best of it, not merely in the sense of enjoying what is best in it but also by spreading cheerfulness and joy as much as we can, by bringing some ray of hope to others". Life he often said, was too short for quarrels and intrigues, for bitterness, malice and hatred.

Vadilal Dagli, editor of *Commerce* and a close friend, described Bapu, after his death, as "An illustrious generalist" who symbolised "dissent, debate, sense of justice and above all a liberal spirit, which is synonymous of an open society. A liberal citizen whose patriotism was expressed in the assertion of those values which make civilised life possible." Bapu was not an industrialist, not a banker, not an economist. What was he then? According to Dagli he was "one of India's most articulate and cultured generalists who brought the riches of a liberal mind to whatever he undertook. This perhaps explains his success in various fields of life including Gujarati literature. He was not an expert in any particular field. His biggest achievement was his emergence as an important public figure in the life of Bombay city. He was always available for such causes as the Social Service League, Consumer Guidance Society, and the movement against commercialisation of reclaimed land and of course a society for civil liberties. His concern for civil liberties was both touching and ennobling." Mr. Warren Unna of the *Washington Post* said "Mr. Mehta was a fearless advocate of right against wrong, of principles against expediency...a warm human being, a fine gentleman". After his death, the Department of Civics and Politics of Bombay University passed a condolence resolution in which it said that "More than anything else, we shall remember the grace and dignity, which marked everything he said and did and his courage of conviction..."

Professor Gangadhar Gadgil said that "G.L. Mehta was a landmark of the city of Bombay like the Rajabai Tower". He was essentially a Bombay man and his last public act was to come from his sick bed to speak from the platform of Save Bombay Committee to halt the desecration of Breach Candy. The *Free Press Journal* wrote, "Mr. Gaganvihari Mehta was one of the fast dwindling generation of distinguished Indians who served the nation with devotion, dedication and honesty. He was a far cry from the usual run of present day public men who are motivated more by self interest than by national good." *Blitz* wrote, that he "touched life at so many points and adored whatever he essayed."

Bapu was an agnostic and wanted a simple cremation without any religious ceremony, no funeral orations, no ashes to be collected or immersed, no public prayers. His simple cremation took place in the presence of captains of industry, educationists, journalists, administrators and leading citizens of Bombay. "My place of pilgrimage is my work and my body should pass by my office before cremation" was his last wish.

10

SELECTED WRITINGS OF G.L. MEHTA

THIS I BELIEVE

This is not a testament of faith nor an avowal of any creed. Life is too complex for any set formula or simple panacea. Besides, it is only very few great persons who can truly be said to have a philosophy of life which they not only preach but practise.

I have come to believe as a result of experience that qualities of mind are more fundamental in life than any doctrines; that feelings are more vital than formulas. In the ultimate analysis, it is how we conduct ourselves and how we behave that matters: not what we profess and enunciate. And our conduct depends on our mental attitude and our feelings–our convictions, our likes and dislikes, and also our conception of our interests.

No man can, in this sense, lay down the law for another. Each one has to formulate his own attitude and cultivate his own feelings. I can, therefore set forth here only what I have come gradually to believe.

To me, peace of mind seems more important than exercise of power or material success. Let me hasten to add that this does not imply a cult of poverty or renunciation of worldly goods. It would be gross hypocrisy if I said so. What I mean is that I would not care for anything if I felt that I would not inwardly be happy by having it or being in it.

We cannot live in harmony with others unless we are at peace with ourselves. This is no metaphysical doctrine, it is plain commonsense. Different people, no doubt, feel happy in different ways and in different degrees. Our own feelings of happiness might also vary from time to time and may change as we grow older. But fundamentally, we have to have sufficient inner harmony before we can achieve anything or even live usefully.

And in order to do this, we must not expect too much of life. The world was not made for us though in our egoism we think so. We must, therefore, cultivate a sense of proportion about men and affairs. This sense of proportion would teach us a certain degree of self-restraint, moderation and even a spirit of resignation in respect of things which cannot be changed and must be endured. Out of such a sense of proportion must grow genuine humility and intellectual honesty.

We must not presume that whatever little we might have achieved is all the result of our own efforts. We might have chosen our parents wisely: some stray incident might have helped us; our education and the cooperation of others who work with us could have been valuable; and apart from the social heritage which has come down to us, conditions beyond our control might have been favourable.

I am all the time conscious of the fact that what little I know is insignificant compared to what I do not know; I am aware that we can, if we will, learn something from everyone; and that we should be somewhat modest in trying to teach and preach. We should be less strict in judging others and less lenient in judging ourselves.

Above all, this sense of proportion is the obverse of a true sense of humour: a sense of humour which enables us to see the ludicrous in life and not to take life too seriously or give trivial things undue importance. I try and console myself with the reflection when anything goes wrong that things could have been much worse; if, for instance, a plane is delayed, that it is better than an air crash.

Only experience can cultivate such an attitude, not copybook maxims. And it can come if we do not fret and fume at the slightest provocation and do not exaggerate our own importance in the scheme of things. In other words, this demands a sense of humour. For, a sense of humour is derived from a sense of values. All human endeavour being short of perfection, we can afford to laugh at ourselves for our inability to achieve it.

We are for a brief moment in this world – beautiful yet sad. In this short time, we must make the best of it, not merely in the sense of enjoying what is best in it but also by spreading cheerfulness and joy as much as we can, by bringing some ray of hope to others. Life is too short, I feel, for quarrels and intrigues, for bitterness and malice and hatred. I must confess I do not have the spirit of the crusader, the zeal of the reformer. It is enough if in the course of my own insignificant life, I can, to some extent, imbibe some of the qualities which I value.

SIX METEOROLOGISTS IN SEARCH OF A GALE

When experts are caught napping our meteorologists' forecasts are usually as accurate as those of our astrologers. On Friday, May 29, both the weather-bureau and the public were taken unawares by what is described in technical terms as "a precursor of the beginnings of the first signs of the monsoon." People were drenched, streets were flooded, trees uprooted, rail traffic was "snarled" (as the Americans say, though I don't know what it literally means).

The weather-bureau experts, dry to the bones in their offices, were caught napping. They felt like our rulers who try to preserve "law and order" (the only function apparently which the British performed) at the outburst of a communal riot. They looked at the weather photographs transmitted by satellite where white clouds signify rain, unlike the real dark clouds in the sky. Were they (I mean the meteorologists, not the clouds) downhearted? Hardly.

Like Churchill at the Battle of .Britain, they picked up the gauntlet. They decided to challenge the weather itself. After a meticulous study and scrutiny of charts and signs, they boldly proclaimed that "the monsoon has arrived at your doorsteps" and that "heavy to very heavy rains" are likely within 24 hours with a "gale-force wind" in the Konkan.

People in Bombay became wary, some were panic-stricken. Since it was a Saturday, many thought it prudent to take "French leave". (By the way, is it true that in France, this is called "English leave"? Does this affect Anglo-French relations?) Many did not stir out of the house. Those who did, went to pray in temples (instead of preying on their neighbours) to propitiate the god (or goddess as the case may be) and offer money to the priest.

The whole idea was to ward off the evil through some kind of financial transaction with the deity.

And all looked anxiously at the sky—in every direction: north-east-north, south-west-south, west-southwest, not to mention due south from where all the brains in India come. But to no purpose. The sky was blue, thin, yellow thin clouds were fleeting across it, the sun shone in all its glory over a city where darkness is only in the hearts of men.

What had happened? People somewhat anxiously, half hopefully asked one another. Will the storm come at night? Will some more buildings collapse—interfering with the city fathers' concern with Cambodia and West Asia? Should not urban property have a sound foundation before it has a ceiling, they asked. No. The night, too, was quiet and unlike a city under prohibition, quite dry.

The weather man was not downcast. He is never defeated. He announced the next day, May 30th, that the cyclonic storm which was to bathe the city in a deluge had suddenly and erratically, almost like a defecting legislator, gone away 200 kilometers south of Bombay. Bless its heart—if a storm has a heart, though it has an eye.

Hurricanes are named (against objection by many women) after women. No wonder. They are capricious and capable of fury. Our gale—I mean the gale which was our due—went away to Verawal side—of all places. Is this evidence of the parochialism of God Indra or of Mother Nature? Was it to deprive Maharashtra or save it? A petition and morcha are in order to clear up the confusion.

The monsoon, which was at our doorstep, went away to the neighbour's backyard. Did the monsoon then strike the west-southwest coast of Saurashtra or even its north-west promontory? No. It did not. Quite inexplicably, it moved on, we were told, on the third day, further west-south.

Did it evaporate? Did it subside into the ocean? Will it form a low depression in the Arabian Sea (a sea of tranquillity not polluted by imperialist fleets) or will it recede to Arabia or retreat to North Africa? One cannot tell now. The weather photographs have disappeared from the paper as suddenly as they came and you cannot locate its epicentre—if that is the right word.

This reminds me that one of our friends always takes an umbrella when the weather forecast is "bright and sunny". But when heavy showers are forecast with "gusty winds", he goes out without any defensive weapon. Some years ago a man saved a whole district from famine by walking without an umbrella (in the face of the weather forecast) and invited "heavy to very heavy rains" with "gusty winds". But such brave people are no more.

People rely on meteorologists who, in turn, have to rely on trial balloons (for winds), storm signals (for storms) horoscopes (for their own future), thumb rockets (at Thumba) and maps sent out by satellites. Better trust out own eyes, our instincts and our luck; they are a surer guide.

—*Times of India,* Sunday, June 21, 1970.

HOW I DECLINED A VICE-CHANCELLORSHIP

It is natural that many conjectures should have been made as to why I did not accept the Vice-Chancellorship of the University of Mandupeshwar despite repeated offers and pressures. I don't know whether anyone is actually making such conjectures, but I guess there must be several rumours afloat. When many of our prominent men and women are unable to obtain a post or an office for which they have tried hard it is not unusual for them to spread discreet reports through friends, admirers, proteges etc. that they were offered Governorship of Orissa, Ambassadorship in Italy, Deputy Ministership in the Centre (Ministry unmentioned); even that there were one or two phone calls from the Prime Minister herself but they had reluctantly to decline. They even had two letters making the offer but through oversight these were destroyed.

But I must plead that this is not true in my case. It will be asked why I have not yet made a statement in the press on this matter so as to scotch all rumours. The answer is simple. Today, there is so much confusion in the public mind, when it is so difficult who is on which side, who has defected from where and who has rebelled against whom; when both sides expel one another and leaders work against their own parties;

when there is bitter conflict between conscience and discipline: in other words, when the atmosphere is so murky that in the midst of statements, counter-statements and counter-counter-statements which are pungent and sensational no one would care to publish my statement — unless I get it published as an advertisement! Besides, when the Delhi University was for some time without a Vice-Chancellor, there were internecine wars in Banaras and Allahabad Universities and the Calcutta University is more closed than open, who will pay the slightest attention to my statement? The facts, however, are stranger than fiction.

On September 21 last, the President of Mandupeshwar University who succeeded in calling himself Mayor, by a majority vote, suddenly turned up at my residence. From his appearance and dress, I first thought he was interested in buying old clothes and furniture. However, I enquired politely the nature of his visit. He observed, "It's a question of life and death." For a moment I thought he was an insurance agent or an amateur astrologer.

But introducing himself, he said rather pompously, "I have come to you for the solution of a vital question of our ancient yet modern land."

I replied: "I am fully conscious of my limitations, Sir. But considering the critical situation of our country, if I can do anything to help I shall certainly try."

The Mayor said: "You surely can. It is our express wish, nay, our ardent desire that you accept the Vice-Chancellorship of our city's University."

I put in rather gently: "I must confess I did not know that your town had a university."

Breaking in, the Mayor rather impatiently said: "Of course there is! We have two thousand students there, we have co-education, play-grounds for tennis, cricket, football, quarters are being put up for professors and teachers, we have many books in the library, apparatus and instruments in laboratories. We contemplate putting up an auditorium. Already we have a mike and radio. What more do you want?"

I said apologetically: "Forgive me, I did not know all this. But what made you think of me in this connection?"

The Mayor said: "We tried several sources, sent people to various places, wrote letters to scores of people but there was no response. No one was willing to come. Some of them were mature and experienced; some were versatile and scholarly. They all gave different reasons but it was evident that these were mere pretexts. One of them had the cheek to write that it is easier to go to the moon or become President of the Congress (Old or New) rather than accept such an offer! After all, you can take a horse to the water but you can't make it drink! When we were sorely disappointed, someone suggested your name. We were then convinced that in the whole country, there was no one more fit for this post! Our eyes are now set on you!

For a moment, I was tempted to say that in that case they should get their eyes examined by a competent specialist but did not have the courage to say so. I simply said: "I am deeply grateful to you for this: but eyes often mislead. Don't we see mirages? Don't we mistake shadow for substance? I have not studied pedagogy nor have any experience of an educational institution."

The Mayor burst out laughing: "Who has such study, knowledge and experience? Let alone Vice-Chancellors, do even our ministers of Education know anything about teaching, training or education? Do Finance Ministers know economics? Do you think Defence Ministers know the difference between a battalion and a regiment or a rifle and a revolver? Aren't you a Graduate? If I am not mistaken, you are even an M.A.!"

I answered: "Yes, sir! But that does not entitle me to give an opinion on education. To have education and to impart it are two different things.

The Mayor again laughed: "What are you talking? When even illiterate people have strong views on education, why not graduates? In a democracy, anyone is entitled to form views on any subject and express them!"

I argued: "To give opinion is one of our Fundamental Rights; neither qualification nor merit is required for it. In fact, the less we know about a subject, the more vehemently we express our views on it. But to conduct an educational institution is a different story altogether."

The Mayor clarified the position: "Institutions and organisations in our country run on their own momentum. For that there are other officers – Registrar, Accountant, members of Senate, professors and assistants etc. etc. Your main work is to maintain your own position in the midst of all of them. How otherwise can a person like myself work in a municipality? This is a unique characteristic of our country. Owing to its ancient religious traditions and spiritual concepts, the country is self-propelled. Our rulers are mostly engrossed in maintaining their offices and posts, in pushing out one another, in manoeuvres and intrigues – and yet is not the country's work going on?"

I said: "That may be so! I understand that a Soviet engineer after a few months' stay in our country said that being a Communist he was an atheist: but after coming here he had begun to believe in some Divine Power – otherwise he could not understand what sustained this country!"

The Mayor said: "Be that as it may! There's no go! You will have to accept this post! You must do your duty the *Geeta* also says so.

This dialogue whether "meaningful" or not would never have ended. So, in order to bring the discussion to a close, I said, "Give me a couple of days to think over this! I shall write to you." The Mayor on departing remarked, "But see that the decision is in the affirmative!"

Next day I sent off a telegram declining the offer.

But matters did not end there. Next week, the Collector of Mandupeshwar (accompanied by his P.A. and peon) came to see me.

I said politely: "Why did you take all this trouble? If you had told me, I would have come over."

The Collector replied: "I was passing this way so I thought I would drop in. It is not proper that you refuse to accept the responsibility of Vice-Chancellorship of our University. You know that it is more difficult to obtain Vice-Chancellors than cooks or motor-drivers! How many V.C.s have resigned during the last few years, how many have been F.T.R.s (Forced to Retire), how many have been assaulted, how many *gheraoed*, how many jumped from the first floor, how many are in hospitals? No one has yet compiled statistics—a task beyond the capacity of even the Indian Statistical Institute! So, there is no option. You will have to agree to serve the nation by accepting this post!"

I said rather haltingly: "I am deeply touched and indebted that you should have thought of me for such a high and responsible position. I thank you with all my heart – I mean the heart though slightly damaged is mine – it has neither been transplanted nor made of plastic so that my thanks are unadulterated and innermost! But I do not consider myself worthy of such an honour."

The Collector thumped his hand on the table and spoke! "Of fitness, unfitness we are the best judges – not you. It is only political leaders who can give assurance of their own fitness and worth. We badly need you. There is indiscipline and discord among the students. Students and teachers are at loggerheads all the time. There are parties even among professors and lecturers. For several months, the University has had to close down."

I interjected, "When the Mayor saw me, he never mentioned this fact to me."

The Collector said: "How can he? He himself backs a faction of students and instigates processions against rival professors! The former Vice-Chancellor was made to go through the town on a donkey with a garland of shoes – he had no option but to resign, although even then he was not prepared to go. Because of the troubles some months ago, the buildings are in a bad shape, doors have been smashed, window panes broken, laboratory equipment destroyed, scores of books burnt!"

I objected gently : "In these conditions what can I do?"

The Collector: "That is precisely why we want you. It is you who have to answer that question– not I. We want a head who will bear patiently and calmly all the insults and abuses of students, would not be worried if professors don't work, assure both sides that he is with them and yet prevent either of them getting the upper hand: we require such a diplomatic, shrewd, determined person who is neither ruffled nor baffled. No doubt, education is important in a university but not all that important as to overshadow other considerations. Indeed, those who have brains and are in earnest will learn – but how many are these any way? And even after that, the question of employment will remain!"

I was speechless for a few moments by this expose of the qualities required of a Vice-Chancellor. When I recovered my speech, I said: "Then I am completely unfit for this job! Anyway who told you that I have ability or capacity to undertake such work?"

The Collector said: "No one! Because we know nothing about you, we felt that you would be most suitable!"

I asked: "But is there not some risk in appointing someone without knowing him or scrutinising his credentials?"

The Collector's reply was immediate: "Where is the risk?

Even when we take someone after considerable trouble and careful examination, don't they turn out to be duds? Do they not prove failures? Success or failure as our scriptures say we should leave to the Almighty: it depends on luck or chance. If you will not succeed in running the University properly, well, we shall think of somebody else!"

After this clarification, I had no further comment to make. So, I gave tea to the Collector (and his P.A. and Peon) and bade them farewell.

Four days later three students came to see me. From their appearance and dress I thought they were not only progressive and "Committed" but highly revolutionary. The two boys had long hair, red eyes and coloured bush-shirts; the girl had bobbed hair, her face was excited, her dress Punjabi style. One of the boys had a short stick – in his hand and the other had some weapon.

On entering all of them shouted together, "We want to speak to you on a very grave matter of importance. Unless you agree to do so, we shall not leave your room – that's our firm and final resolve!"

I interrupted: "But when did I decline to see you? Please sit down and tell me what you want!"

One young man said: "No! We shall not sit down! Without standing on our feet, we cannot be self-reliant and we cannot maintain our revolutionary spirit. It is only imperialists, reactionaries, monopolists and feudalists who always sit down on the heads and bodies of the exploited proletariat!"

The girl said in a shrill, high-pitched voice: "If we stand, we can walk, if we walk, we can run. Those who sit do not serve, they stagnate, they deteriorate and decay. Mao-tse-Tung has said that even the longest journey begins with the first step."

The other young man proclaimed: "In fact, neither shall we sit nor shall we allow anyone else to sit at rest. We have yet a long way to go. We have to burn many newspapers and books!"

Somewhat bored I said "That may be, but what have you come to see me for?"

The first young man answered: "It is our firm and ultimate demand – indeed, an ultimatum that you accept the post of Vice-Chancellorship of the Mandupeshwar University here and now!"

I was thunderstruck. Disbelieving I said "Really? Even you want this? But why?"

The second youth replied: "Since there is no head of our University, it is impossible for us to revolt against anybody!"

The first youth added: "We cannot *gherao* anyone's office or residence."

The girl put in: "We cannot burn anyone's effigy!"

The first youth again said: "We badly need a symbol of our rotten, corrupt, degenerate Establishment whom we can attack!"

The second youth supplemented: "Without a Vice-Chancellor whose prestige we can undermine, whom can we dishonour?"

And the girl quipped: "And without that how can we maintain our revolutionary zeal and ardour?"

So as to find a way out, I suggested: "But surely, you must have a temporary head?"

Both the young men said: "That's the main difficulty! No one is prepared to accept the post even in an acting capacity."

And the girl said: "The Registrar is there but on the pretext of ill-health, he has gone on leave for three months. Whose files can we burn in the courtyard?"

I enquired: "Then who looks after the work of the University – the campus – classes etc.?"

All the three replied together: "We ourselves, of course! But we cannot revolt against ourselves!"

I ventured to offer advice: "Then start parties, divide yourselves into groups and factions. Proclaim your opponents as reactionary, C.I.A. aided, obstacles to progress like the Syndicate men! Lead processions against them! Convene meetings, challenge them! It will be quite exciting, exhilaerating!"

The girl lost her temper: "What are you talking! You seem to be a Fascist! You seem to be a Social Imperialist, a Soviet Revisionist! How otherwise can you suggest a course of discord among students?"

The first youth said excitedly: "We shall certainly have discord. We already have it. But it would be of our own making, self-motivated, spontaneous – not taught, imposed, instigated by others."

The second youth said: "We are prepared to accept the guidance of leaders who have no relations with our University, who know nothing about it – not of our own administrators and teachers."

The girl explained: Because they are all guilty men, hypocrites, self-seeking, opportunistic. The outsider would be impartial and neutral."

I gathered enough courage to say "then why do you invite me?"

All the three replied simultaneously: "So that we can defy your orders, we can resist you, we can lower you in public estimation, and in the end, you will be defeated and will have to offer your resignation! Or, Government will appoint a Committee of enquiry and force your resignation! That will be our proudest day, our Day of Triumph!"

I said briefly: "I regret I am unable to be the recipient of so much attention and honour."

I might have forgotten this whole episode when a few days later, I had a trunk call from Mandupeshwar.

The Voice at the other hand said, "Are you Gaganvihari

Mehta?"

I answered back: "I have now begun to doubt most things in life including life itself, but of that I am quite certain."

The Voice was visibly or rather vocally irritated: "What did you say? Please reply 'yes' or 'no'!"

I retorted: "This is not a Law Court or a viva voce that I have to reply one way or the other. In many complex subjects, the simple affirmative and negative are half truths and tend to mislead."

The Voice: "For heaven's sake, will you tell me your name? The Education Minister wants to speak to you –

I butted in: "I thought he had already resigned and defected!" Unperturbed by this disrespectful interjection, the Voice went on: "The Honourable Minister has very urgent and important work about which he wishes to speak."

Unruffled I said: "I am myself even if this be an illusion. I am ready to speak also."

The Voice: "Then call that gentleman. Until he comes on the phone I can't put through the call to the Minister. He has issued strict orders."

I said: "How can I call myself from another place? Both physical laws and spiritual existence make that impossible!"

The Voice was now really angry: "Why do you go on speaking nothing at length."

I put in "I learnt that from politicians' speeches!"

Ignoring me, the Voice proceeded : "I can't follow your rigmarole. The Honourable Saheb's time is limited. He has just to leave for opening a new ward in a mental hospital."

I protested: "How am I preventing him from doing so?"

The Voice (completely losing temper): "Then why don't you call Gaganvihari Mehta?"

I replied: "But for the fifth time I am telling you that I am that person whom you want!"

The Voice: "Then why don't you say it clearly and

promptly? Here's the Honourable Saheb."

The Minister asked: "How are you? How is your health?"

I said: "I have had a bad cold, Sir. Before that I had 'flu which developed into hepatitis."

The Minister: "Very sorry to hear that. But apart from these illnesses, you are keeping well isn't it?"

I said: "Yes, Sir, except that I am getting old."

The Minister consoled me: "We are all doing that. No one can escape the ravages of time."

I asked: "Sir, why did you remember me today? Is there anything I can do?"

The Minister replied: "Yes. It is my earnest desire that you accept the Vice-Chancellorship of this University this is not a request, not an offer, but a command!"

I said: "I am most grateful. Mayor Saheb and the Collector Saheb had approached me –"

Interrupting me the Minister said rather loudly: "You can refuse them. You can't refuse me! We are really in a predicament and badly need you. Otherwise, do you think I would leave all my heavy work and phone you?"

I said: "I fully appreciate that but –"

He said: "No 'buts' and 'ifs'. We have decided to appoint a Committee of enquiry to go into the affairs of the University. Now how could the Committee function if there is no Vice-Chancellor in the University? What can we say to it? We have to throw the responsibility on someone at least! How can I otherwise show my face to the public and face the electorate in future? The elections are not far-off, you know!"

I protested: "But, Mr. Minister, how can I undertake the responsibility of an institution about whose affairs, management or mismanagement I know absolutely nothing."

He replied: "Your ignorance will ensure your impartiality. Besides, someone has to take the responsibility. If the Committee reports against you, you may immediately resign and we shall unhesitatingly accept your resignation."

Before I could reply to such an unusual offer, the telephone was fortunately cut off and our conversation abruptly terminated.

Next day, I wired to the Minister: "Grateful for your most unique offer. Because of adverse circumstances and personal reasons regret inability to accept. My blood pressure has gone up to 210/125 after our phone conversation."

—*Illustrated Weekly of India,* March 9, 1971, Bombay.

AN EXTINGUISHED VIP

New Delhi, August 15

News has just been received that President Batuta of Pong Ping is paying a four-day visit to the capital followed by a fortnight tour of several cities in the country—PTI

New Delhi, August 16

It is authoritatively stated by well-informed sources that Pong Ping is a small but independent state in the Arctic Circle, north north-east of the northernmost tip of North Korea.

This country has a population of 7001 persons (male and female adults) and 699 children. The state is sovereign, non-aligned and committed to socialism.

One of our junior ministers when visiting Outer Mongolia to explain our stand on Bangladesh last year is reported to have met President Batuta and was impressed with this enlightened ruler in the heart of the Polar region. On the minister telling him about India's policy in relation to Vietnam, Israel, Kashmir, etc., the President asked to be shown where these places were on a world atlas which was procured with some difficulty.

However, the President immediately issued a statement stating that he wanted friendship with all, had malice only towards some but enmity towards none. Whereupon he was invited to visit India, an invitation which was instantly and gratefully accepted. No date was set on that day.

Tokyo: August 17

The state of Pong Ping is said to be in a state of domestic crisis. It is authentically rumoured that the President has five wives (in addition to two concubines and three mistresses) and there is a regular (or irregular) fight between them as to who (or how many) should accompany the President on his trip abroad.

On being informed by his Secretary of State (temporary) that the people in India were by and large monogamous (though they thought it was rather monotonous), the President called the official astrologer (who forecasts as desired) for consultation.

The astrologer after looking at the relative horoscopes and throwing some pebbles in the snow came to the conclusion that the Fourth Lady should accompany the President. It was also an auspicious number. This set the controversy at rest.—*U.P.A.*

Seoul: August 18

Reliable reports indicate that Pong Ping is in a condition of acute financial crisis because of the prospective visit of the President to India. The treasury was found empty by the Chancellor of Exchequer (officiating) when he opened it this morning.

After an urgent cabinet meeting when some ministers were absent on tour and others were asleep at home, the President has cabled to President Nixon of the U.S.A. asking for aid under A.I.D. and to Mr. McNamara of the World Bank for a soft loan in hard currency to enable him to meet the cost of his journey.

Replies are eagerly awaited—*A.P.A.*

Washington, D.C. : August 19.

An unofficial spokesman of the White House said that the request of the President of Pong Ping is under active and urgent consideration.

Meanwhile, the state Department and C.I.A. are trying to find out whether there are any communists in Pong Ping which would facilitate their giving aid to combat them: If not, whether the President was prepared to import some communists from other countries.

He was also asked what he thought of two Chinas being merged into one Ex-Red China: and whether he was prepared to give moral and verbal support to Thieu and Bhutto.—*Reuter.*

Pong Ping: August 20

It is authentically stated that the President has sent a secret message to Mr. Brezhnev, First Secretary of the U.S.S.R. requesting him to spare a few communists to create trouble in his State.

He said they would be warmly welcomed, properly looked after, suitably compensated and returned to the Soviet Union after American aid was obtained.

The President (whose real name is Batuta Chin-tai and not merely Batuta as previously reported) has given Dr. Kissinger and Mr. Roberts to understand that he was willing and ready to recognise three Chinas if necessary, including Hong Kong and support their amalgamation.

He said he had always been of the view that the genocide in East Pakistan was "an internal matter" of West Pakistan which should have been solved by negotiations between Pakistan and India.—*A.F.*

Moscow: August 21

The Supreme Soviet today turned down Pong Ping

President's appeal for sending some communists to that country.

Official sources in the Kremlin commented that communists are not capitalistic currency or commodities to be loaned temporarily; they must be in sufficient numbers and should stay in a country long enough to take it over so as to make it sovereign democratic, peaceful, socialistic and non-aligned as well as tied to Soviet Rusia.—*Tass*

Vladivastock: August 22

President Batuta (etc.) has been sorely disappointed by the Kremlin's negative and discouraging reply. He proposes approaching Peking for deputing some dedicated Maoists and his Minister of External Affairs (permanent until dismissed) is drafting a suitable *aide memoire.—N.C.N.A.*

New York: August 23

A consortium of American banks has agreed to bear the cost of the foreign visit of the President of Pong Ping. This, it has been explained, is being done to further the cause of democracy in the polar region and counteract the spread of communism among penguins.

President Batuta is expected to fly by Pan American to New York collect the funds, go back by TWA to Pong Ping (both free passages for him and his retinue) and then proceed to India and South Asia. – *O.P.A.*

New Delhi: August 27

President Batuta (whose real name it is now learnt is Tamuta Bin-kai) and his wife (no. 4), Her Excellency Presticia Kin-natchi (weighing 270 lbs and 210 lbs respectively) received a warm welcome this morning at the Palam airport where the President, the Prime Minister, Cabinet Ministers, Ministers of

State, Deputy Ministers and a large number of leading citizens, headed by the Mayor were present.

As it was not known what was the ideological slant of the state, the entire diplomatic corps was present.

Since the national anthem of the State was not known, the band played "It's a long way to Tipperary" and everybody stood (with some difficulty) to attention.

The President found it difficult to get out of the door of the plane (it is not known how he was able to enter it). At one stage, it was feared that the door would have to be broken open; subsequently, there were anxious moments when it was feared the gangway would give way under the combined weight of the President and his fourth Lady (totalling 480 lbs).

The Minister of Civil Aviation was seen rushing towards a nearby ambulance reciting some Sanskrit verses of prayer.

As soon as the President touched the soil of India. he was greeted by a salute of 21 guns—two of which, however, did not go off.

The President of India in his welcome speech said: "Pong Ping and India are connected by ancient and unbreakable ties;" and that their relations were most cordial and friendly and they had no problems between them.

He mentioned the fact that the national language of Pong Ping (which he regretted he did not know and could not understand) contained three Sanskrit words and one Tamil expression which fact "the Chief Minister of Tamilnadu will, I am sure, be glad to know." He added parenthetically, this showed their age old relationship on a free and equal basis.

"The approach of both Pong Ping where people are peace loving (except when they are at war) and India to national, international and space problems is similar, if not identical.

"We both believe in democracy socialism, secularism and want peaceful co-operation, non interference in each other's (or any body else's) affairs. We are prepared to conclude a treaty till eternity."

President Batuta (or Tamuta) in the reply warmly and sincerely thanked the Indian Government and people for their hospitality (which he was yet to enjoy) and for their good will.

He brought with him (free) the cordial greetings of the 7003 persons of Pong Ping (there had been two more births since he left) as well as the children of the country (who were praying when he was leaving).

He assured the people and the Government of India that his people were equally—if not more—anxious to know something of the ancient culture of the great Indian nation and also learn something about their planning (in public) and plotting (in private).

He added that his lovely wife and he had been eagerly looking forward to this visit for which he had explored all avenues (including the Park and Madison Avenues in New York) to make it possible.

The Presidential party then left for Rashtrapati Bhavan. Since there was some uncertainty about the flag of Pong Ping State, a mixture of stars and stripes and hammer and sickle had been put up.

It is understood that special chairs, sofas and beds had to be made. The work was entrusted to the State Trading Corporation and the P.W.D. and was completed just as the Presidential party arrived.

New Delhi, August 27

There was a sensation in the capital this morning when it was found that the President and his wife were missing. They seemed to have disappeared after midnight and have not yet been traced.

The police are making vigorous inquiries—airports, railway stations and mental hospitals have been alerted.

A delayed message from Tokyo said that there is some mix-up in the name of the kingdom and the Indian Minister might have landed elsewhere.

New Delhi, August 28

An adjournment motion in expected in tomorrow's session of Lok Sabha and Rajya Sabha.

Mr. Atal Behari Vajpayee has issued a statement declaring that Indira Gandhi's Government should resign immediately because of the humiliating fiasco which had compromised India's prestige and had weakened our position vis-a-vis Pakistan.

Rajaji writing in *Swarajya* states that this tragi-comedy is the direct result of the Permit Licence Raj and stressed the need of a national government.

The Communist Party of India has strongly condemned the action of American bankers in providing funds to a renegade lackey stooge of imperialism. This proves the need of taking over all monopoly houses.

The Communist Party (Marxist) after six hours deliberations had issued a declaration that nothing better could be expected of the reactionary government of Indira Gandhi.

It is no wonder such a Government rigs elections and bullies voters which outrages all true Marxists who firmly believe in democratic procedures.

While Mr. Nijlingappa declined to comment, the Congress (O) President, Mr. Sadiq Ali said that this was one more false promise which the Prime Minister had not been able to fulfil.

The incident expresses not only the political bankruptcy of Government but its utter unreliability.

No official comment was available on the whole incident.

—*Sunday Standard,* 22 October, 1972.

LEADEROPSIS, PAISA-PAISA: NEW INDIAN DISEASES AND THEIR CURE

A mysterious epidemic is raging; the symptoms are disturbing—garulity, money-grabbing and a mania for limelight. We've just discovered a vaccine which might make a dramatic breakthrough.

Over eighty years ago, the ruler of a Princely State in what is now Saurashtra called his personal physician and told him that he had a severe pain as his belly had burst. The physician mildly protested: "Your Highness, such a thing is unknown! Stomachs don't burst." His Highness was irritated and retorted, "Cannot there be new diseases?" The physician was, no doubt, dumbfounded.

But surely, there is a point here. Have we not new diseases with the spread of civilization– cancer, ulcers, meningitis, applexy (owing to over centralisation), anaemia (owing to loss of position), etc., etc.? Or, is it that these diseases were there but their appropriate names not known so that our ancestors died without even knowing the cause of their death? We are, in this respect, more fortunate. Not only can we die beyond our means, as Oscar Wilde remarked, but we can know precisely what our doctors can't cure.

Our country has been in the past a land of epidemics– plague, cholera, canker, malaria, splits, kala-azar and so forth. Some of these have been controlled, some eliminated others are being fought. But apart from these recognised and quite respectable diseases, numerous other maladies prevail which should be treated and when curable, cured. These maladies might be regarded as psychological; but that is why they are more, and not less, catching and dangerous. They are widely prevalent and are contagious as well as infectious. I know I am rushing in where doctors and psychiatrists fear to tread. I will mention only a few of these new ailements which are rapidly developing into epidemics. Others will no doubt, be able to supplement and enlarge the list of incidental and consequential complaints and complications and side effects from their own experience, observation, errors, etc.

A widely prevalent disease is technically called Leaderopsis or the Burning Desire To Be A Leader in some sphere or the other but especially in what is called "public life." This affects the young and the old alike; persons of all ages and in all stations of life become victims of this fell disease; women are also (unfortunately) not free from it.

Symptoms: The patient in the early stages shows a marked weakness for reading newspapers and attending public meetings. After having been "among those present", he begins to write letters to the press and even articles; he also develops a tendency to deliver speeches and unburden himself by being a burden on various audiences. He also gets an attack of *photogenia*— to sneak in where prominent leaders are being photographed for the next day's paper. If he cannot stand in the group, he will peep from behind. Gradually he has an irresistible desire to join some organisation or other and try to become its office-bearer. If he cannot succeeed in one association or society, he joins another or alternatively starts a new one; in this condition, he has a rash on his face when he begins to denounce his previous colleagues as cliquish, factious autocrats and charges them with corruption, nepotism and Fascism.

Supplementary complaints: When the disease becomes pronounced, the patient usually has several ancillary complaints. One of them is *Postophilia* or a feverish craving for some office or post. In this condition, the patient gets into a municipal body, tries to get into all possible standing committees and subsequently becomes their chairman, ending up with nightmares of mayoralty. And if elected to a legislature, he wishes to becomes a Deputy Minister and then Minister. This is usually accompanied by (red eyes with anxiety and anger), green spots on the body (through envy) and sudden fluctuations in blood pressure. The patient also develops a mania for going abroad on various delegations and conferences. This is accompanied by insomnia at the apprehension of being left out.

Urban Susceptibility

Another serious complaint which arises out of *leaderopsis* is *Statitis* or the Itch to Issue Statements to the Press and the news agencies on every conceivable and inconceivable occasion. Not merely all politicians and public men catch this infection but even business men cannot escape the scourge. The result is that a person issues statements at the slightest provocation or even without any provocation at all. This complaint is particularly prevalent in an overheated climate like that of New Delhi, Bombay, Calcutta and Madras. On the whole, rural areas are free from this complaint except when public men visit there. On the evening and late night of the presentation of the Union Budget every year, scores of business men get caught by this mini-epidemic and condemn various taxation proposals in diverse statement. Since July-August last year, this malady has broken out in a virulent form in the national capital and has virtually become uncontrollable. The patient suffers from *headlines* instead of headaches — which readers get.

In an advanced stage of *Leaderopsis*, the patient is often attacked by *Partysthenia* when he is prone to start a rival faction or a new party or group or section so as to become its leader. Oscillation between two rival parties or factions not infrequently produces somnambulism when the patient walks over from one party to another even in his sleep. The complaint is easily recognisable by its frequency and regularity. Very often, in several parties and places there are more "leaders" than followers. Indeed, it is hard to find many followers nowadays. "Leaders" have to scour and hunt and advertise for them.

Incurable Stages

In the last stages, the patient frequently develops *Osteoporosis* or swelling condition of the head when *Leaderopsis* becomes practically incurable. It is accompanied by delirium. It is during this stage, that in certain cases, the public has to suffer the minutest details of the movements, arrivals, departures, warm receptions as well as the health of leaders. If, unfortunately, a "leader" falls ill or suffers from *Fastestria*, the hapless public is compelled to learn particulars of his blood pressure, the intensity of heart throbs, the quantity of albumin, sugar and acid; and a grateful (if rather bored) nation has to read day after day what is the present state of the nose, lungs, throat, eyes and teeth of these high personages. (Bertrand Russell, however, says that he got throat trouble trying to swallow the words of politicians). Fortunately, the tongues and hands of the patient are so affected by *Statitis* that nothing prevents the issue of daily statements, contradictions, explanations, manifestoes, appeals, messages, "clarion calls"— not to mention interviews subsequently modified and corrected by supplementary statements and interviews. In political parlance, this is called active participation in "public life."

Another disease which has a somewhat complementary complication is *plutograstria* (commonly known as *Paisa-Paisa* and to be distinguished from *beriberi*) or the quasimania for Money and More Money which affects the rich and the poor alike. The first symptoms are evident in the patient's dissatisfaction with his earnings. But the very rich also suffer from this and cannot rest without exploring every avenue (and by-lane) for multiplying their wealth. Once the germ of the disease gets into the system, the corpuscles transform the man into a living corpse. He develops speculation fever (or *marketomania*) which is as bad as claustrophobia, as also *turfophobia*, that is, backing the wrong horse which is worse than hydrophobia or being bitten by the wrong dog. More recently, in some of the States an endemic trouble has been *ticketsy* or the craze to purchase lottery tickets and the zeal to obtain a ticket from a political party.

For nearly half a century many people have suffered from *Fastestria* or the *Fasting Hysteria* as a protest against anything or anybody or to get something—be it a refinery, a steel plant, a new college or university, dismissal or reinstatement of a principal or a manager; be it to obtain decisions on boundary disputes or even against a rival fast. Fasts have been undertaken to have a railway station, to start a bus service, to bring about compromise at elections to Congress Committees, to collect funds, to prevent misuse of funds, to protest against increase in rates, fares, fees, electricity and telephone charges. This malady usually results from Being Fed Up with a particular grievance or wrong so that the patient feels that by not feeding himself, he can get the grievance redressed or the wrong righted. One possible cure in such cases is for a number of opponents to sit opposite the patient and over eat.

Treatment: If a case of *Leaderopsis* is taken in hand early enough, there may be some chances of cure. The patient should be warned not to attend too many meetings (where he might also catch flu) or deliver too many speeches (which might develop throat trouble for the speaker or sleeping sickness for the audience). He must not get himself photographed (which is bad for the face and the eyes). The patient must be advised day in and day out not to be impatient in his pursuit of leadership.

In order to fight the epidemic, the Union Government should (one day before the parliament meets) pass an

Ordinance enjoining journalists and other press organisations not to publish in a month more than one statement of a leader. The All India Radio must also be called upon to treat such statements and speeches as "views" and not "news". The Government should also take strong preventive action prohibiting photographs of foundation laying ceremonies, "leaders" embracing one another on their birthdays, VIPs being mobbed, politicians emerging from party meetings or business leaders giving orations (which no one listens to). New Committees to enquire into what everyone knows by now and whose reports no one reads or acts upon should be strictly banned for ten years. No delegation should be permitted to go abroad nor anyone allowed to attend international conferences. The epidemic might then gradually subside.

"Grave" Results

It is difficult to suggest a cure for *Partysthenia*. But in an attempt to safeguard public health (and sanity), legislation should be undertaken, laying down that no one can assume the title of a "leader" unless he can show at least one thousand (or ten thousand) faithful and consistent followers whose heads could be counted (and, if necessary, broken) and who, in turn, would not try to be "leaders" themselves for a period of five years from the time they are accounted as followers.

If the patient develops *Osteoporosis* (or a Swollen Head) there is unhappily no known remedy. The head must be allowed to shrink to its original size by its own action or hard knocking by opponents. The processes of this illness, like the path of glory, lead but to the grave.

—*The Illustrated Weekly of India,* March 29, 1970, Bombay.

NEW NURSERY RHYMES

(Revised and Brought up-to-date for the very modern children in the Nuclear Age of Not Very Peaceful Co-existence)

1.

Humpty Dumpty sat on a Cuban wall
Humpty Dumpty had a big fall
All Uncle Sam's planes and all his men
Could not put Humpty Dumpty together again.

(This was written at the time of the Cuban Crisis in 1962).

2.

Nikita Krushchev could eat no fat
And his Chinese Comrade could eat no lean
And so between them both, you see,
They licked the continents clean.

3.

I'll tell you a story
About the Crisis –
And now my story's begun:
I'll tell you another
About changes in our Frontier
And now my story's done!

(Refers to Cuban Crisis and war between China and India over the frontier—1962)

4.

Chou-en-Lai, Chou-en-Lai, the Peaceful man,
Get me some territory as fast as you can;
Pick it and pocket it and mark it with a C
And put it under the Red Flag
For Mao and me.

5.

Hey Diddle Diddle
The Earth is a riddle
The Lunik jumped over the moon
The Lieka laughed to see such sport
And the Sickle ran away with the Tycoon.

6.

Subversion of lands be Liberation
Infiltration of peoples is not bad
True Socialism's expansion doth please me
Only imperialist obstruction drives me mad.

7.

If wishes had axis
Dag would still try
If aeroplanes were taxis
He would all the time fly!

(Dag Hammarskjold- U.N. Secretary General)

8.

Dillon, Dillon, Nice Man, have you any dollars?
Yes sir, Yes sir, I keep them for the callers.
Some for the poor nations, and some for the tame.
But none for the naughty ones who live in Red hued lane.
(Donglas Dillon, U.S. Secretary of the Treasury)

9.

Simple Simon met a Highman
Going to the World Fair
Said Simple Simon to the Highman
"Let me taste your ware."
Said the Highman to Simple Simon

"How shall I be paid?"
Said Simple Simon to the High Man
"That'll count against your Aid!"

10.

Planner, Planner, pass my scheme
If you do not, I shall scream.
Give me grants and give me plenty
Even if your means are scanty.

11.

Delegate, Delegate, where have you been?
I've been to countries to increase my trade.
Delegate, Delegate, what did you do there?
I enjoyed all my dinners and drinks being paid.

-*Financial Express*, 2 May, 1961.

INDEX